Against Death: 35 Essays on Living

Books to Prisoners
P.O. Box 78005
1755 East Broadway
Vancouver, BC, V5N 5W1

Against Death: 35 Essays on Living

Edited by
Elee Kraljii Gardiner

ANVIL PRESS 2019

2nd printing: February 2020

Anvil Press Publishers Inc.
P.O. Box 3008, Main Post Office
Vancouver, B.C. V6B 3X5 CANADA
www.anvilpress.com

Library and Archives Canada Cataloguing in Publication

Title: Against death : 35 essays on living / edited by Elee Kraljii Gardiner.
Names: Gardiner, Elee Kraljii, 1970- editor.
Identifiers: Canadiana 20190082682 | ISBN 9781772141276 (softcover)

Subjects: LCSH: Death — Psychological aspects. | CSH: Creative nonfiction,

Canadian (English)
Classification: LCC PS8373.1 .A43 2019 | DDC C814/.60803548—dc23

Cover design by Rayola.com
Interior by HeimatHouse
Represented in Canada by Publishers Group Canada
Distributed by Raincoast Books

The publisher gratefully acknowledges the financial assistance of the Canada Council for the Arts, the Canada Book Fund, and the Province of British Columbia through the B.C. Arts Council and the Book Publishing Tax Credit.

PRINTED AND BOUND IN CANADA

Nou tout a p mache ak sèkèy nou anba bra nou.

We're all carrying our coffins with us every day.

—Edwidge Danticat, *The Art of Death*

TABLE OF CONTENTS

Origins

Elee Kraljii Gardiner

I grew up with a mother, uncle, and grandfather, all surgeons, for whom the durability of the body and its marvels are a practical matter. In a home filled with medical journals, where lab samples were frequently stored in the fridge, mortality was familiar. Death was neither negative (cruel robber) nor positive (sweet release); it was knit into daily life as fact. Our busy, loving, sporty house was full of movement and spontaneity. Lively. And still the bloom of death took precedence over everything: any conversation or family moment could be interrupted by a beep from my mother's pager calling her to an emergency. We lived five minutes from the hospital for precisely this reason.

I knew the nurses' station as well as I knew my friends' homes. I knew, on turning the corner into a patient's room, how to push forward through the reflexive pause of apprehension. By age five, I could count tubes and discern a catheter from an iv. I held hands with patients while sutures were removed and pulled curtains around beds. I complimented well-healing amputations from a perch on the bed where a leg had once been. I played with needleless syringes in the tub and did homework with purple surgical markers printed with a ruler on the side for measuring incisions. Reminders of the body's fragility — and its persistence — were omnipresent.

My bedtime stories about the day's medical mysteries were just as dramatic, just as somatic as my father's Greek mythology tales. He told me about Medusa's gaze turning people to stone while my mother explained the same predicament in the form of ALS, a degenerative neurological condition rather than a moral one. I interrupted both their stories to focus on the point of inflection where things went right or wrong, asking for the story beside the story: What did the characters do, how did they go on? What happened next?

This is all to say that death has never been a strange character; I thought I knew it. My father's death when I was fifteen pushed me through the grapplings of first grief and demystified another aspect of what one can choose and not choose. Soon, my own experiences with coming close to death added another layer of meaning. Yet, it was not the parachuting accident with a failed chute when I was twenty that altered me, even though I did experience the hackneyed "life flashing before me" as I fell. It was not the near-drowning with my family swimming too far under a coral reef against tide and current, either. Nor was it the murder of a man in the movie theatre three rows ahead of me who was shot in the head at close range. I still check exits in auditoriums, but I can't say his murder changed me. Neither was it the smoke-filled airplane cabin with my husband and young children on an emergency landing, although I suspect I'll never shake the tang of sadness in the look he and I exchanged over their heads as we assumed crash position.

Each of us is an idiosyncratic bundle of experiences, and what registers as monumental for one may be negligible for another. What matters is where we put meaning. One person's crisis is another's party anecdote. My training in literature urges me to consider Borges' idea of never being able to read the same text twice: each time we approach the text we are a new self, a unique bundle of thoughts at a precise cultural moment; each reading becomes absolutely its own iteration. Certainly, if I were to parachute out of a plane this afternoon and had to cut away my chute I would have a different reaction than I did at twenty. At forty-eight, I have more to lose, or at least a better sense of what I don't want to lose.

I began this anthology to find community with those who have come close to death. When I was about to turn forty-one, a blood clot went to my brainstem. It was entirely out of the blue — I was fit, unmedicated, healthy. I was working out at the park when a twitch in my left eye not unlike one from computer fatigue took hold and instantly spread to my cheek. Within a second, the left hemisphere of my head and arm was frozen. Nothing in me changed except the ability to move and feel my left side. My thinking remained cogent; I was not confused but I couldn't talk because of partial paralysis. I knew instantly I was experiencing a stroke but refused to name it to the EMTs.

I refused to name it in the ER after the feeling and use of my left side returned. I flexed and unflexed my hand as I told and retold the story to various neurologists and refused to name what had happened because I didn't want it. Stroke was invisible, unpredictable, and unnecessary, so went my magical thinking. Days later, tests revealed I had torn the tunica intima, or lining, of the vertebral artery. Maybe, neurologists posited, the clot that had lodged in my brainstem originated from this undetected injury. It made me feel better to have a cause, and also so much worse.

A bottle of baby aspirin, instructions to keep my head above my heart and my pulse even were all the tools I was given. For a year I had a migraine every day. My pupils dilated independently. I had mild face drop and numbness down my arm, which reappears when I am stressed or tired. I had trouble processing incoming information. These were unpleasant nuisances. Primarily, during my recovery and beyond, I was a captive of fear. I knew enough of medicine to predict the worst. That's what doctors do: start at the worst-case scenario and rule out, rule out. I cast a wide net on calamity.

My entire relationship with fear changed after I was injured. Previously, fear had been a friend. In the comfortable, protected life I led, sheltered by copious resources and fuelled by high capacity and athleticism, fear was merely an indicator of something interesting, something I should try. Butterflies in my stomach meant "ooh!" rather than "uh oh." I walked toward those scenarios that elicited nerves rather than away. I was extroverted, social, confident to the point that a room full of strangers didn't inhibit me; rather, it looked like an energizing playland! And then my capacity shifted.

I don't know if the mini-stroke in my brainstem, the area of the brain that controls the flight or fight response, contributed or if this reaction was state-based, but as soon as the clot blocked the blood flow to my brain, I began experiencing fear differently. My pulse raced, I hyperventilated; I couldn't calm down even when the feelings of paralysis passed and it was clear I was out of immediate danger. I began looping through a circle of fear and anxiety.

The neurologists cautioned me that the first year after an event like this is the riskiest. Other clots, if they are going to occur, generally manifest within a year. I listened acutely to each ping and snap in my body. Was that it? The big one? Meanwhile, I had trouble organizing sensory information — I could listen to one person talk, but not track visuals at the same time. Or, I could touch something but not talk. Watching TV was impossible. So was reading more than a paragraph. Certain radio stations or electronic noises were painful; the frequency drilled into my brain. Perhaps this was from the daily migraine, but I struggled to understand the massive shifts in myself as physical rather than mental. I couldn't rely on myself. My brain hurt. My brain was tired. There was a real but invisible and untouchable injury — the lining of the artery wouldn't repair (it remains separated to-day), but the neurologists were unconcerned as long as blood flow was not obstructed. Microsurgery was not an option. They couldn't fix it even if they needed to.

I sat in a heightened state of panic, counting breaths, reaching for comfort wherever I could find it along the radius from my couch. Even the familiar world was rife with risk and terror. If I walked around the block, I was spent afterwards and needed to sleep for an hour. During this era I was aware of how unmy-self I was. A friend on the phone mentioned I sounded toneless, bored. True, I hardly laughed for a year. I flatlined emotionally only to flinch in the middle of a "nothing" moment. It felt as if the colour would drain from the frame and the angle of the world would shift into threat. A situation would be fine until it SUDDENLY WASN'T. Abruptly, I would leave the dinner table for bed, overcome and crying, or I'd exit a conversation mid-comment. Nothing on the outside had changed, everything on the inside had. This non-negotiable limit taught me how often it is OK to say no (always!) and how easy it is for people to accept a "no" when there is no other option. To say this was a revela-tion is an understatement.

As I healed, I managed to catch a phrase or thought every so often and jot it down, sometimes just one word on a page. If I hadn't, I never would have believed who I was then and how I came to be now. A year to the day of the injury I saw I had filled an entire journal with a record of my thoughts, a notation of my un-me-ness. These notes evolved into a memoir in poetry, *Trauma Head*. While living the experience was sad and uncomfortable, the creative exercise that took place much later to build the book was playful, exciting, and happy. Then and now I hold my re-covery as a lottery ticket. How senseless and wonderful that I am OK! Closing my eyes, I pictured walking away from a crash in a

Hollywood movie. But when I opened them I knew there was a subtle mark on me, at least in my psyche. This perspective came later. During the healing I was anything but curious.

The notes I took of the year of healing were a shorthand text completely devoid of image or metaphor. I then set about making it weirder, turning it into poetry. Returning to these truncated, bizarre notes proposed an etiological question. Etiology, the study of the cause of illness, featured in my thinking. How much of this condition did I manifest myself? In recording the year, did I unwittingly create any of the situations I suffered? I chewed up my fear with art, breaking patterns and conventions that were holding me. The change in my writing process was absolute, as impossible to ignore as the impulse to escape an over-stimulating environment when I was recovering. I had to respect my impulse (get out of here!) and isn't it the best thing for a writer to listen to her intuition? I couldn't think about what an audience might like, or what might "make sense." I absolutely had to do what felt right to me. This artistic authority served me in so many ways.

I used every bit of medical training-by-proxy to maneuvre convalescence. Paradoxically, what I wanted most was to manage the one thing I was powerless over: my recovery. Tension and vigilance reefed on my musculature. A massage therapist tried to help but I was so nervous about my neck being compromised, I panicked, literally rising off the table. During this recovery I listened entirely and only to my feedback system. An artery thrummed in my left ear and each swoosh of blood flow scared me. The tinnitus in both ears became so loud it woke me up in the middle of the night. My temperature soared and plummeted. I went from moving, lifting, bending, and running to an absolute sit-still. My body softened. I wanted it to soften; I was afraid of edges.

Everything is edged, though. Abrasions with family members, conflict with parking lot drivers, even trying to open the front door with too many bags in my hand, never mind the fact that serious larger socio-political issues are all about contact, about rasping up against something or someone else. At times, every emotional or physical contact was painful, even previously enjoyable experiences. For an extroverted and gregarious person this was my hell. I couldn't figure out who I was when my entire slate of options had changed. I didn't know if it would or wouldn't be permanent. I'm not returned to the original, unknowing person I was, of course. I see my own edges more clearly and perhaps this event accelerated the process of thinking through rather than acting out the familiar midlife crisis. It was helpful to do some sessions of EMDR with a counsellor to help me process the fear and uncouple it from the signals my body gave me.

It turns out I am not afraid of death or even dying, but the unpredictable loss of control. The injury was spontaneous, and untouchable — I couldn't see my brainstem, wrap it in a bandage or ice it, or monitor the healing visually. I've been cleared health-wise for everything except roller coasters, which I can live without although they were the only reason I went to amusement parks! I celebrated the all-clear by doing one back flip off the diving board — a sort of slap in the face to illness — and tried not to freak out afterwards about what that might have done to blood vessels. Now I watch my body progress through aging, a natural process maligned and criticized by media, and think *at least I am here to witness the rot*!

During the healing, it was hard to convey my reactions in a way that made sense. Some people, despite their gentleness and care, did not recognize how out of sorts I was or know how to be around me. Some of the unlikeliest, gruffest, roughest people did. The common denominator in the ones most easy to be with was a profound experience of their own of coming into contact with death. I began to think I could recognize a shadow, a reverberation, almost see a psychic watermark on the people who had been next to death themselves and I wanted to know their stories.

To be against something can be to reject or refute it. But to be against death can also mean to be in contact with, pressed up next to, to be intimately proximate with mortality. This anthology gathers a community of people who self-identify as having come close. Some pieces may touch on similar details, in fact, it was only late in the editing that I recognized a magical twinning that runs through the collection. Here again I feel Borges tap me on the shoulder. There are echoes, point of view contrasts, alterations on strangely intimate stories that one could not plan or solicit on purpose: two pieces written by people who were actively dying, two by elder women ready for what is coming, two by young widowers about fatherhood, two by people negotiating suicidal thoughts, two hospice volunteers, two mothers relating their sons' dangerous addictions.... While I recognize the magic involved in a text finding its companion, each piece is particular and peculiar in all the best ways.

So often the meaning of an anthology becomes clear only as the pieces form a whole. This assembly of responses confirms that there is no one way to be; no matter how common an ailment or predicament, we each navigate our irreproducible way using the tools we have picked up through the years. We come up against death and it is brand new, and yet nothing is new. We have been dying for eons.

I sent a call for essays to as many communities as possible, aware that even the submission call could be jarring for people, especially those still at-risk or in vulnerable communities. To that end, I offered to brainstorm, chat, answer questions, and read drafts with prospective authors. This is not typical editorial behaviour, but I could only commit to this project by believing this exploration could be gentle on us as we figured out how to get these lightning bolt stories safely to the page. Although I was open to republishing texts, each author decided to produce a new piece, which I believe speaks to the need for a collection like this. I left it to authors to determine what experience they consider foundational or transformational. Who am I to judge the impact of accompanying a beloved through an awful situation? Or to insist an injury isn't severe enough to "count" when my own pivotal scare more or less evaporated within a short period?

If you are squeamish you may find these pieces psychologically (but not graphically) brutal. This is not a book that pulls punches and offers platitudes. This anthology is deeply philosophical: as Laurie Lewis writes, "it's the night again and all the lives I didn't live are here with me, living here in the dark."

In many cases it *won't* be OK and the authors are figuring out how to live with that knowledge or prepare for the final change. Sometimes this falls onto the page as the recognition that life is ridiculous, just as ridiculous as aspects of "untimely" death. The authors are frank witnesses to all that makes us human, including our capacity for humour. Moira MacDougall, faced with an avalanche of multiplying health crises, writes, "I decided if I couldn't dictate Nature's capricious whims or control the cellular chaos of our bodies, I could organize our closets."

Each author articulates their concerns with the idiosyncrasies not only of their craft (some include poetic or photographic interventions), but also according to their mental state during the events. The difficulty of understanding death sometimes demands surrealism or hyperrealism, or both: there are many layers at play here; how could it be otherwise?

Spending time reading these texts as I renegotiated my own position against death made me more tender and more fierce. I have this wish for you, the reader. I hope these essays help you connect with the humanity you see in front of you, and within you, even during dangerous or challenging times. I hope you find comfort in the idea that as lonely as it may be standing near death, someone has stood in a similar position before. I am grateful to these authors and for the craft of writing that has made these questions more answerable in my own life. As Aislinn Hunter writes here, "The narrative is a survival mechanism I've used in order to live with uncertainty."

Three contributors knew they would die before they could see their words in print and I send my condolences to their friends and communities, hoping their words here might be a comfort through their absences. My friend John Asfour, with whom I co-edited *V6A: Writing from Vancouver's Downtown Eastside* and who taught me about being a writer, answered my nosey questions about his life and gave me leeway to do with his words what I wanted.

Harry Langen said yes to writing his piece while in a bed at Vancouver General Hospital, post-terminal diagnosis. Harry's enthusiasm for the project is evident in his expansive acceptance of love in his last days. He also offered me editorial freedom to conduct his message to the page.

Connecting with Susan Briscoe, who was actively dying while creating her contribution, was, from what I have heard from her friends, illustrative of her: Susan was frank, funny, and professional in our correspondences. Her curiosity about the process she was witnessing bloomed with love for her life and I am so happy to have been in conversation with her.

Contributor Aislinn Hunter, who writes so beautifully about her love and life with husband Glenn, accompanied him through his last days just before the manuscript was set. Their mandate to, "drink the good wine now," is one to enact in appreciation of any love that surrounds us.

With this end we also celebrate a beginning: I send a warm hello to little Runa, who was born to contributor Ben Gallagher and mom Brinleigh just as Ben filed his final version.

An Introduction

Kiera Miller

Truth: I can't talk about mortality without talking about addiction and I can't talk about addiction without talking about violence and I can't talk about violence without talking about being a woman and I can't talk about being a woman without talking about being a wife and a mother and I can't talk about being a wife and mother without talking about my husband and his own press against death right after my clutch and shiver, and, dear God, I will have to talk about my son, and to talk about my son means to admit he is affected by all of my experiences with these personal subjects certainly made more public in the past ten years, but remain, to me, privately intertwined. They are braided together. It's impossible for me to pull out one strand. You must see the entire braid. It's the only way to explain how invisible pulls awakened me to the essential holds in my life.

Did this insight come from my press against mortality? Oh, how easy it would be to say yes. Yes, it did. But that would be a lie, and I don't lie for ease anymore. It's a decision I've consciously made because it winds back to attention. How I spend my attention is how I spend my time. If I lie, my attention is directed away from the truth of my past, present, and future, and to spend time away from the truth is to fall down the rabbit hole, dress billowing around face inhibiting vision and ending up in some strange place uncertain of who I am, where I am, or even what size shoe I might wear in this land of inconsistencies.

I am asking for your attention, the most valuable thing we have: we experience only what we pay attention to. We remember only what we pay attention to. When we decide what to pay attention to in the moment, we are making a broader decision about how we want to spend our lives.

Once Upon a Holly Tree

Susan Cormier

Friends envy their pastoral lifestyle. They call her Snow
White, a rural damsel surrounded by rabbits and deer and
crooked trees bearing red fruit. Snow White and the Prince,
happily ever after.

One summer afternoon while the Prince is at work, she finds
another dead rabbit in the garden, its soft body stiff and twisted
from a neighbour's rat poison. Deer gather in the backyard, wide
eyes and down-filled ears turned towards her in a curious audience as she scoops the small body with a shovel, avoiding the
fleas and ticks that might be seeking warmer blood, and moves
it to a forest grove for the nighttime scavengers to address.

※　※　※

Perhaps this is the afterlife. Or, more appropriately, the after-
death.

※　※　※

Once upon a time, there was a teenage girl, as sad and dark as
she was quiet. She lived in a small town surrounded by few
friends and many people who said ugly words to her, and she felt

alone. She fell down a lot. She always felt like she was falling. She wrote dark poetry, listened to angry songs on repeat, and collected sharp objects and reasons to die, or leave, or simply to not exist.

On a bright spring day, a friend drove her to a party. The car engine squealed, the wheels skidded, and everything was blood and broken. The falling, dark girl fell further into darkness. No happily ever after.

But a few days, a few weeks later — the blip of a heart monitor. A blink into consciousness. Here. Now.

And the years turned by. And the falling, dark girl fell no further into the darkness.

But she knew that Death stayed close. Every footstep across a busy intersection could meet a speeding car. Every swallow of food could clog a trachea; every climb up a ladder could slip and sever a spine. And she knows all the spells to conjure up Death: the razors, hoarded pills, knives, poisons. The high places with hard landings. The dark, deep lake water. She leaves her notebook closed, does not read her old writings. The last pages are yet blank, the last sentence unfinished, ending in a semicolon.

There is no happily ever after. But there is an after — this time. This is not always so.

※　※　※

At forty-seven, he slipped sideways from consciousness into some other world characterized by bright lights — familiar faces — strange conversations with those long gone. He woke in a bed surrounded by tubes and wires, his face smashed by the sudden collapse, ribs cracked and back bruised from aggressive CPR pounded into his chest.

There is no memory of death itself. Only that of before, and after. Between, there are dreams, stories written by angels, myths, oxygen-deprived brains.

※ ※ ※

If you are reading this, you have likely been there. You have leaned across or been pushed through that dark doorway, that black maw pit — you've felt the hot breath-stench rushing up into your face, felt your fingers curl around the edges — and you are here, with the long stare and quiet of those who have travelled a long distance alone.

We can only describe the journey back if we know where we've been.

※ ※ ※

Healing is not a reversal of damage, a negation of what has happened. It is not a backwards movement. It is a movement forward.

In their backyard there is a holly tree that was broken in a windstorm. Its trunk had cracked, split, and the tree fell over; its top branches came to rest pressed atop a small grove of pines. The holly tree survived — the cracked and broken trunk oozed sap, grew new wood and bark, closed. The tree grew new waxy green spiky leaves, and each spring it starts a new crop of red berries. The tree is healed and healthy. But its top still rests against the grove of pines. In healing, the tree did not reverse its fall, pull itself back upright. It is healed and healthy, but it will never be the same.

The human body has an incredible capacity for growing new tissue and recovering from wounds. But it does not rearrange the cells; it grows new ones. The ends of a broken bone will generate new bone tissue, cover the distance between the pieces and heal. But the body cannot pull misaligned bone fragments back into their original positions — they heal where they are: crooked, lopsided, misaligned. A bone broken by impact does not just break and stay stable: it shifts within the tissue around it and in the joints it is part of. So when these bone pieces have grown back together, if they are misaligned by even the tiniest fraction of a millimetre, they will heal into that new position. And that change in position, be it ever so slight, will affect the body's kinetic dynamics: how the muscles move, the angle of the joint, how the nerves and tissues configure themselves.

So too for the flow of blood through severed veins, the electric spark of neurons across frayed spinal cords, the flex and thud of torn muscle and heart tissue. We will never be the same.

※   ※   ※

In the autumn she collects seeds from her flowers to save for the winter birds, as she has done since childhood. In the parched, dry summer, he digs a hole, lays a waterline so the night animals can drink. She brews thick syrup for the hummingbirds in the winter, thin syrup in the summer. He builds birdhouses, bat houses, and rearranges his workshop renovation plans to accommodate the nests he finds in the rafters.

Some say they should build a fence to keep the rabbits and deer from her garden, but she shakes her head. She does not mind the nibbled leaves, the torn-up roots, the heart-shaped hoof prints that punctuate her soil. She is amused by the tiny paw prints, the quiet eyes that watch from the grass, pretending to be invisible.

In the spring she picks tiny carcasses from the melting snow, arranges their bones to weather and dry. In the spring, he lifts lids from beehives, breathes in the scent of warm wax or cold musty death. Hawks turn above, hunting tiny rabbits and quick-darting mice.

※ ※ ※

Fireman. Man of fire. A man who seeks fire, is created and shaped by fire, broken by fire.

An acquaintance overhears the name of their rural home-town, laughs, comments that the Prince must have a pretty quiet job because there aren't many buildings to catch fire.

But when the old lady's hearts seizes, the gas leak sputters and flows, the highway bridge cracks and falls tossing cars about like pebbles, the airplanes crash into buildings — it is not the ambulance or police who rush first to the rescue, but the firefighters. Who else has towering extending ladders, heavy hydraulic tools and jaws of life, layers of muscle and sinew tensed for action and trained in navigating destroyed buildings and hauling deadweight bodies. Who else can free the crum-pled children from car wrecks, the buried bodies from broken buildings, so the paramedics can wrap them with bandages and splints, or the police with handcuffs and paperwork, or the coroner with resolution and bodybags.

Who else can choose to bear the weight of moments that leave the mind twisted and broken. The gruesome smear of innards across a car dashboard. The rasping breath of a crushed and dying body. The scream of a child calling for his mother. How much violence can a body endure and still survive. How much grief can a mind carry and still awaken in the morning, fill out paperwork, brew coffee. A hand slammed on a counter in frustration. A back bent, jaw clenched, with the shudder of unspoken rage.

When Timmy falls down the well, you can picture bright red cartoon fire trucks racing to the rescue. It is not the whole truth, but it is truth enough.

※ ※ ※

Friends ask her, how has your life changed since the accident?
And she cannot answer. She does not know how to compare
the life she has with the one that does not exist. And it has been
so many years now.

Is this the afterlife, or a dream, perhaps. This strange and fascinating world characterized by the surreal brightness of colours,
the delightful déjà vu of small familiar things. Fresh water tastes
like the smell of wet dog, clocks' hands seem to turn backwards,
and sunshine on her face feels so deliciously fresh. She wonders
how to distinguish between the shift in perception and attitude
caused by the brush with death, and the shift in cognition
caused by the brain injury. And does it really matter.

Or perhaps she was sleeping, and is now awake, trying to recon-
cile her experiences with fading dreams. The moment of confusion
when a dream is recounted as fact: *Don't you remember? We spoke
just yesterday.*

After returning from a long journey to a strange land, one's
home seems familiar but odd; well-wandered streets seem stilted
and bright, as though from a movie. The process of reconnect-
ing is a disconnect. A long stare, remembering.

※　※　※

When they part ways, even briefly, they always share an embrace
and *I love you.* They have both been there, and returned. And
they have seen those who did not. Next time, they might not.

The boy whose heart stopped suddenly during soccer practice. The man whose tractor tipped, crushing him in a distant
field. The woman who slept through a gas leak, dreams slipping
into deeper dreams.

The man who went walking at night, darted into the road
to pull his dog back from a speeding truck — his shoe left
lonely by the road as the ambulance sped pointlessly away.

His wife recounts their last conversation, sharp and bitter as frozen mud.

These could be your last words. What will they be. The slammed door. Anything could be the last thing you say to her. *I'm going to the store; back in five. I love you.*

※ ※ ※

Touching death is not like going on a journey and returning home to the same place. It is stepping out of the room to walk into a confusing and many-angled hallway, then through another door into a room that looks familiar. Is it the same room from a different angle? Or another room that looks similar?

Trying to decipher the truth is like comparing two pictures in a child's magazine — something is different, but what. The furniture has been rearranged, the walls repainted, but is it the same room.

※ ※ ※

They call him hero. They praise him for his bravery, for saving lives. But after decades of hauling bodies from burning buildings, breathing air into bruised smoke-clogged lungs, palming tourniquets against severed limbs and pumping blood wounds, he cannot claim to have saved a single life. The patient is loaded onto a stretcher, the ambulance lights flash, the sirens scream away — and the firefighters are left to pick up hoses, wash blood from the pavement, fill out forms for an incident they will never know the outcome of.

※ ※ ※

While picking blackberries on a sun-bleached afternoon, she realizes she forgot to check the rat traps that morning. They have been trying to catch the pests that live under the porch, to eradicate them before the house becomes infested with chewed wires, mangled insulation. Every morning, she empties the hand-sized traps tied to the fence and disposes of the dead as needed.

The rat is standing up like a little bright-eyed man, one front paw resting on the closed jaw of the black trap, the other folded softly as though about to reach out and open. Beneath it, its hind leg is twisted at too many angles, caught, snapped. The rat stares at her with round dark eyes. She is touched by the curve of its tail draped softly over the fence's bottom wire. She is sorry for the heavy dry heat, her negligence, the hours of struggle and pain.

She calls out to the Prince. They speak a moment. Their eyes are guarded with the echoes of a restless night of aching bones, broken sleep, muttered disagreements, a morning marred by short-tempered words. She returns to her garden.

She glances over her shoulder and sees him walking towards the rat with a heavy fencepost balanced on his shoulder. His muscles flex. His face is solemn, his head bowed. She turns her back, picks blackberries.

Thump.

※　※　※

Like birth, death is rarely quick, elegant, or silent. When the family members ask, he always tells them their beloved went instantly, knew no pain, did not suffer. Why would he say anything else.

Suicides. Heart attacks. Car accidents. Death slips into his workdays like unscheduled meetings, brushing aside schedules, plans, commitments. The pager goes off at noon, dinnertime, 3:00 AM, and it's work gear on sirens screaming engines steaming down roads clotted with ice cars bodies to save lives pronounce death witness the struggle between one and the next.

In a fairytale, death would not be nonexistent. It would come quiet and easy, and always be welcomed, or deserved. It would be given, and received, as a gift, or a long-awaited resolution.

※　※　※

As the Prince sleeps she keeps one hand on him, or a quiet outstretched foot. When she wakes, she feels his warmth, pauses and listens for the quiet hush of breath. Mothers of young children do the same. *Are you alive, are you alive.*

She turns the stove off, adds lids to the pots. When he will be late from work, he usually calls, sends a message. Her hand shakes as she pours another cup of tea. He knows a delayed dinner or a shift in evening plans is but a mere inconvenience — it is reassurance he needs to urgently convey. *I'm alive, I'm alive. At this moment I am alive.* She turns her back to the clock, busies herself with small inconsequential tasks, tries not to hold her breath and listen for the crunch of tires on the gravel driveway. *Are you alive, are you alive. At this moment are you alive.*

※　※　※

Scientists and human rights activists argue about when life begins and ends. As though it were binary, a light switch. Is the heart beating. Are the nerves responding. Is there brain activity. But what we are afraid of is not muscle or neurons failing, but consciousness — or the lack of it. We do not fear the body dying so much as that of the mind surviving. We fear nightmares, a conscious mind trapped in an unresponsive body; we shudder at tales of anesthetized patients frozen and awake under the surgeon's knife, theories of autopsied cadavers sensing the sharpness of the coroner's scalpel.

We ask those who have touched death: *What do you remember?* As though they had taken a journey, we expect tales of some strange land. Their scars and mending bones are souvenirs that tell truncated and unsatisfying stories.

※ ※ ※

He thrashes in dreams, yells out, caught in the half-world of those he has seen crushed, mauled, tangled in the tentacles of disfiguration and death. Dead children. Disembowelled men. An elderly couple, crushed. Decapitation. So many dead children. She tries to wake him, pull him back. Sometimes she cannot. There are those who watch the dying, and those who watch the watchers.

In the mornings they snarl and pace like restless monsters, fanged beasts conjured up by broken sleep and the anxious uncertainty of aging scar tissue. She squints through the blinding scotoma of seizures and migraines; he limps through the gauntlet of old injuries. He tries not to yell. She tries not to leave. They cling to each other with clawed hands, hissing and crying quietly, struggling to not drown in their own shadows. There are those who tame the monsters, and those who try not to become them.

※ ※ ※

Touching one's own death does not leave one unscarred, or unbroken. Death works in tandem with a sidekick named Trauma. Trauma carries two weapons: one to break bodies, one to break minds.

Death touches the dying. Trauma touches all: both those who survived, and those who bear witness.

He brings back stories from the siren-filled battlefields of first responder front lines. Respectful of Trauma's reach, he chooses his words carefully, avoids adjectives when describing victims. She suggests vague descriptors of injuries and deaths: *insides on the outside, bits and pieces, crispy chicken.*

For them, injuries and fatalities are not pictures on a computer screen, news reports to be ogled and discussed like staged reality show entertainment. Death and Trauma are as real as the scars on their hands, the blood in the toilet bowl — and they are cautious not to look too close.

※ ※ ※

Her friend misquotes doctors and insists that once healed, the body returns to a stable normality and all injury is reversed. Two years, the friend says, the body continues to heal for up to two years. After that, it's done.

The arthritic bone spur in her neck grates as she shakes her head in disagreement. She thinks of the medicine cabinet filled with painkillers and herbal remedies, remembers years of ongoing chiropractic therapy and neurology tests.

She holds her face calm against the urge to grind her teeth and shriek, to tear at her hair and fling claws of fury against the skies. How to explain. How to describe the endless desperate search for relief from a body that betrays her, that falls apart in strange and unexpected ways. The experiments with magnets, heat, strange ritualistic stretches. The daydreams of smashing aching bones with a hammer to ease the swelling pain. The nightmare of waking into unresponsive limbs cold and heavy with the sharp ache of neuralgia. The nightmare of a glass coffin body that cracks and stabs her with shards as she lies within it, screaming silently.

She leans to one side to ease pressure off a nerve pinched in her twisted back, and mentions the holly tree.

※ ※ ※

He counts the deer on his bent, heavily-scarred fingers. The dark fungus of arthritis in his knuckles keeps him awake at night. In the mornings, the deer watch him from beneath the apple trees with huge dark eyes and soft attentive ears, stepping elegantly through the weeds like stiletto-heeled dancers.

He counts the deer, compares the number to memory. Is anyone missing. Are there more. The wild-eyed doe who leapt from the shadows, too close as headlights flashed her flank, a screeching thump then a staggering limp into the forest. The fawn whose twin was taken down by coyotes. The buck who regally steps into the forest on his annual migration route: each time, the Prince hopes he'll return, never knowing until, never certain.

※　※　※

She stands by the holly tree, raises her lily-white hands to the clear blue sky, and sings, picturing a candy-red fire truck passing by with smiling firefighters leaning out the windows, waving. The birds do not land on her and twitter in harmony; the forest creatures do not gather at her feet. Her back is crooked with mishealed broken bones; his neck is bent with the weight of memories. They are holly trees, reincarnated.

She carries quiet ghosts, is haunted. The Prince carries a gun. Their bones chatter and creak with the aching language of the undead Otherworld. They wrap their arms around each other and look long into the sunset, drink fresh clear water, watch for the deer. There is no happily ever after. This is the after.

The Things She Left Behind

Adrian M. Zytkoskee

My wife Danae left behind a pair of black Adidas tennis shoes with pink trim that continue to sit on the front porch. They're far too big for my daughter but too small for either of Danae's sisters. I should move them, but I don't. Instead, I see them when I come home from work sitting next to the pumpkins the kids decorated with glitter — as if she were right inside. The sneakers get dusted by snow and still I leave them. No one comments on the lonely shoes. Perhaps they fear any words will fall short.

※　※　※

She left behind paperwork that continues to come to our address in her name. Mostly bills as the people who matter are aware that she's gone. One day, I decide to call the half-dozen hospitals who want money from us — from me. The bills sit, growing like the cancer they represent, in a file cabinet covered with free stickers from sports equipment we bought together.

I'm put on hold. I'm transferred. I talk to a woman who says she cannot talk to me because I do not have power of attorney. "So," I ask, "then I'm not liable for these bills?" "Unfortunately, you are," she replies. "You can make a payment; I just can't tell you the amount or any other details. I suggest you contact your wife's insurance company directly." So, I do. They transfer me three times, disconnect me twice, and finally, after an hour and twenty minutes, a woman says, "I understand your situation sir, but I'll have to speak directly to your wife." I tell her something colder than I've ever said in my life. "Ma'am, I hope that you get to watch your husband or whoever the fuck you love slowly die!" Before she can respond, I hurl the phone against the wall where it breaks into pieces. Instantly, I feel stupid and helpless. Rather than calming down, I scream into a pillow and then throw a tantrum worthy of a two-year-old. Afterward, I dig around the garage until I find some old, dry tobacco and sit on the back porch smoking an awful-tasting cigarette while listening to sad indie music.

※　※　※

She left behind her territory under the sink in the master bathroom. Really, the entire bathroom was her territory, but I've reclaimed a majority of the lost ground...except for under the sink. Crammed to nearly overflowing, it was too daunting a task until one day I put on loud music and got to work — and by "put on," I mean dialled up to house-rattling levels. She has space-saving baskets overflowing with unfamiliar things. The first one I pull out has maybe twenty different nail polishes. In her last months, she became obsessed with doing her nails and anyone else's who would let her; it was something she could do even in the hospital. I put them in a pile to give to family and friends. One sparkly, blue colour catches my eye and I set it aside for my daughter. Does nail polish spoil, I wonder. All the emery boards go in the trash; they disturb me, especially remembering the infections she got on her feet towards the end, infections that I told her weren't gross when she cried about how disgusting her cute toes had become. Another basket contains hospital masks; these remind me of death. Into the trash they go. I discover a box filled with small vials of essential oils for aroma therapy, vials that proclaim healing potential for just about every ailment. A memory flashes through my mind of a mocking comment I'd made to her about "stupid hippie products." Why did I feel the need to put down her excitement? Fuck. I keep sorting and find nail clippers, an eyelash curler, two hair driers, boxes of unused contact lenses, laxatives, an old toiletry kit from Emirates airlines, a Beanie Baby seal, and a neti pot. Some of it I keep. Some of it I set aside for her mom and sisters. A lot goes in the trash. I feel pulled between a desire to keep it all and to throw it all away.

She left behind her preferences for little things. At WinCo, I grab Fuji apples because those are the kind she likes. This is not sentimentality. It's habit. Not until three months after she's gone do I grab Granny Smiths, carefully selecting each green apple and feeling a sinking in my stomach as I do. Likewise, when I dress my two-year-old daughter Arya one morning, Danae's good-humoured criticism of my outfit choices echoes, and I find myself deciding against a particular pair of leggings because "stripes and plaids don't belong in the same ensemble." I put on *Buffy the Vampire Slayer* one night when I can't find something to watch — this was always her go-to when we couldn't decide on something. But when the character Angel utters some ridiculously moody line, she's not there to hear my teasing, to laugh and tell me, "I can't help it Matt! I love this show!" So I turn it off, the fun gone. And it goes like this. I wipe up water from the bathroom floor after my shower because it bugs her. The Alfredo sauce remains off the pizzas I bring home from Papa Murphy's because it makes her feel bloated. In the used bookstore, I automatically reach for a title from the *Outlander* series in case it's one she hasn't read. Fourteen years of a shared, intimate life leaves deep patterns, like old familiar ruts on a country road, and I'm not really sure how "to be" without her.

※   ※   ※

She left behind the walk-in closet. Like the bathroom, the closet was her domain for the most part, and is filled with hat boxes, small treasure chests, plastic organizing drawers, shoe racks, and a wrapping station. To me, a wrapping station was just one of those "female things" that served as a place from which to steal scissors and tape when the need arose (an action that seriously pissed her off). Now, when my four-year-old boy Finn is invited to a birthday party, I scour the wrapping station and find themed gift bags and colourful tissue paper. Thank you, Danae! And rather than leaving the scissors and tape out, I carefully put them away — I want them handy for the next time. I also find myself saving gift bags that are given to the kids, thinking, "Hey, I bet I could use them later." In the past, I couldn't chuck them into the recycling bin fast enough.

※   ※   ※

She left behind boxes of carefully-wrapped holiday decorations. It was always "clutter" in my mind, and if I was left in charge of putting it away, things got recklessly tossed into the garage (or even the trash if I could get away with it). This year, on January 5, I tenderly pull Christmas ornaments off the increasingly flammable tree, carefully wrapping each one in tissue paper and packing them away for next year. Some of the ornaments are new, gifts from friends and family at Danae's memorial service, and some carry the energy of her loving stewardship. They are my responsibility now, and I will not treat them with the same careless disregard as the ghost of my Christmases past. While I perform this task, it occurs to me that I used to consider it a "task" as well, not realizing that having her by my side, listening to music, chatting, and sharing in the holiday effort was the real Christmas gift.

※　※　※

She left behind her words in different forms like beautiful ghosts, ghosts who exact tears from me even when I believe my reservoir to be dry. In a stack of old letters, I find a homemade birthday card she made for me out of a map of Paris. She writes, "Happy Birthday Matt! Life with you is an adventure and I look forward to many, many more years of exploring. I love you! Yours, D." Another night, I find the courage to open up my old Yahoo email account. There are close to a hundred emails from Danae spanning the first seven years of our marriage. The messages range from everyday life details to love letters like this one she sent to me while I was commercial fishing in Alaska:

"My love, I miss you. I want to cuddle in your arms, kiss your sweet lips, hear your melodic voice in my ears. I want to talk about life and the thrills and woes that drop into my head and swim about at night. I want to roll over in the morning and put my arms around you and feel the warmth of your body heating me up...devouring me. Most of all, I want to see you, just look into your blue, daisy eyes, clasp your hand in mine and walk along the water...Roy running ahead and then turning to see if we are still heading in the same direction. You are my love forever and for always...enjoy the fish and tundra. Yours, Danae."

※ ※ ※

She left behind her presence in home movies. Whereas her writing is mystical and sentimental, the Danae caught on tape is usually laughing and telling stories that bubble over with valley-girl cheer. Arya likes one in particular and asks to see it regularly. It's a video taken at a family vacation, a clip I filmed without Danae's knowledge. She's telling my mom about her and my dad's experience killing time at a local karaoke bar. She's wearing a funny tie-dyed shirt and her hair, streaked with summer reds, is long. Voice teetering on laughter, she says, "This guy is older, wearing glasses, and is — I don't know — maybe sixty. And he gets up on the stage and is singing this song like, 'I stroke it to the east, I stroke it to the west, I stroke it to the girl, I like the best,' and he's dancing all sexy, like doing all this kind of stuff." At this point in the movie, Danae jumps up and starts gyrating her hips in imitation. "I mean it was sooo hard for us not to laugh! And after the guy finished, the DJ's like, 'I don't know about east and west, but I got north and south down!'" As Danae and my mom crack up on the video, Arya laughs loudly too, her eyes glued to the computer screen, her little mouth forming smiles. She doesn't understand a thing from the video, but she likes seeing mommy, likes hearing mommy laugh. It tears my soul in half, but when she says, "Again!" I start it over.

※ ※ ※

War journalist and filmmaker Sebastian Junger writes that for soldiers who have seen action, seen death, "It's coming home that's actually the trauma." They return to a place that no longer exists, to a world that moves forward without them. I am not a soldier and have heard arguments against the war analogy for cancer. But, war seems to be the only fitting analogy for the violence cancer inflicted upon our lives. I have seen incredible suffering, shrieking in pain, puking blood, lying naked on the floor in shit and urine after she fell on the way to the bathroom. I have seen maggots crawl out of her nostril after feasting on rotting tissue, the humiliation and horror unbearable for her. I have watched dreams wither and fear spread like a virus. I have lived with the threat of death on a daily basis for prolonged periods of time. I watched the love of my life die on a hospital bed, blood trickling out of her eyes, her swollen, unmoving hand lifeless in mine. And, like some soldiers, I know what it means to find that home no longer exists, at least not in the way it did.

※　※　※

So, the kids and I rebuild, salvaging what we can and scavenging the rest. And some days I see that she's left behind immense love and two thriving children. Other days, I see that she's left behind a deeply wounded man with one foot in this life and one forever on the other side.

Untethered

Kerri Power

It's like going to war. And coming back and sitting at the kitchen table, and not being able to say anything to anybody that becomes recognizable to them. And the embarrassed silence that ensues is not that welcome.

— Stephen Jenkinson

My body feels unaccountably soft — my face, flesh, hair, even my bones are softening from within. It is the softness of decay, the slow elegance of autumn leaves turned to powder. Perhaps my fear has softened too, because I feel only a tender curiosity towards this sweet, mysterious decomposition. Is this what a decaying body feels like?

It's the second day after my first chemotherapy treatment. I lie in a lawn chair on the back patio, screened by thick hedges, alone except for the apple tree my husband planted thirty years ago when his children were small, and a density of suburban birds. A cardinal holds daily concerts on the telephone wire over my head; chickadees inspect every crevice of the deck for moths — even the goldfinches and catbirds come close enough that their proximity feels slightly off balance. The giant ash trees where many of our southern Ontario birds once lived have fallen in recent years to the emerald ash borer, forcing the birds to descend to our level. The beetles themselves are living jewels — I've found loose metallic clusters congregating on the cedars, apparently mating. The beauty of destruction.

Throughout my bones and tissues, molecules of three different chemotherapy drugs are destroying any fast-growing cells, just as the beetles destroy the inner bark of the growing ash trees. Hopefully, any stray cancer cells that evaded the surgeon's knife will be among those they destroy. No one knows for sure.

One thing is certain: the drugs, and everything that came before, have dissolved something — some veil of self that hangs between me and the world in normal consciousness — and everything streams in unfiltered. The backyard is a joyous riot of light and life. The apple tree with its leaf rot is almost too vivid for my eyes in the midday sun. Crumbled, mossy patio stones... light off cedar needles... brilliant.

Does anyone realize how crazily alive the world is?

※　※　※

That was almost three years ago. And while the brilliance of the world has dimmed, much remains. An encounter with the ending of your days is like a visit to the land of Oz: you tumble and spin till you lose all perspective, eventually finding yourself upended into a world you never knew existed, in dizzying technicolor. It's a world where dying is real, complete with statistics, where joy and grief dwell together in your heart, and where loving life means loving all of it, including its ending.

In this world, you see beauty and humour all around you. A quote from my pathology report reads like poetry:

Vesicular nuclei,
  often with prominent nucleoli,

exhibiting marked variation in size
and shape, occasionally with very large
and bizarre forms.

The "bizarre" pleases me — a touch of human awe in an otherwise passionless account of whether I might live or die. I picture the variant cells as Dr. Seuss characters — some with gangly giraffe bodies, others stubby like tennis balls — running amuck with their prominent nucleoli balanced on poles, like spinning plates.

But I am deep in Oz territory here, and I try to orient myself, to grasp the boon at the end of this road and bring it back with me to my normal life. Though I have survived, I live now with a daily, visceral knowledge of the reality of my dying that I couldn't have imagined before. This includes deep joy, and deep grief. It also means I feel much less afraid of dying than I used to.

A gift, surely. But a challenge too. The things that used to matter don't as much. The goals that used to motivate me ring hollow. I struggle to find a way forward. I've become untethered from my old world. Where am I? And where do I go now?

The truth is that to know where I am, I need to understand how I got here. When I look back, I realize that my first day in Oz was June 8, 2015.

My surgeon is young with Lady Godiva hair and earthy green eyes — not the jade of new life, but the mossy hue of forest pools, of things that live and grow in darkness. An unsettling colour. Under the sterile glare of the examining room, she pulls my gown aside and presses her fingertips along the length of the scar that runs from midline of my chest to just under the right armpit. On the left side, my remaining breast, an oddity now in its newly un-twinned state, hangs pale and uninvolved. The good twin.

With a last prod, she lowers her hand. "Beautiful," she says under her breath, her eyes still on her workmanship. It's one of those otherworldly compliments that are common in the land of Oz. Others will come later, such as when we ask my oncologist whether I should have a "port" installed for the duration of my treatments, to give the nurses easier access to my veins. "I don't' think you'll need it," he says, glancing at my thin arms. "You have beautiful veins." He means that my prominent veins, like mountain ridges on a globe, offer an easy target.

But today it's my scar that is beautiful. My husband shifts on the plastic chair as we wait for the real pronouncement. We're here to discuss the latest update on what type of cancer I have, and how bad it is.

A cancer diagnosis doesn't happen all at once; rather it's a slow-motion event, unfolding in a series of painfully cranked-out verdicts delivered by diagnostic machine and unseen inter-preters. It's like entering into a mystery — ritualized, boring, terrifying. But in the end, inarguable.

For me, it went something like this:

> You positively do not have cancer.
> Relax.
> Those are just cysts. Normal for women
> your age.
> Try evening primrose oil for the pain
> > > pain
> > pain
> > pain
> Actually, something looks off here.
> We can't quite rule out cancer.
> The biopsy is negative
>
> but
> we want to be positive.
> So we'll check again
> > again
> (again)

Hmm.
We were all quite puzzled.

Yes it is indeed a true cancer (like true love?)
You have the invasive type of cancer.
You have the type of cancer we call triple positive.
This is not a positive thing

but
your ten-year survival rate is not
        too bad.

On this, our first post-surgery appointment, my surgeon tells us that the five lymph nodes she removed along with my tumour-riddled breast tested negative for cancer. This may mean that I don't have cancer elsewhere in my body. Or it may not. No one can say with certainty. I see this in the faces of the doctors: deflated arrogance — youthful confidence worn away by time, and failure.

I've been handling this well, I think. My years as a science writer for the government have provided my main coping strategy: research the hell out of everything. Track down survival statistics for every type of cancer, question the efficacy of every chemo drug, find cutting-edge doctors with different opinions. I've spoken with an integrative cancer centre in the US where I can get personalized care; I've found a pharmacologist who advises me on which blood tests to demand, to ensure that my particular metabolism can process the drugs they want to give me. I'm impressed with my own initiative.

From medical file glimpsed in chemo unit:
Patient seems to be having trouble accepting diagnosis.

I was still in coping mode then. Like a diagnosis, coming un-tethered is a slow process, like pulling the stitches from a hem. But there is a moment when the last stitch falls.

If I were to pinpoint that moment, it wouldn't be during the weeks of ultrasounds, MRIs, biopsies, false negatives, retest-ing, or even the final diagnosis itself. It would be a phone call I received on July 7, 2015 — six weeks after surgery.

My oncologist, an elegant man of late middle years, has a per-sonal charm that is well calibrated to soothe the fears of his female patients (several women I met raved when they heard I was seeing him). The treatment he advises for me will last almost a year: six rounds of chemotherapy and eighteen rounds of a drug called Herceptin, to treat a mutation called HER2. Because I have a movement disorder called dystonia (the delightful term for this is "comorbidity"), I will receive one of the less harsh chemotherapies, so as not to worsen my condition. As he explains all this, he sprinkles his medical opinions with the language of love. "And if you decide not to do chemotherapy, I'll still love you and take care of you," he assures me.

Honestly, the man could talk a woman into anything.

His charm is in full force on the July day when he calls with a cheery update — my new pathology results are in. Up to now, I have bargained myself onto shaky ground: I don't have the absolute worst type of cancer, it doesn't seem to have spread, and my chance of recurrence is between seventeen and thirty per cent, which will improve with treatment. I am handling things.

I'm on the back patio when I take his call. The latest results confirm the original diagnosis of triple-positive cancer, he says. I start to ask a question: "So — "

He interrupts. "I'm sorry! I was reading the first page. Ah, it looks like your final result was actually negative for the HER2 mutation."

That's one positive turned into a negative. "Oh," I say. "And what about the estrogen and progesterone?"

I hear pages flipping. "Those biomarkers are negative as well."

A long pause. This is a complete reversal of my "triple-positive" diagnosis. A different type of cancer altogether. "You mean — I'm triple negative?"

"It looks that way."

He launches into an explanation of why I should still take Herceptin, even with these results. My thoughts reel. Why is he talking about Herceptin? What does this mean? Triple negative means one thing — this is a much worse type of cancer than we thought.

"This may change things," he says finally, then hangs up. I won't see him for more than a week.

A friend in my support group — a petite mother of two from Guadalajara — is triple negative, and she has told me what that means. An aggressive cancer with a high risk of recurrence, and no treatment options except the toughest of chemotherapies. "We're going to give you the Cadillac treatment," her oncologist said when her gave her the news. That meant eight rounds of chemo, so toxic she had to be hospitalized for most of them. Fingernails blackened and falling off. The skin on her hands darkened like a bruise. Stabbing nerve pain in her fingers, so bad that she would stand in the shower and let the water run over her, unable to wash or even touch the faucet.

Within the space of a phone call, I go from a reasonably good prognosis to what sounds like a bad one. A very bad one.

I stumble from the backyard into the kitchen and put the phone back in the charger. I try to write some notes on a pad. Trip-le neg-a-tive. Trip…neg…the counter gleams and rears. For three months I've been hanging over a cliff, taking a long hard look at the possibility of my dying. Coping, but stretched so far, all I needed was a nudge. Three months of handling things.

But not this. I c a n
                   n
                    o
                     t
                      h
                     a n
                      d
                      l
                      e
                      t
                      h
                      i
                      s
                      . .
                    . .
                    .

What happens when you take that final step beyond your capacity to cope, and the illusion of control finally falls away? Fear tips over into something else. There is a moment when I can no longer see myself — when I was forced through the narrowest of doorways and passed beyond my own view to a place where grief and love and pain and joy coexist, where everything, even my own death, is okay. I struggle to describe it.

But it has changed everything.

In the years since, I've searched for ways to live out of that moment and bring this new understanding into my "post-cancer" life. I've sought guides — people who have walked this way before, who can help me understand the rules of this new world.

Stephen Jenkinson is one of those guides. His book *Die Wise* is a manifesto for a "wisdom" approach to the end of life, one that acknowledges grief and dying as sacred parts of our living. It's his response to twenty years of working in palliative care with dying people and their families — what he calls "the death trade."

In *Die Wise*, Jenkinson marvels that in our entitled Western culture, we wake up every day "expecting to live." We see it as our right — unassailable, proper, and natural:

> *I have seen 'waking up expecting to live' every day on the job, and I've seen what it does for us. I have seen that there is a diminished ability to suffer. There is little instinct or capacity for grieving. There is a headlong flight away from discomfort, hardship, dying .... In a culture that wakes up every day demanding to live, dying is a failure, at least temporarily, of the way that culture lives.*

When I first began to share the news of my diagnosis, kind people with good intentions told me stories about their friends and relatives who had "beaten" cancer. Who hadn't failed by dying. The wife of a church friend cornered me one afternoon in her living room and handed me a copy of a cartoon she got from a friend, an "amazing woman who has had cancer seven times." The cartoon shows a pelican swallowing a frog. The frog's head is halfway down the pelican's throat, but its arms are still free and wrapped around the bird's neck. The caption reads "Never Give Up."

It's a lonely experience, to grieve the possibility of your dying in a culture like this. We prefer to think that life always finds a way.

The BBC series *Planet Earth* is a good way to picture this. I had watched the series a couple of years before the cancer diagnosis. As a survey of the natural world, it's breathtaking, but what struck me most was the unstoppable force of life on Earth — penguins in Antarctica; snow lions in the Himalayas; blind sea creatures in the blackest depths of the ocean. No matter how hostile the conditions, life was there, adapting and persisting, finding a path.

It was an image I returned to during treatment, as I sought understanding from the science of cancer. In his book, *Foods That Fight Cancer*, Canadian biochemist Dr. Richard Béliveau explains, from an evolutionary perspective, why cancerous cells behave the way they do. He writes: "As in any traditional psychological analysis, the answers are to be found in the cell's infancy."

Béliveau speaks of cancer with the respect one accords a formidable enemy. The origin of cancer, he explains, is found in the origin of life itself — the first cell. Since its emergence more than three billion years ago, the primitive cell has faced bombardment with uv rays, shifts in oxygen levels, and many other changes in the environment. To survive, the cell has continuously modified its genes — or mutated — creating new proteins that help it to face new challenges. "This ability that cells have to mutate their genes is thus an essential characteristic of life, without which we would not exist," Béliveau writes.

About 600 million years ago, cells made what Béliveau calls the "decision" to cohabit and form multicellular organisms. This meant that the survival instincts of individual cells had to be repressed in favour of the larger organism. But the balance is a fragile one, and when a cell is under attack, such as from repeated exposure to carcinogens, it may revert to its childhood instincts: mutate in order to survive.

A cancerous cell, then, is doing what evolution does — adapting to changes in the environment. This is how life survives — clustered around geothermal vents in the depths of the ocean, frozen in glacial ice, or even thriving in radioactive waste dumps. As Béliveau writes:

> *This is what makes cancer so difficult to fight: trying to destroy these primitive cells is like trying to snuff out the very adaptation skills and strengths that*

let us evolve into what we are. It means trying to
destroy the forces at the very heart of life.

How can I despise the cancer cell? It is driven by the same force of adaptation that made me, that made all life. The force that drives cancer is the impersonal and unstoppable power of life itself to evade, evolve, survive.

This doesn't necessarily mean that I will survive.

I feel compelled now to find myself within a larger whole. I'm in awe of the power of cancer, the power of evolution itself. It is beautiful, in the way something can be beautiful and terrible at the same time.

※　※　※

A month after my final chemotherapy, during a live podcast, I have the chance to ask Stephen Jenkinson the question that leaves me adrift: once we have travelled to that country where the reality of our dying resides, and tasted the bitterness of grief, and joy, how do we return? What happens when we find ourselves back at the door of the farm in Kansas, bruised and disheveled but still alive? When the world is black and white again, but we are not?

Stephen's answer is simple yet inescapable. "The mistake," he says, "is thinking we can return to our 'normal life'."

"Your normal life — that is, the normal life as an idea — is one of the first casualties of your encounter with a terminal disease. Your normal life ain't there anymore, and it ain't coming back.... That makes you a stranger amongst people you share DNA with.... And that's the grief I'm talking about. That nothing survived your encounter with the ending of your days. And apparently it's in the natural order of things that it not do so."

※　※　※

It's a sunny Friday in August. In the front garden, the last of the bleeding hearts release their petals to the soil; the black-eyed Susans watch and sway in silence.

Someone has brought me a quilt — because I'm a cancer patient. A woman whose face I will never see, the wife of an acquaintance, asked her husband to drop it at our door. It's twenty-three degrees celsius out, and I'm in shorts and a tank top as I unfold the quilt. It's handmade, lightweight with alternating squares of sky blue and rusty autumn red, bordered by a dark floral pattern. It's lovely. Yet it leaves me confused, and a little sad. I want to be grateful for this gesture of kindness from a stranger, yet it fails so utterly to meet my true human need, which is for people to put aside their fear and face me — face the possibility of my death, and by extension, their own. Walk the path with me, at least as far as you are able. Share my grief, and let it transform your heart.

I fold up the quilt and put it away.

Only recently, when cleaning out the closet, did I notice the bible quote stitched into the quilt's white cotton backing:

> *Be strong and of good courage, do not be*
> *afraid, nor dismayed, for the Lord your*
> *God is with you wherever you go.*
> — Joshua 1:9

There is another guide on my journey. Dr. James Finley is a former Trappist monk and spiritual teacher. He speaks often of the god encountered by the Christian mystics, a god who "protects me from nothing, but sustains me in everything." I wonder if this is what the bible quote refers to — not the god of answered prayers, but the ocean that sustains our very being.

When the bottom drops out, and there is absolutely nothing there to catch you — no belief, no bargaining, no idea of God, even (God forbid) no hope — in that moment, only then, in the very absence of grounding, does something change. Something dissolves into that greater ocean. Our death grip on life — our "expecting to live" — exhales in a sigh big enough to envelope the whole world. The emptiness opens out into something infinite, which I can feel, thought not see. It's very different from resignation. The only word is trust.

That stupid frog relaxes its grip.

The Christian path that Finley teaches is one of letting go. But I didn't choose to let go — I was forced into the crucible of fear, and nothing survived the trip except acceptance. I learned the end of my capacity. And it was freedom.

The encounter with death is a gift, and perhaps an invitation — to extend a hand to others, to invite them, if they are willing, to walk the path with us, at least for a while, till we must walk it alone. To point out the scenery — it's more beautiful than you think. As beautiful as a healed scar, or a grieving heart.

How do I live now? The question pulses through my days. To be untethered, one foot on the dock, the other on the drifting boat, ready to jump. And fear almost gone. And life too beautiful to bear, and yet beloved beyond words. I only know that what has been untethered can't be restored. And it's in the natural order of things that it not be.

WORKS CITED

Béliveau, Richard. *Foods that Fight Cancer: Preventing Cancer Through Diet*. McClelland & Stewart, 2006.

Jenkinson, Stephen. *Die Wise: A Manifesto for Sanity and Soul*. North Atlantic Books, 2015.

Patten, Terry, host. "Stephen Jenkinson — Death Phobia and Grief Illiteracy: How They Distance Us from One Another, Our Planet, and Our World Crisis." *Beyond Awakening* podcast, 10 January 2016. www.beyondawakeningseries. com/archive/

After Survival

Amanda Earl

like a highway over hills eight inches of stitches &
staples of bifurcated flesh torn apart by almost death I
can still see the reaper the hood over its eyes I am
stretched out on the narrow metal table hands in
restraints as its claws come down

— Amanda Earl, *Beast Body Epic**

BACKGROUND

In November, 2009, at forty-six, I became deathly ill for no reason. I had pneumonia; I was intubated and placed in the Intensive Care Unit of the Ottawa General Hospital. My pneumonia was cured, but I continued to deteriorate. The doctors told my husband I could either die in the ICU or on an operating table during exploratory surgery. They gave me no chance for survival. Thankfully, he chose the surgery and I am here today. I had full body sepsis and a toxic megacolon that had to be removed. For fourteen months I had an ileostomy bag until reattachment surgery in 2011.

While I wasn't in a coma, the drugs I had been given: Versed, Morphine and Dilaudid, coupled with ICU psychosis, resulted in a loss of short term memory so that I was unaware of what was happening to me. I was in the throes of delusion and paranoia. Medical staff appeared in my delusions as crack addicts, sexual predators, and power-hungry exploiters. I believed they were all out to get me. They tied me to hospital furniture and left me stranded. They belittled me and made fun of me.

One of the most horrifying delusions involved a shadow I sensed from my basement room where I lay in a hospital bed unable to move or escape. I heard the creaking of the stairs as the creature descended. Between my bed and the threshold was a veil. The creature's hand reached out. I wasn't sure whether I should take it or not. The creature said the word, "silence." I did not take its hand. It was a frightening experience. Could this have been Death, coming to take me to the Underworld?

Another ghost had a New York accent and sounded like an old woman. Later when I heard the hospital's heating system, I recognized her moan. My world was a disturbing mix of real and delusion. And it was never ending. I had no sense of time passing. I was caught in a repeated, disoriented loop of nightmares. I can still sometimes feel the presence of these ghosts.

> in one version of the story Persephone is lured away from home in another she goes willingly was I tired I felt anxious had I made plans to pack to run away my first delusion where I sat on a bus bound for Toronto did I change my name to black & white leech the colour from my stories taste the bland of my own volition put unsalted crackers in my mouth to break the bones of my own longing
>
> — *Beast Body Epic*

The nurses told my husband to surround me with familiar items in the ICU. They asked for my regular shampoo. In every delusion, the green Fructis bottle appeared. I was always in a hospital gown with no other clothing, barefoot and without possessions. In many of the delusions, I couldn't move and asked people to help me, but everyone laughed at me. No one did a thing to help.

I was in the ICU for about ten days or so then moved to the general ward on the seventh floor where I recovered slowly with the help of physio and occupational therapists, dietitians, my surgeon and his staff, and my husband.

I was so disoriented that I wasn't sure for a while what was real and what was a delusion. I figured out that when there were two sets of hands on the clock on the wall facing my hospital bed, and one set was going backwards, I was back in the scary nightmare world. Once I could consciously realize this, I could get back to reality.

> *bloody paw of cartoon rabbit I hung there*
> *no shotguns fired just wild-eyed girl trapped in snare*
> *of nightmare open wound bloody gauze anaesthesia*
> *scalpels catheters oxygen antibiotics saline bags moni-*
> *tors bedpans the murmur of innumerable doctors*
> — *Beast Body Epic*

I still don't know whether the cruel treatment I received from the orderlies who took me down to the basement for X-rays was real or a delusion. I find it unsettling to have been so confused by what was real and what wasn't. I have a profound sense of empathy and sadness for all who experience psychotic break-downs all their lives.

I had to hear about everything that happened to me from my husband. I had no idea. Somehow I knew about the ileostomy bag, but otherwise, I was confused. At one point I noticed dressings over my right breast and on the side of my chest. My husband informed me that my lung had collapsed in icu and they'd put in a chest tube. A major health issue normally, this was something that was incidental in my situation because my health was so precarious. I have the sense even now that I am not in control of what happens to me.

> *embalming is the practice of ancient Egyptians I*
> *was stuffed with gauze rag dolled kept on a slab for*
> *later autopsy a renovation project insulated with*
> *formaldehyde I'm toxic now will bite back at you with*
> *mean words because what the fuck do I care*
> — *Beast Body Epic*

When I went back for my reattachment surgery I was in the hospital for only a few days, but the surgery was another long procedure due to adhesions from the previous surgery. Residents came to see me one afternoon on the ward. They were young and inexperienced. The Ottawa General is a teaching hospital. They removed my dressings to take a look at my open stoma wound. It had been packed with gauze. They did their examination and left the room quickly, leaving my wound open and me unable to move for fear of causing blood loss.

I have never felt so vulnerable in my life. I pressed the call button and eventually a nurse came. She redressed the wound and called one of the residents back to apologize. The resident felt terrible. I am pretty sure she will never make that mistake again and for that I was relieved, but it was such a scary moment for me. My heart goes out to those who are vulnerable. It is a terrible feeling to be helpless.

> *the nurse pulled the bloody gauze out of me & kept*
> *pulling I was the hat with the long trail of colourful*
> *scarves but this one was only red & it stung its string*

of scarlet bell rings making me squirm in pain
— *Beast Body Epic*

TODAY

It has been eight years since my near death. I am in peri-menopause. I am outspoken and emotional. Some of this has to do with my hormonal state, but I can't deny that my strong sense of justice, not wanting to waste time and my heated emotions also come from the knowledge of how short life is, from a sense of urgency. Some people compliment me on my vivacity, while others are wary of my intensity. I don't want anything to do with poseurs, ass kissers, or those who don't have integrity.

I am grateful to be alive. I don't waste time on bullshit and I'm impatient when it comes to dealing with bureaucracy, the cruel, and the inauthentic. Sometimes my reactions are sharper than I intend. I've had to apologize numerous times when I've hurt or confused people with this sharpness. I can sometimes have a short fuse or be triggered by things I didn't realize had anything to do with my health crisis. Or I can be so grateful to be alive that the sight of the first crocus or cherry blossoms in the spring causes me burst into tears.

I know for a fact that at any moment life is taken away, just like that, without reason. My relationship with my husband, which has always been strong, is now ferociously strong. He saved my life. He sat by my bedside in the ICU and had to deal with the inevitability of my death, as the doctors told him. Yet he didn't give up hope. Nurses told my husband that some patients' partners do not visit them in the ICU. There have even been instances of divorce. But he never wavered.

I have been polyamorous for years, but now I'm especially open to love and desire. I want to give as much love as I can and in the process, I've been lucky to have enjoyed numerous loving relationships, whether they last for a long time or just for a moment. This openness leads to criticism and mockery from others, but I know now that there is no point in following convention or succumbing to societal pressure to conform to rules that don't work for me. I am a rule-breaker par excellence now. I question social dictates and mores. I speak against convention more easily than I ever did before my health crisis and I was pretty candid before.

I haven't seen a psychologist but I believe that I have some aspects of PTSD. I still grit my teeth and wake up curled in a ball. My husband says I sometimes scream in the night. The teeth gritting probably has to do with the intubation tube I had in ICU. Apparently I bit down on the tube to try to remove it. The screams are probably still reverberations from the delusions.

> *I heard the jangle of chain it pulled me down I was transfixed turned to stone could not escape the chasm that had opened up for how long I did not exist did not resist the pull until metal taste in my tongue waked by the metal taste of blood on my tongue & the backwards clock on the hospital wall*
>
> — *Beast Body Epic*

I am extremely claustrophobic now. I was a little bit before, but the condition has become debilitating and terrifying. In ICU, they had to restrain me so I wouldn't remove the intubation tube or pull out all the lines attached to my body. I can't lock the door in a tiny bathroom because I have panic attacks and can't remember how to open it. Elevators are scary but I live on the nineteenth floor so I have to face my fear daily. I haven't flown since long before my health crisis and I'm not sure that I'd be able to. Sometimes I wake up gasping for breath.

I have a terrible fear of falling. Recently I was doing some physiotherapy for issues with my foot. Some of the exercises required me to try to balance on a plank with a ball beneath. My hands were sweaty and I clung to a nearby vertical beam. The sweat was pouring off me and I trembled. I know this made no sense to my physiotherapist and I didn't know how to explain. To this day I have an irrational fear that a fall will cause my scars to open up and what's left of my guts will spill out.

While I was recuperating, I walked our apartment hallway daily, first only our floor, then up and down the stairs over each floor as my strength grew. At first I could barely walk, I was very weak. I had a feeling as if the ground wasn't solid at all, as if I would fall through at any moment. I always feel precarious now. I always have a sense of no longer being on solid ground. I tend to avoid experiences that increase this precarious feeling.

Even standing in the shower required effort. For the first while I had a shower chair because I couldn't even stand long enough to take a shower. My husband had to do everything for me. He did all the chores, went to work, and took care of me. It was hard not to feel guilty and helpless. I feel guilty for all that my husband had to suffer while I was in hospital. When I moved from the ICU to the seventh floor of the hospital and started to make sense of things again, I was confused when I saw him. He had bags under his eyes, grey hair that hadn't been there before, and he'd lost weight. This was my fault.

My stomach still gets occasional hives, extreme itchiness, and dry skin discolouration. I have to moisturize in winter a lot more than I ever did. This itchiness can drive me bats at times. I've had to learn how to focus on other things, on the nonphysical. Fortunately, I have a limitless imagination. In the hospital, especially at night, I had a lot of trouble sleeping when I was fully aware of my circumstances. I tried to find places on my body that were not in pain. I began an inventory, starting with my little toe on my right foot and moving upward. This has been my strategy for dealing with feelings of anxiety since that moment when I learned how to focus.

> *limbs needled & pinned until numb quasimodoed,*
> *cactus-hived skin itch my flesh brushed with nettles I*
> *want to drink poison to rub my flesh against a wall of*
> *spikes*

— Beast Body Epic

I get occasional blockages and have had to return to hospital twice for CT scans, once as an emergency when my vomiting and diarrhea didn't stop and there was a serious risk of dehydration. I have to eat small meals and chew my food very carefully to avoid blockages. I must avoid a few old favourites such as sunflower seeds and raw oysters. If food is bad, it is dangerous for me due to dehydration and bowel issues. I have only eight inches of colon left, my sigmoid. This also leaves me with a feeling of precariousness, a reminder that at any moment I could die or get seriously ill. I sometimes have anxiety about eating because of this.

When medical staff meet me now, they are confused. I am healthy. When they read my file or see my scans, they look at me as if I am Lazarus risen from the dead. I wasn't supposed to survive and it makes no medical sense that I did. The looks on their faces tell me all I need to know about how miraculous it is that I'm still here.

I am now afraid of death or more specifically, of oblivion. I never was before my health crisis. Aside from the delusions, there were moments where I sensed nothingness, white blanks of time where I felt I no longer existed, where I felt that the world and those close to me were going on without me. These were more frightening and sad to me than the delusions. In fact, maybe they were also delusions. I'm just realizing this now.

Sometimes I feel guilty for having survived. I'm not particularly valuable except to loved ones. I have no unique skills. I write and I publish others. When I was in hospital, it was the time of the HINI crisis. Many young people were dying. I heard about a university professor in his thirties who died in the ICU. I was in my late forties. Still relatively young, but I'd lived a good life.

I feel almost as if I am two people: the woman who survived and the one who lay dying on her ICU bed. I feel as if I abandoned her somehow. Maybe I am not even real. Maybe I am still having delusions. Maybe I never woke up. I have a sense of otherliness now that is disturbing to me and also interesting to me as a writer. Even writing this makes me shiver. I feel her presence, this ghost of myself.

Other times I feel almost evangelical in my zest for life. I have no patience for people who are leading lives that are making them unhappy. I have a hard time being around friends in bad relationships or jobs they hate. I want to shake them and tell them to get out, that life shouldn't be a trap. There's always a way out of a tough situation. Put on your own oxygen mask first, and all of that.

I want to do good in the world. I am as generous as I can afford to be with money, but if I had more, I would give a sizeable donation to the Ottawa General Hospital. I do what I can. I publish others and consider it to be a labour of love. In my own writing, I'm trying to connect with kindreds: people who don't fit in with the status quo, who speak their minds, who make art, who value connections with others over material goods. I am defiant as hell. I will fight to stay alive. I will fight for those I care for. I won't put up with bullshit. I have no idea when the end is coming or how I will die. All I know is that I will. It's out of my control.

AGAINST DEATH

don't let them possess you:
the clock, the highway, the coffee pot
I am supple, feathered, ready for fight

— Beast Body Epic

*Beast Body Epic is an unpublished manuscript written a few
years after my health crisis.

Mapping Resilience

Moira MacDougall

A ten-year sojourn along the River of Malady in the County of Cancer[1] transformed me from a highly independent, competent, and competitive individual into a misshapen prowler who grew round, fierce, and tender. Navigating this tributary as caregiver and patient, I learned to move to its distinct currents and rhythm. Realizing you have lost your footing, time slows. If you relax, it won't hurt quite so bad. Maybe.

Those who survive choose to rise like Lazarus, perhaps stiff and slow, roll back the stone of patienthood, and step back into daily life, or, remain cocooned, defined by the disease, and waterproofing through every subsequent crisis. Of course, it's never either/or. Some days the body cooperates and supports your decision to rise. Some days it does not. Solitude and quiet are now my oxygen.

The choice to begin again felt much like the task of unhooking my grandmother's fully-lined drapes from the living room windows to send for dry cleaning. I worked one heavy handful at a time, methodically setting myself to repetitive steps. Some days it felt as if I was lugging a bag of saplings to replenish the radiated forest by the river, heavy with moisture and hope. I was Sisyphus and the rock trying to roll uphill. Though I never rolled over into self-pity, the one moment I wailed, *I want my life back!* a clear voice from within responded, *Then you are going to have to go and get it.*

It has been ten years and only recently has daily life has become less onerous: switched up thrice-a-week visits to the gym for a tap dance class and a plunge in the pool — something shifted. The music, a return to childhood tunes I sang with my dad at the piano and the space I once knew as home, the dance studio. The concentration required to execute a sequence of steps in time with music awakened a part of my brain that was in a deep slumber. Had never liked swimming, but suddenly it was refreshing and meditative as I built my capacity to complete lengths.

The shock and grief of losing my beloved older brother to multiple myeloma, baby sister to locally advanced breast cancer, our eighty-six-year-old father, then my beloved dog, all within eighteen months made my bit of cellular chaos seem small.

Sure as the fire-bellied toad lying limp on a leaf, appearing dead so predators will pass her by, I sat with barely a twitch of muscle. If I was still enough perhaps it would all pass over and I might remain invisible to cancer's wandering eye. In the Dominican Republic on a work furlough six weeks later, my cell phone rang — it was my doctor asking me to come in. The oldest evolutionary trick in the book hadn't worked.[2] The arc of our family story — athleticism, health, success, and independence, lay empty as the carapace of a dead beetle. My husband's Stage IV Hodgkin's lymphoma followed swiftly a year after my own illness. We were everyone's worst medical nightmare.

In the most literal sense, cancer changed the shape of my body: seven years of sitting in chemo clinics with siblings, self, and husband were evidenced in my glutes as the only kind of running I had time for was between bedsides. With a flattened chest because of a bilateral mastectomy, I could not have been happier. As a former dancer who grew up in an era of very tightly prescribed body types, my breasts had been an impediment. Their loss set me free of every kind of harness, harassment, and future mammograms. While my chest now resembles the rippled body of a Shar Pei puppy, *The New York Times* headline, "Flat and Fabulous" (October 16, 2016), buoyed my choice to avoid reconstruction and wearing prostheses. Surviving on chicken-fried rice and beer for six months during chemo grew a roundness of belly I'd never experienced, but I could not bring myself to care — it was the only food that tasted like something other than cardboard and the only beverage that quenched my thirst. Over-developed dancer's calves drooped, the weight of small bowling balls around my ankles. Chipmunk cheeks folded over themselves with every dose of steroids and my wonderfully symmetrical, bald skull shone in the fall light. I was a Buddhist's dream girl!

Cancer also kindled a ferocity that continues to burn brightly in the face of life's daily challenges — transit breakdowns, weather, cost of living, aggressive drivers — it's been difficult to know how to enter conversation concerning these daily woes without sounding like a self-righteous prig. Best I can do some days is remark to myself how grateful I am for not sitting in a leaking zodiac out on the Mediterranean. Seriously. Yes, my family suffered great sorrow, but we had access to the best care in Canada. We grieved, but there was no worry as to affording medical bills. Employers were accommodating and generous. If this reads to you as if I am minimizing circumstances, I write only to communicate the privilege we lived that afforded me a small degree of equanimity as Nature unleashed her forces.

My ferocity was forged into a custom-sized sledgehammer that I used judiciously in conversation with medical students. Wandering into the consulting room in white coats, my file in hand, behaving as if they had studied it. "I see your sister has had breast cancer. How is she?" "She died." A humble "oh" would follow, much fumbling amongst the paperwork. "And your brother I see is also ill with cancer? How is he?" "He died just before my sister."

When not needing to swing it at medical students, Ferocity stood watch. My own oncologist, not six weeks after the end of chemo, and without looking up, asked when I was scheduled for my next mammogram. I was so stunned, I played stupid, "What?" She was impatient, "Has your surgeon not scheduled a follow-up mammogram?" Leaning forward, hands ready to part my clinic gown, I asked, "And what exactly would they be scanning?" She paused, cheeks burning bright and mumbled an apology. But her need to re-establish her power overtook as she gleefully corrected the spelling error on the typed list of vitamin supplements I'd asked her to review. Her young resident offered up precisely the same question the next year. I asked her to close her file and insisted on eye contact saying, "Look at me. Seriously, look at me." "Oh, well, we are trained to always ask," she chirped. "Ridiculous," I lashed back, "that as a scientist you have forgotten to use your eyes!"

Ferocity, of course, masks an equal portion of fragility and tenderness. I cry at any prompt: the death of a child, the sighting of a standard poodle resembling my own former companion, the slaughter of elephants. Colleagues at work stop to chat, often to tell me of their family sufferings. I can't fathom the anxiety of parenthood and a sick child.

All of which whittles the paddle we use to move downriver to questions of belief and suffering. A preacher's kid gone sideways, I have landed alongside my dead brother as an agnostic-Buddhist. For Buddhists, life-death is daily: molecular degeneration and regeneration. Nature never rests. Learning how to die, a life's lesson, perhaps the lesson because it is hard work to endure a body dying and its indignities; because the instinct to cling like an oyster to moorings, enduring. Letting go is profoundly contrary to everything this culture values, and yet it is so necessary. It is a state we have only known in the arms of our mothers or lovers. If you are lucky, you practice corpse pose at the end of your yoga class.

Only astrophysicists and astronomers offered comfort as they helped me see our earth for what it is: a tiny, spinning orb in the vast darkness of the universe. Their discoveries filled me with wonder. Don McKay's poetic meditations on deep time provided solace. While this may appear to be heady space to retreat to, Cancer was busy growing me a second skin of compassion and kindness. The humanity behind what we so quickly refer to as "systems" came to the foreground — nurses, technicians, hospital porters, doctors — their dedication to care, their own defences in the face of a relentless enemy that often overpowered, and the deep weariness etched on their faces.

My sense of self opened with the kindness and generosity of the people around us as I recognized how interdependent my well-being was on institutions and networks: health care, an employer, those I had lost, and now those family and friends remaining. Flowers left on the front porch, the card in the mail, dinners delivered, the email or text — lifted my spirits. The River of Malady may have rerouted me through unexpectedly rough waters, but there was hope.

Husband and I organized a small team, fundraised, and cycled two-hundred kilometres in two days at the end of my treatment for a cancer foundation. Exhausted, he went home to bed while I partied with our team and close friends. Four days later he insisted I take him to the ER. Our family doctor out of town, we went, though with great trepidation at being laughed out of the place: of course you are tired and have back pain, you just cycled two-hundred kilometres. We were dismissed the first time. Next morning, husband insisted we go back. This time an older physician actually examined him and in ten minutes he was in line for a CT scan: "not good," the doctor murmured. Admitted that day, two weeks and eighteen diagnostics later, he was engaged with stage-four Hodgkin's lymphoma. The oncologist thought we should get a refund on our fundraising!

We had arrived at Level Five rapids in Cancer's tributary. Edges worn away, soaked to the core with fear and grief, I saw how porous I was. The only question was whether I would disintegrate: for the sixth time in as many years, I understood I had no control. His only family, I called my boss to delay my return to work. The silence at the other end of the line was deafening — he didn't know what to say. Who would?

Back to being caregiver — and a better one for having been sick. Even better for the time I'd spent with my baby sister. What she taught me was timeless and essential. She was a "blocker" when it came to information about her disease; I am her opposite, a "pursuer." Both strategies are effective in allowing one to have some sense of control. Knowing wasn't helping her and in my role as supporter, I was only undermining her confidence by believing I knew better — the plight of every older sister. Recognizing my husband as another "blocker" and having learned to support, mutual trust was less challenging.

There is hierarchy in the cancer world: better stage-four Hodgkin's than stage-one lung cancer. Hodgkin's they can cure, even late stage, but they may kill you in the process. Level-six rapids — didn't know they existed. During his first chemo treatment, husband suffered bleomycin pulmonary toxicity and landed in the ICU. For five days, a parade of specialists from three hospitals were bedside. Home alone at night, the expanse of our bed was Arctic tundra: dark, vast, and cold. Widowhood raised her icy head and winked: the floor fell out from under me.

A lifelong girlfriend who had devoted herself to palliative care and who had accompanied me to chemo, reached out to her favourite colleague. The cancer psychiatrist poked his head around the curtain of my husband's bed. He is owed a badge of honour for this one intervention: he saw the suffering and sat down with us, unhurried.

Husband survived and we began the slow paddle toward daily life. During our time at home together, I decided if I couldn't dictate Nature's capricious whims or control the cellular chaos of our bodies, I could organize our closets. Coping strategies abound! By the time we are eight or nine years of age, we have figured out that by being sweet, the class clown, the bully, or the whiner, adults respond, and a negative response is better than no response. Experiencing serious illness as adults puts these instinctual strategies into full deployment as we respond to the loss of control over our health. For those of us who learned we had to downplay need, up-play our competence and independence so as to not burden parents already overwhelmed, the best strategy a health care team can respond with is to let the patient take the lead.[3]

Radiation specialist began our relationship with a very simple query: "what do you understand about your cancer?" Then he shut up and listened. Given the average physician can only maintain silence for eighteen seconds,[4] I was floored by the elegance in his clinical skill: it opened the door for both of us to be people who knew things. As he listened, he calibrated the information he shared with me. Genuine partnership with a medical professional was possible.

As a published poet and poetry editor for a Canadian literary journal, my chief strategy for coping with the river I was paddling was to write. I knew the value of scribbling, hoping good words might act as a fulcrum and gently lift the boulder of shock off my chest so I could breathe and grieve.

Late night calls from my brother and emergency runs to the hospital with my sister had put my adrenals and startle reflex on full alert. I didn't know how to shut down. Sleep was a two-hour cycle. Drugs offered four hours and a hangover. I became a full-fledged insomniac over these years, prowling at night, shining a light on every memory, moment, and regret.

Ten years later and a manuscript, *Vanishing Acts*, is with a publisher.[5] I have grown less round, curly hair is now straight. Ferocity's sledgehammer sits quietly by my side, ready. Clarity about what is important is unfailing. Quiet weekends at home are our new normal. My dear mom, now eighty-nine, has disappeared into the fog of dementia. I prowl less. Waking after a solid eight-hour sleep, feel I have won the lottery. The joy is visceral and immense. Lazarus accomplished this in three days. Me? With a lot of help, in 3,295 days, but who's counting?

[1] Christopher Hitchens' phrase from *Mortality*, 2012 (Atlantic Books)

[2] It doesn't for twenty per cent of the wee beasts who try this defense and die, because they slow their own systems too much.

[3] *Love, Fear and Health* by Robert Maunder and Jonathan Hunter, 2015 (University of Toronto Press)

[4] Beckman & Frankel, 1984 research cited in the *New York Times*, January 4, 2015, Dr. Nirmal Joshi

[5] Pedlar Press, Spring 2019

How to Make Art Out of This

Joe Average

I was randomly tested for HIV in 1984 when I was twenty-seven. A few weeks later I went for the results and my doctor said, "You're HIV positive." And I said, "Oh. Okay. What does that mean? How long do I have?" Because, at that point, it was a death sentence. And he said, "You've got the virus, and we don't know exactly when it's going to kick in. You could have six weeks. You could have six months. You could have a year. You could — I don't know — live forever." And I said, "Okay, I'll take that last one."

For three years, I felt fine. I wasn't on any medication, because my viral load was still good. My helper cells were all good. I was feeling pretty cocky about myself. But I had the virus. And all of a sudden I lost a bunch of weight, got a few opportunistic infections. I had thrush, which is a real sign that your helper cells are low and your immune system isn't working. My numbers were all crashing and they put me on the only thing they had at the time, which was AZT plus a wide-spectrum antibiotic.

My doctor said, "I'm not going to lie. Things are not looking great. The AZT isn't doing much. You've probably got six months."

There was that "six months" thing again. At the time I was unemployed, and collecting unemployment cheques, which is demeaning on its own. So, I thought to myself, "Okay, Joe Average. If you've only got six months to live, do you really want to spend your last six months standing in an unemployment line? You have to change all this, so that you have a reason to live."

Now, my art, up to that point, was just something I had fun with. I never in my wildest thoughts considered making a career out of it, because, I had some self-esteem issues. And seriously, all I did was cartoony things. But I thought, "Okay, challenge yourself to see if you can live off this art."

I didn't have any money. My boyfriend, who was an elementary school teacher, would bring home boxes of coloured chalkboard chalk for me, and I bought some charcoal. I was making little charcoal and pastel drawings and tacking them on the walls of my apartment, and having little shows.

And I didn't die! Six months went by, and I was still kicking. I knew a lot of people in the gay community that were HIV positive, and who let that dictate everything in their lives. And they were dying. And I thought, "If I keep telling my brain it's HIV positive, it's going to believe me." If people wanted to know, I was very open with them. But I wasn't that "I'm Mr. HIV-Positive" guy. Cause, I didn't want my brain to have the okay to go ahead and let my body die.

We all have a survival mode in us that turns on when it's needed. I wanted to live. I mean, there's some people I know that are going, "I don't care. I don't have anybody who loves me, and I just want to die." They die. Real quick. I had to make sure that my brain was operating as positively as possible.

I still felt like a fraud. Still, to this day, I feel like a fraud. My art is really just doodles that I anthropomorphize. When I was a kid, we didn't have a TV. And in grade 3, I got invited to some classmate's birthday party. They had one of those giant console colour TVs, with Saturday morning cartoons. The colours just burnt into my retina. And ever since, I've been trying to recreate colours that look like they're coming off that goddamn console colour TV screen. To figure out how to make them go that bright.

I just kept doing that. And the response was starting to be pretty good, which I didn't understand. But it was making me money. And there I was, surviving. I had accomplished the challenge that I set out before myself, which made me feel happy and in charge.

It was years later, when I was thirty, that I got the first "Get your affairs in order." They'd put me on drugs and, in two years, I would become immune to them. Faster than they could make new ones. My doctor, Julio Montaner, got compassionate access to drugs for me, on quite a few occasions.

I'd been to so many funerals and seen what a nightmare a death can be, for loved ones and relatives. Especially the whole money part. So, with every show that I had, I would take ten or twenty percent of it and cash it, and put it in a safety deposit box, at the bank. And it was my Dying Fund, so that when I die, in my will, there's instructions that there's money set aside.

I wanted to take care of the people around me that were going to have to deal with me dying. I'd been through the survivor's guilt. I couldn't figure out why I was still alive while all my buddies, back in Toronto, were all dead. And it was like, "Well, I guess it's my turn." I'd see how brave other people were, and I'd think, "Well, be brave! You've just got to be brave. It's going to happen. Just be brave. But, make sure that everybody else is taken care of."

When I first started getting notoriety in the nineties — enough that people wanted to interview me about my art, and stuff — I was very open about the fact that I was HIV positive.

I understood that I'd become Vancouver's little darling, and there was a lot of love and respect out there for me. I thought,

"Okay. A lot of those people that love me probably don't know anybody that's HIV positive. I've got an opportunity here to ease their minds." So, I was very open about it, to the point where they started referring to me as "the HIV-positive artist." I know it's good for headlines, but I'm not really an HIV-positive artist. I don't draw things that are HIV — you know, that's not my genre of art.

But being "the HIV-positive artist" gave me some fantastic opportunities. There was a poster competition for the very first national AIDS Awareness Week. I did this image, and it got selected. And Gerda Hnatyshyn — the wife of Ramon Hnatyshyn, who was the Governor General of Canada at the time — her platform was HIV and AIDS. So she flew out from Ottawa, to unveil the poster with my image at the Vancouver Art Gallery. So, there I was, standing with Gerda Hnatyshyn. Mounties on either side of us. And I was very nervous. Photo ops, right? We were given a break, and I whispered to her, "Am I doing okay?" She put her arm around me, and said, "You're doing great." We kind of bonded, right there.

Six months later, I got this really fancy, embossed envelope in the mail — an invitation to Rideau Hall, to be one of fifty Canadians to have lunch with Princess Diana and Prince Charles. I mean — Moshe Safdie, David Suzuki...half the people were in the arts — like, famous ballet dancers — and the other half were architects and scientists and people in AIDS research.

We all went into the giant tent room, for petits fours and coffee. Gerda sat me down with Princess Diana, and I got to chat with her for ten minutes. The first thing I said was, "You must be missing your kids." And she went, "Aww." So we start talking about her kids. And she goes, "You know, I have looked at your art. And I like it a lot." She did her research on me. And it just made me feel so good.

And I got to meet Elizabeth Taylor, right after the World AIDS conference. They asked me to do the image for it, the "One

World, One Hope". There were banners of it all over the city. Shortly after that, we had done a limited edition set of prints. I got a call from Elizabeth Taylor's people, saying that she was coming into town, to promote her perfume, Black Diamonds, at Eaton's. And every stop she does on this promotional tour, she likes to do something for the AIDS community of each city. She and I both signed the prints and gave them to three different AIDS organizations in town, and they auctioned them off, which was cool.

Right at the very beginning of my notoriety in Vancouver as a popular artist, David van Berckel — the fellow who started Opus — and his wife came to my show. His wife fell in love with one of my pieces, and they bought it. A few weeks later, David and I went out for lunch. He said, "I think you're going to have longevity, with your career. I think your stuff is awesome. But, here's my advice. When you have enough money, invest in reproductions."

Back then, the reproductions were offset lithograph. An edition of three hundred of one print cost twelve grand or something. I put out a lot of money for a really slow return. But I kept on doing it, so I'd have an inventory. I got up to about eleven different prints.

And, in 2000, I stopped painting. Part of my regimen at the doctor's office was testosterone injections. The doctor said it was to keep my muscle mass, energy, and appetite up. That doctor eventually started screwing up on me. Like, he — I would ask him about something that we'd talked about previously, and he'd say, "I never said that to you." And I went, "Yes, you did." And he did that quite a few times, to the point where he said, "I think you're getting dementia." He set me up with a psychiatrist. I felt like Mia Farrow in Rosemary's Baby. And I ended up having a panic attack, and collapsed in my apartment. Didn't know what the fuck was going on. Dragged the phone off the counter.

Called an ambulance. They put me on Ativan, and said, "You just had a panic attack." So I fired that doctor.

The next doctor I got — a young, kind of hip doctor — said, "I don't agree with this four-week-on, four-week-off thing, with the testosterone. I think it's too hard on your body. So I think we'll give you a lower dosage, one a week. Just keep it going." So, that was going on for eight or nine years, and during that time, I had maybe five or six unexplainable medical weirdnesses and no one had a clue why they were happening to me.

I was getting really frustrated. These were things that were screwing up my life. And it went against everything I've heard: "Do not diagnose yourself on Google." But I went and tried to find some information on hormones, and testosterone. I found out that nobody really knows anything about hormones. I kind of gave up for a while. But I went back and finally found this one thread where this one guy was complaining about similar things he had, and he said it was definitely because of the testosterone.

So, I went to my doctor, and he said, "Ready for your shot?" And I said, "I'm not doing shots anymore." He got mad at me. He raised his voice. And I said, "I'm trying to take care of me. Nobody else seems to be caring about all these weird things."

A month later, every unexplainable thing disappeared. But, at the same time, I went through andropause. Complete male menopause. Everything that every woman I know that has gone through menopause described to me — "Ah! It's happening to me." I didn't know who I was anymore. I thought, "I don't feel like drawing those cartoony characters with big lips. It's just not in me anymore." And so, all of a sudden, I was a different person, without a Plan B.

I was kind of panicking, a bit. But, thanks to David van Berckel, I have this inventory of prints. And while I was on the testosterone, I started losing body fat. And I asked my doctor,

"What is going on? Why is my face sinking in?" And he explained, "There is a class of HIV drugs called antiretroviral drugs that you are on. Long-term use of those causes lipoatrophy. It eats your body fat up. Nothing you can do about it." I said, "What happens when there's no more body fat?" He said, "Then it starts on your muscles."

So I hired a trainer. I was with him for eight years. I went from this, like, scrawny little, cute little boy, to this — I was 150 pounds. I was ripped. Plus, I had no body fat. My trainer loved me. He could point out muscle groups on my body.

But then, when I went off the testosterone, I did not care about working out, at all. Cause I had all this aggression, too. Plus, I had kind of run out of money a year earlier, and said to my trainer, "I've got to quit. I have no more money." "He said, "We can't go there. I won't charge you from now on." So he trained me for free, for a year after that.

I was kind of a good "advertisement" for him. We had become pretty good friends. But then, after I quit the testosterone, I said, "I don't even have the urge to come down and do it." So, that was kind of weird to get through. But I'm comfortable with it now.

About five years ago, I found this guy who could build me a site I could manage, myself. And now I had a whole inventory of really good reproductions. I had most of my things photographed, so I could offer people a lot of new images. And that went pretty good, for a while. But, still, people aren't buying like they used to.

Last year I was whining to my friend Sherree about only having three thousand left in my account. She said, "Remind me again why you're not on Disability?" I said, "Well, I'm not disabled." And she said, "Joe, could you stand at a job for eight hours?" And I went, "No." "Could you sit at a job for eight hours?" "No." "Honey, you're fuckin' disabled." [Laughter] So, she got all the forms. We applied. And, a few months later – I'm on Disability. Whaaaat?

Another friend of ours said, "Has Joe applied to Wings?"

Wings is an organization that was set up by a man who was HIV-positive. He was watching his friends having to move into subsidized housing. Having to leave their homes and move into these crappy little units. And it made them a little unhappy. So, he set up a thing with the government, where they give him money that he allocates to people. They subsidize my rent.

So, I applied for that, and I only have to pay a third of what my rent is. My friend Doug said to me, "You know what this means, don't you? Dude, you're retired!" I only have to come up with 375 bucks a month for my rent. My groceries are paid for. I only have to sell one print a month to cover my rent, kind of thing.

It took me a while for my head to wrap around that. Because, as an artist, I'm hardwired to constantly be in a panic. "Where the fuck is my next cheque coming from?" I kept on thinking, "it's going to all be pulled away from me." I stressed about it for a few months. But lately I've been sleeping better. All of a sudden I don't have to worry about anything. And that is the closest I think I've gotten to happiness. So, thanks to my friend Sherree — who all my friends call my wife — I'm sitting pretty!

Last year I called up my lawyer to redo my will. Now I have an itemized list of things that I want people to have. My affairs are completely in order right now, and I'm so healthy, it's stupid. It's just a matter of organizing.

There were a lot of times, before that, where I was, like, "Okay. Take me. I don't care." I did go through a really hard period, while I was in this space.

I was on this difficult drug called T-20, which had to be injected into body fat — which I had none of — twice a day. Once in my abdomen and once in my back. With a hypodermic needle. My friend Anne came to the hospital with me when I just needed some moral support. So, we went down there, and we're sitting with Julio. And he says, "Yeah, well, we've got you a drug, Joe." And I go, "Really?!" "Yep. You're going to be the first guy to use it.

And so, I walk into this room, and there's this chair, and there's this little table, with a white towel on it, with hypodermic needles laid out. And I went, "That's not for me, is it?" And they went, "Oh, yeah. So let's test it, right now." And I was, like, seriously? Because, for me, even blood tests, I couldn't look. I would have to stare at the "Hang in there, Kitty" poster on the wall until it's done.

I was never good at needles. Ever. And, I had no body fat. Just skin. So I had to get the needle on an angle parallel with the skin, get it in, just get it under, and then slowly inject it. Sometimes it would all just come shooting out through the pores of my skin, which was so gross! I'd be sitting in my bathroom, going, "Oh, isn't this glamorous." I would do it in my abdomen, and, evenings, my friend Anne would come over and do it in my back.

The stuff was really toxic, and it hurt like shit. So, I'd be standing with my hands gripped on the counter. She'd be behind me. I'd be shaking. And she would cry, almost every time.

I would comfort her a lot, afterwards. She'd say, "I hate hurting you." And I'd say, "Honey, you're not hurting me. It's the drug that's hurting me. After two years, she got really burnt out. My friend Sherree took over from Anne.

With this drug, each injection site would swell up, for four days or so, and it would be very painful. I literally had no position I was comfortable in. I was ready to give up. I'd been in pain for so long, it was, like, I don't want to be in pain anymore. It got to the point where it was so uncomfortable, I went up to Julio, and I said, "Julio? It's been a good run, buddy..." And Julio said, "No. Noooo."

And the pill that I got — seamless switch, from the T-20 to this. My body didn't react in any way. And I've been on it for ten years. I got to get rid of all the rubbing alcohol, all the hypodermic needles that filled my cupboards. It was crazy. It's been a journey. I don't think of it as anything unusual.

For me, it's just my reality. I'm used to being the anomaly. It's frustrating sometimes. After I noticed my body fat disappearing, I got very self-conscious about my appearance. I did not go anywhere. I just became very reclusive, and kind of depressed. And I thought, "Okay, why don't we try and turn this into art?"

The Georgia Straight or somebody was doing a story on me, and they sent a photographer over — Jamie Griffiths. We'd clicked immediately, and the photo she took of me was awesome. So, I called up Jamie, and I said, "I want to document this." She was like, "Absolutely." So, maybe once a month, for a couple of years, I'd go over to her studio, first thing in the morning. We'd sit, have tea, chat, see how I was feeling, talk about what was going on. And then I would just take off all my clothes, and she would just photograph me, for a couple of hours, and document the changes, what was going on in my body.

I trusted her so much, in photographing me. And she's awesome. I love her dearly. Documenting all of this helped me through the whole thing. And the gay and lesbian film festival Out On Screen contacted Jamie — because she's a filmmaker as well — and asked her to submit something to the festival. So, she came to me, and she said, "Joe, this might be a perfect opportunity to put something together with all the work we've been doing."

Because, sometimes, she wouldn't just photograph me. I'd usually come from the gym after boxing and sparring with my trainer. I had the gloves with me, and she said, "Can I just film you, just doing that?" So, we have a lot of material: still photos, and moving images...

And some of the photos of me, I had manipulated, in Photoshop, depending on how I was feeling. We sat here for a month, put it all together, and put it in the festival, and got a really good response. The piece was about lipoatrophy.

I say in the film, *I See the Fear*, that I was at Safeway once. Safeway opens at seven. I'd be there right at seven, so there were the fewest people I could see. Did everything early. I'm kind of used to being alone. I've been alone most of my life. It's not big thing for me. But I was at the checkout once, and there was a woman and her daughter, right in front of me. The daughter looked up at me and said, "Why do you have holes in your face?" The mother looked at me, and I could see the fear in her eyes. And she kind of shushed her daughter, and whisked her out of there as quickly as possible. And I thought, "Oh my god, she was frightened of me." Because she saw something she didn't understand. She might have thought I was a junkie, or something.

Another time, I was walking down Davie Street, and I hear this "Eh! Joe Average!" — from the other side of the street. "I don't know what you're on, but you'd better get your act together soon, before you die." Them, thinking I was on crystal meth, or something like that. So, I knew that everyone was looking at me, thinking I looked frightening.

So, I just hid. A lot. You know? But this whole — it got me to the point where I decided, "I'm just going to own this. These are my battle scars. I'm going to be proud of this." That was a challenging thing for me... really challenging.

The name of the film was *I See The Fear*. That was the trick — it's, like, how do we — how do — oh! Let's make art out of this! Art makes everything better.

It's in My Head: A Resurrection Story

Jennie Chantal Duguay

There is a difference between rebirth and resurrection. With rebirth, we make a choice — to be born again. We start a new life: cleansed and whole. With resurrection, we come back from the dead, wounded and estranged, to resume the lives we left.

I wasn't reborn. I was resurrected.

❋ ❋ ❋

The room constricts. The ceiling drops. I lie on the bed and I cannot move. My eyes meet a corner of the ceiling and fixate. I leave my body. I leave the pain and the fear of what the pain is doing to me. There is no sound, temperature, or sensation: only the calm of inertia. I don't know how much time passes before I get up, wash my face, and resume the daily work of pushing against the invisible force that is slowly encompassing so much of my life.

❋ ❋ ❋

"It's in your head." The blotches of white on the MRI. My surprise. The bafflement of neurologists. Their reckoning: that maybe in a hundred years they will have answers.

For fifteen years "it's in your head" has meant dismissal and scorn. I am used to medical professionals treating me like a fraud, refusing treatment. But I am done with weeping. Instead, I wrestle to understand the physiology of this essential organ, floating like a wounded bird in the cage of my skull.

It's in my head, and yet it is my body that feels a terrible intimacy with pain.

※　※　※

My body is not my body.

I refuse this body, refuse to be in this body, refuse to accept the illness this body carries. What I refuse claims me, even as I push against it, all fists and teeth in my effort to cure.

※　※　※

The yard is covered in morning glory. It chokes everything it touches: the laurel hedge, the lilac tree, the lawn. Do you know that every time you cut a piece it comes back? It is the way of vines. I know this and yet I pull at it, desperately rip it from the bushes in handfuls, tear it from the grass. Little pieces swarm around me like bees. It is a focused madness, interrupted only when searing pain sends me weak and shaking to my bed. I promise my body I will stop. But I can't give up. I have to get all the morning glory out of the yard if anything else is ever going to grow. I fill bag after bag. No matter what I do, it comes back.

※　※　※

There was no emergency. No sudden trauma. No doctors brought me back from the brink or gave me three months to live. There was no tunnel, no bright light, not even a broken bone. Not even a bruise.

※ ※ ※

Death took its time with me. So did resurrection. There was no gasping breath. No sudden hunger. My fist did not break through the wood of my coffin to spray dirt from my grave. For three years I wrote my body into story, gave it shape and weight, my words searching for an exit to what felt like endless mourning. I remember the first year through a haze of medication, nervous breakdown, and the devotion of a person who would not leave me. I was infected with grief; illness had won. I would never recover.

In the second year, months of recounting over two decades of chronic mental and physical illness led to the realization that I had been ill nearly all my life, that my losses and griefs seemed to have no real beginning or end. Like waves slowly eroding the shore of my body, death came for me: turned my bones to sand.

Somewhere in the third year, I was resurrected.

※ ※ ※

It hurts to come back to life.

※ ※ ※

Disabling invisible chronic illness has its own logic. Its own mathematics, dictionaries, and theories. It inhabits its own dimension, a parallel world where the agreements of the twenty-four-hour day and the seven-day week only come into play for appointments, medication times, and trips to the grocery store or the pharmacy. My resurrection opened a portal to this world, where everything looks the same — my body, my scars, my hands held out before me. But when I look up I see all my little deaths cast out like constellations, every loss condensed into memory — my stories — bright, fixed, and out of focus. I spin on my axis. From here my past stretches out like a rocky shore, every memory of survival the shape of a stone, and every stone a story I must tell, eventually, or at least, a name I must speak.

※　※　※

It's in my head. Ableism. The blotches of white. Ingrained. Years of denial. The pressure of inhabiting a sick body in a world that does not tolerate chronic illness. Resurrected, I feel such tenderness for that stubborn person, so afraid of the truth of her body. I imagine my brain: not a wounded bird, but a vine — resilient and adaptable. Pushing against death.

※　※　※

For seven months, I walk every day to the park near my house to sit on the mossy roots of a big leaf maple. Some days, I imagine its trunk conforming to my body until I feel like a child, safe in the embrace of a loving ancestor. Other days, I imagine a throne, and myself a witch. I close my eyes and feel the transformation — frozen to frazil, slush to stream, vapour to cloud. There is only sound, temperature, sensation. All fall and winter I practice feeling alive in my body, practice stirring and trembling, like spring awakening under a shroud of soil and snow.

※　※　※

My body has accepted all my apologies.

※   ※   ※

When I press my lips to the soft flesh in the crook of my elbow and feel the melt of meeting my body, I am excited as a new lover. How do you like to be touched? I slide my fingers up and down my limbs, feel the hair lift, the gooseflesh bump. Resurrected, I learn my body of pain can feel pleasure: a gust of wind that picks hair up off the head and tosses it around. A breeze shivering up a pant leg. Water tickling down skin. Hands cupping the base of my skull. Touch that doesn't want, or need, anything from me. I take to wearing ankle socks. Sitting on benches in the rain, my face tilted up, reverent.

※   ※   ※

Illness is the physical place where I live. Here, rest is work and work is symptom management, and I don't have to produce to consume or to be deserving of care. People want to do things for me. My dishes, my laundry, my groceries. They like to do things for me. The modes of production that sustain me are also the skills I must learn and teach: Receive. Offer. Ask. Decline. I feel the gravity of this world pushing my body into a shape made for survival — sick, ill, disabled, crip, weak, broken — and liberating my mind from the shame and guilt I feel about how much care I need to survive. It recalibrates my days and movements into units of rest and energy, orienting me to a world where force does not create movement and movement is not necessary for change.

※   ※   ※

Ableism is why we say to ourselves, and each other: Stay strong. No pain, no gain. Mind over matter. Don't give up. It's why we see illness as something to fight until it goes away and death as preferable to disability.

I know death is not finished with me. My chronic illnesses are too unpredictable, too ravenous. But resurrection shows me how to keep living with a body I know will not be healed. I must give up — again and again — any story that binds my worth to my productivity, erases my claim to pleasure and connection, denies my right to be here — sick, disabled, and alive — my power inherent not in what I can do but in who I am.

※　※　※

Resurrection can only bring me back to life; it can't keep me alive.

※　※　※

It's in my head. I turn myself around and around, shake all my limbs. I twist and contort myself until the belief that I am unworthy drips out like dirty water from an old rag. Until words bounce into an alphabet at my feet, just letters.

※　※　※

I reach out my hand. My body reaches out too. We pick the bright blue flowers of the morning glory, rub the soft petals on our cheeks, place them on our fingers like little hats. We lie down, resurrection between us like a covenant. When the stars appear, we point at constellations and remember how we died and what illness has taken from us. Under our bodies we feel the earth, gravity grounding us into our stories of survival. The vines dominate our landscape, turning ruins into rolling hills, its leaves shaped like hearts.

An Expectant Dissembler Tours Tijuana

Rebecca Fredrickson

SKULLS AND WATER

Sometimes I miss my cozy, asbestos basement. I was there. Two minutes ago, I was there. I had just brewed the ideal espresso in my stovetop machine.

Coffee steam on my top lip. Saturday in my muddled apartment. Grounded to a tree with roots I might have said two minutes ago. But steam fogged my glasses, and when I wiped them clear I was in the wrong city. Mislaid. Emails bouncing back.

I know that I've been moved and mislaid, uprooted like a late-fall tuber, when I look out the kitchen window to a sky full of sugar and wet breath. Two minutes ago, snow and wool hats.

Local television says the San Diego fires have thankfully expired. Fires now swim like sooty ghosts in ruined backyard pools.

My new place is clean and decorated by Ikea. The maid uses Pine-Sol. She has placed a suitcase on my new bed, so I begin to unpack. I empty my belongings, singing a Van Morrison favourite about starting a new life. A holiday. Who doesn't enjoy a holiday? Kittens in a gunny sack, I guess, would not enjoy. But

I expect recovery and adventure, good treatment and sympathy. My girlfriend has sent along a hardcover journal. *Dear darling: write a masterpiece, would ya?*

Outside my window, an enormous flag waves hello. It's the first day of November and white buildings perch on a hill, like sugar skulls in the fog. Sugar skulls in the market because death is the one thing. A twenty-four-hour guard, handgun on his hip, stalks the double-glass doors of the clinic below, and, three floors up, I unpack.

In the hallway, an elevator. I ride to the main floor.

The receptionist wears high heels. She wears a balloon tied to her wrist. *Felicidades*, says the balloon.

"Your birthday?" I ask.

"Yes," she smiles. "The doctor will see you tomorrow at ten."

"Thanks." I have questions but can't formulate them. "See you then," I say. "Happy birthday." What doctor?

What fine antebellum is this? A formula. What formula? What secret cage?

My brand-new journal opens pencilled and banal, a few questions for the doctor vis-à-vis bursting internal organs and spinning, pocket-sized hatchets. Must remember to ask how these houses grow exoskeletons like the hard drop cloths over cages. Must ask the doc if I can I eat my way out of this clinic.

Did I mention my girlfriend has left me for her makeup artist? My girlfriend with very white teeth sings in an alto voice. You should really see her dance. She wears smudged eyeliner and a boyish beard. I love her like a laptop loves the rainbow underside of a compact disc. But I have a secret lover who calls nightly.

Must ask how ghostly sugar water escapes Petri dishes, slips from the cozy little beds of threatening cells, and takes shape for the Day of the Dead.

To my list of medical questions, I add a poem, inspired by a modern opera:

Mushroom Moon on Red Water

Guilty! To drown in a private,
sooty pool, immaculate lab.
My remarkable brain
floats on epoxy water. A scale full
of woodsy and paranoid. Blud! Blud! Marie!

"You're not the first and you won't be the last," says the in-house pharmacist. In the age-old rivalry between doctors and pharmacists, too little attention has been given to the category of bedside manner.

PHOTOS

Mornings, the nurses hook me up to an intravenous drip. Afternoons, I wander with a camera and my new journal. I copy things down in a poetic collage, a few catcalls and canned songs like,

hey beautiful lady from Hollywood. *¿Qué haría sin ti? Sin ti mi vida no podría existir.* Hey lady, come and look. When negativity won't pull you through. When I was in Santa Ana. When I got deported. Soon hit the harder stuff. Started out with my chest hurting. Now I don't have the strength to get up and take another shot.

My best friend, my doctor has lost my X-rays. My ears itch and ache and I wonder how many of these very friendly vendors also have ripped up driveways in them, tectonic geography, ghosties doing laps in their hearts. The usual: breaststroke and freestyle. Sooty cinderblock whirlpools.

Good news, three tumours have developed and vanished. G-tubes and tracheotomies have flown. God's hand came down and thankfully swiped away my Jamaican friend's breast. Good news, one man came in with two weeks to live. That was ten years ago and he's still on the right side of grass. Good news. You are never alone.

※　※　※

Avenida Revolución boasts twelve donkeys masquerading as zebras. They are sickly creatures, permanently ridiculous. Illness parties or gets ready to party in their beastly cells. These animals are pathetic. They are wildly tacky. Spray-painted ponies. I name all of them Tito.

"Come and see the donkey show," says Tito's master. "Oh you think that's funny, yes?" Tito's master has been standing here, on the corner of Third and Revolución, for seven hours. Seven times seventy-seven. "I've been waiting for you," he says. Camera's in focus, but I find Tito embarrassing and turn away.

From Tijuana to San Cristobal, a very young Frida Kahlo lights incense for her own altar, lights a cigarette, or smokes it unlit. She is what I've been looking for.

Dogs

Edgar is a cross-town driver and X-ray tech, and he drives me to the imaging centre, through barrios and barrios. Who is Edgar?

Edgar is a health care professional. He deals in isotopes. The ceiling in the X-ray room is splotched with water like a mis-shapen Doberman. A small dog must appear on every altar of the dead for protection. From a different angle, my Doberman could be the chunk of flesh they roast at taco stands.

Edgar wears a technician's jacket and shoots up his patient with five syringes of dye. I survey the room. On my back and wearing an airy, blue gown. A drum beats, but it's just the machine, almost relaxing me. Arms held over my head at Edgar's command,

I survey the room. The pipes and breaker boxes take me back in time to my dad's shop and his old lunch kits of wringers and bolts.

"Breath deep," says Edgar, who speaks only laboratory English. "Hold. Breath deep. Hold. Relax." Clicking and spinning, inching up my pelvis, past my pancreas, and over my lovely brain. My body feels heavy and stoned, like I have eaten a batch of something baked with butter and THC. This I convey to Edgar. Pot, body, and strange, I say. But Edgar says this is normal. *"Mi cuerpo,"* I say. *"Qué extraño. Es como si me hubiera comido una galleta con mota."*

"Es normal," says Edgar. *"No te preocupes. Es normal."*

CANDLES

Thanks for sending the blessed oil of St. Nectarios. Father Gregory has told me to anoint myself daily for seven days and then burn the oil-bearing cotton ball by candle flame. I was fascinated to learn how your kidney stones poured out of you like so much water. This is encouraging!

Please don't misread my tone. Myself, I have no faith, but the saints have so much. The oil has a very pleasing smell. I believe in the intersession of St. Nectarios. I believe his dead body has never corrupted.

CEMPASÚCHIL, LA FLOR DE LA MUERTE

Marigolds and rosaries. Four-hundred fallen petals to guide the dead. Alongside these petals, in a kiosk near the border, El Santo's wrestling mask is empty and laced tightly.

I heat up on complimentary radishes at a shiny taco stand. Radishes make my eyes water, but I freely admit to freeloading. Everything on the menu is strictly taboo. Can't order any of these deathly meats. The doctor forbids all forms of animal fat.

The doctor has lost my X-rays. He has suggested I try not to bounce up and down. The doctor has his fingers crossed. He is hopeful. He has a framed picture in which he is shaking the hand of the living. He concurs with Father Gregory re: burning the cotton ball.

A few stands down, I order tripe and avocado, planning to save it for Ignacio López Tarso.

I will honour his altar because I have just written a story about him in my new journal. Here's a rough draft:

My Real-life Macario

Tarso plays the US Open. He is greasy with sweat and obese with grease. The crowd mocks. They toss rubber chickens onto the court. Their placards accuse Tarso of pandering to North American taste. "Go ahead," the crowd chants. "Hack up another chicken for Death!"

"But he is a great actor!" I scream. Death sits next to me, sucking on oily bones. It is then that I realize I have just disagreed with God.

Is this story confusing? Yesterday, in a basement store that sells door handles, they were watching Macario on TV. I watched with them as Tarso took a machete to a roast chicken and shared a mangled half with Death. I wanted to allude to the film, but maybe I've been too obscure.

SALT AND COLOURED PAPER

Have you heard of a Type C personality? Brand-new friends have been lending me books, and these books are telling me that I'm Type C. I must learn how to say no.

Gentle Edgar scratches at my door. Edgar does not seem to

care that the nurses have attached an intravenous port to each of my breasts. These ports do not intrigue him, but they don't discourage him either. His lips are not dexterous. He is brackish and a bit nauseating.

"Now you can tell your friends you've had a Mexican boyfriend," he says.

"Where are you from?" I ask. I don't tell him I have had many from many places. Some with arms like hard candy. One with horn-rimmed glasses. One with five-hundred different neckties and a sleek wit. One in a furniture warehouse.

"Guanajuato."

"I can tell them I once had a boyfriend from Guanajuato."

"I just had to come up here and see you." I put on his light-blue technician's jacket. November is chilly, and this boyfriend is metallic and rattling like skeleton teeth.

A secret lover calls nightly. Maxim Maximytch is what I must call him. He has unearthed my location. Not another soul knows where I am hidden. Emails are ricocheting off springs and chrome in someone's rumpus room. God is playing handball with the ASCII system. Somewhere in China, they are trying to figure it out, smashing up every motherboard I've ever owned, but they only make themselves sick. I attempt calls to old friends, but the phone line crosses the border, and people step on it, make too much static. Can they not watch where they put their boots? They kick up a real racket. Have you seen that high, barbed-wire fence? What a work of sinister engineering. Maxim believes he can get me out, back to my asbestos basement.

Once, I flew to meet him in Winnipeg. I rode the escalator to arrivals, shaking. Daisies excite me. Carnations depress. Roses embarrass.

Tonight, Maxim calls my room with the touching story of stealing a mannequin. Headless and poised, she stands in his closet. "Such small round breasts," he says. "So much like yours." Maxim tastes like cucumbers and radishes. He floats in stainless steel bowls at the taco stands, and tasting him there makes me weepy.

I am not depressed because of my condition. I have always tended toward ample melancholy. I have always noticed coloured paper, and it's always made me sad.

On July 4, in demonstrations across the northern country, people rally in their bathrobes. They distribute rattling buttons. "Depressed?" the buttons ask. "It might be political."

SIPPING TEQUILA

I meet Maxim at a side-street bar. He's still sure he can get me out. We meet for drinks. We always meet for drinks. Oatmeal stout. Lager of organic summer wheat. Tequila so sweet it is best when sipped.

What do you like best about being drunk? Myself, I like dancing with Maxim in an orange kitchen. I like kissing obnoxiously at other people's parties. So drunk I can barely walk and watching snowflakes snap like a thousand falling cameras. Tiny paparazzi catching me and Maxim kissing. A row of pretty houses. Amplified footsteps and awkward mittens.

"Meet me in Montauk," he says, margarita glass on his lips. But I know he will not erase me from his lovely head, will not rub me out the way those crazy lovers erased each other in a very sad film.

"You never seem drunk," I observe. "Even when you are."

"I hate it when they put sugar on the rim."

"They've done that again?" Coloured paper, cut-out of a skeleton couple, wavers by the window. "Tell me again, darling, what does sugar taste like?" Sugar is much like water. Tasteless, more or less. Good for hummingbirds, or maybe very bad for hummingbirds. Maxim gets up and packs his belongings, his sparkling accordion and his cell phone. He puts on a wool hat.

I order more tequila, and a small girl brings me a steel bowl. I dunk my fingers. The wool hat is gone like the wind. The water in this bowl is warm. The body is warm. Remember?

The Reboot Diary

Becky Blake

Nine months after I finish the chemo that was supposed to cure me, my doctor informs me that I've relapsed. My chance of surviving Hodgkin's lymphoma has decreased from ninety percent to fifty per cent, and I need a stem cell transplant. When I don't respond, he tries to explain the transplant to me in more detail — as if it's the medical procedure I'm having trouble understanding, rather than my bad luck. "We're basically going to reboot you," he says. This analogy seems a little cold, but it allows me to ask him a terrifying question. "Is there a chance I might be completely shut down?" My doctor looks at me blankly for a moment — sustaining metaphor is not his area of specialty. Finally, he answers, "No. That shouldn't happen. The transplant procedure is pretty safe." He hands me a consent form, and I sign it.

At home, I review the pages of a spiral-bound booklet I've been given: *Preparing for an Autologous Stem Cell Transplant.* Inside is a daunting list of both space-age and medieval-sounding procedures that need to be checked off before Transplant Day: a bone marrow extraction, daily injections of biotech meds, the harvesting of my stem cells, and a surgery to insert a catheter tube that will run from a vein in my neck down to an exit point below my collarbone. The catheter scares me the most; the idea of having a portal installed between my inner and outer worlds disturbs me. During the surgery, I try to get up off the table even though I'm heavily sedated. For days after, I can barely look at the long tube hanging from my chest; it's so alien. I worry that the plastic valve on its end might pop open while I'm sleeping — that I'll wake up in a pool of blood, that I might empty out completely. As a writer, my imagination has always been an asset. As a patient, it's become a liability, a disruptive force that needs to be controlled as I try to work through the nightmarish items on my Pre-Transplant Checklist.

Three days before my stem cell harvest, I develop a high fever and have to go to the ER. At triage, the nurse asks me if I'm feeling short of breath. I answer: "Yes. But it's probably just anxiety." This innocent oversharing of my mental state sets in motion a response that will detain me for the next seventy-two hours. I have unwittingly activated Protocol Droplet, a precaution to isolate incoming patients who might have contracted a new super-flu; fever and shortness of breath are its symptoms.

At my regular cancer treatment hospital, where I am transferred by ambulance, I discover that the one good thing about being "on Droplet" is that you get a private room. Mine has an excellent view. Anyone who comes to see me is required to wear hazmat garb. Each doctor who visits agrees I shouldn't be on Droplet, but there is nothing anyone can do to deactivate the protocol; it's the weekend, and a government official has to sign off. The situation would be almost comical except I've had six-thousand dollars worth of biotech meds injected into my stomach this past week in preparation for having my stem cells harvested. This process is time-sensitive, and the injections can't be repeated. Even so, I am not allowed to leave my room on Monday morning to go downstairs for my collection appointment. Not until a Russian doctor — who I will never forget;

who I develop immediate romantic feelings for even though he is a rotund and sweaty older man — comes into my room and, breaking all North American protocol, puts the back of his hand on my forehead briefly and then tells me to just wheel myself to the elevator and go.

The questionnaire I'm given before my stem-cell collection asks: Are you seeing double? Are you feeling anxious? Are you feeling combative? Do you have diarrhea? Only four questions, but after my experience with the ER nurse, I'm nervous about giving a wrong answer. Carefully, I check off: NO / YES / NO / NO. Then the tube in my chest is hooked up to a machine. "You might not want to look at this," says the technician as the first cup of my blood whooshes out of my body and starts whipping around in the centrifuge. The process of separating and collecting my stem cells will take a few hours. "Do you want a magazine?" asks the technician. This time I opt for NO; I don't think I'll be able to read. Instead I sit wondering about how many cups of blood are inside me, and trying to distract myself with fantasies of the Russian doctor. Will I ever see him again? Spoiler: I won't.

After my release from the hospital, I go home for a few days to wait until a bed opens up in the transplant ward where I will need to spend three weeks. When I get the phone call to return, it's evening, and the main hospital entrance is closed. Outside the after-hours door, I pause. What if the reboot doesn't work? What if this breath — no, this breath, no, this one — is the last I ever take of fresh outdoor air? I stand there for a long time before I'm ready to push open the door and check in.

The next morning, I begin a regimen of extreme chemo to prepare me for Transplant Day — a square marked "Day Zero" on the calendar at the end of my bed. The purpose of this treatment is to kill off any cancer cells in my body before the transplant reboots me. My bone marrow and soft tissue are also being destroyed. After the second day, my doctor visits and says, "Those cancer cells must be in their final death throes by now." He means to sound encouraging, but the image of cancer cells dying slow, dramatic deaths is a little battle-scarred for my taste. My doctor senses he's missed the mark, but I give him a small smile to let him know it's okay. Cancer imagery is hard to get right for both doctors and patients. We all need visuals to make our invisible goals imaginable, and hopefully achievable, but nothing we use as a comparator ever seems quite right.

Post-chemo, my blood counts are dangerously low and I need a transfusion. After receiving my new blood, I'm trying to sleep when I hear a gruff, female voice coming from the right side of my stomach. It sounds like a belly gurgle, only more articulate. "I'm down here," the voice says. At the same time, my bed shifts lower as though the weight of an extra person has been added. My fingers reach toward the call button, but stop short. Earlier, I'd overheard a conversation between another patient and her doctor. They'd decided that although her body was strengthening, the treatment had left her cognition too damaged to return home. She was having delusions and would need to move into an assisted-care facility. It wasn't what she wanted — what I would ever want. I wait through the next quiet minutes and tell myself I'm fine. But then the voice comes again. "He's cheating on me, you know. With that whore of an understudy." "I'm so sorry," I whisper, medicated and uncertain. There is silence after that.

On Day Zero, the day they're calling my "new birthday," a technician with a moustache and a white lab coat enters my room pushing a trolley. I've been warned that the transplant procedure might feel anticlimactic, but the technician seems determined to make it memorable. With the showmanship of a magician, he lifts his rubber-gloved hands to the sky, then digs deep into a crate and pulls out a metal book that bears my name. Liquid nitrous rolls from the tome and scrolls out through my room, eddies around my bedside. "Is this you?" he asks. I nod, impressed. He goes out to thaw the specimen and returns with a small clear bag. Inside, the contents slosh: a cream of tomato soup. The nurse hangs the bag on an IV pole beside my bed and then attaches it to the catheter in my chest. My family watches as the soup moves down the tube to meet me. On impact, I choke: a metallic, corn taste scours the back of my throat. My whole body gags and then the cells are in me, racing. I've been told that these cells are equipped with a homing device — that they'll move through my blood until they reach the bone marrow, then settle in, and begin to create a whole new immune system for me. Stem cells are like pure potential — they can grow to be anything. It is June 14, 2013; I am rebooted as a Gemini, a twin for my other Aquarian self.

This ward is a place of stasis — a remote space station of beeping machines and patients who have fallen out of pace with regular life. Since check in, I have been attached to a mechanical pump on a pole. Together we circle the nurses' station on our mandatory "walk around the block." The mask I wear fogs up my glasses in rhythm to my breathing. In and out. The respiratory sound reminds me of snorkelling off the coast of Florida, my breath speeding up inside my mask as I contemplated shark life — another day, another fear. Past moments like this one ping on me constantly, a stream of memories interrupted only by my occasional effort to refocus my attention on future goals: to share love, to write books, to be healthy and strong, and do good in the world. What's missing from Ward 14C is the present. In this moment, almost nothing exists — nothing except the tall, thin pole pumping liquids into my body. And my breathing. In and out.

When I'm back in my bed, a bag of strong painkillers is added to my IV pole, and a nurse explains how I can increase my dose by pushing a button. Part of me hopes this might be fun — if I have to be stuck in the hospital, I might as well be high. I press the button a couple of times and start to feel sleepy. When I close my eyes, I am expecting to drift off into a pastel-coloured fog, but instead, I'm smack in the middle of a construction site, a bustling, futuristic world populated by bald, androgynous beings. "Are you a scribe?" one of them asks, running by. "Um, yes." "Well, come on! We need you." I hurry to catch up and am hired on the spot. My job is to keep track of everything they're building; it's a full-time position. Any time I open my eyes, I find my hands typing against my bedsheets or writing in the air. If I try to search for paper, it's always too far away. Closing my eyes, I'm back in the exact same place. "Where have you been?" the workers always ask, tugging on my pyjama sleeve. Then we're off again to see some new structure: a bridge or a high-rise.

For two days, I pick my way through debris, ducking under beams and squinting up at Escher-esque scaffolding, trying to take down notes on all the progress they're making. By the third morning, I'm overtired. A line from a poem I'd memorized in grade school keeps repeating in my head: "In Xanadu did Kubla Khan a stately pleasure-dome decree." Xanadu was an idyllic world that the poet, Coleridge, had imagined while on opiates. When I Google him on my tablet, I learn that he described his narcotic experiences as a kind of repose without sleep. "I don't think you should be giving laudanum to writers," I tell the doctor who is on duty that day. "It's way too exhausting for us." "Why would I be giving you a drug from the nineteenth century?" he asks, perplexed. "You're on hydromorphone. It's like morphine, but stronger." Hydromorphone. The name of the drug sounds familiar, like maybe I've been told it before. I think about writing it down this time so I won't forget, but as usual there is no paper within reach. The doctor squints at me. "Is everything okay?" "Fine," I say.

It's Day Eight and I've had no food and only the smallest sips of water since Day Zero. My throat and stomach lining, damaged by the chemo, need time to heal. The antibiotics I'm taking until my immune system regrows, Moxyfloxacin and Acyclovir, sound like Beatrix Potter characters: Moxy, Floxy, and Cottontail. When I try to swallow the pills, I choke, and a whole part of my esophagus comes hurtling out into the sink — a disgusting piece of tortured viscera that seems like it could be my cancer itself. I'm pretty sure that's not possible, but I can't be certain. I've been employed for a week in a futuristic world; my rules of reality are in flux.

At the construction site that evening, I'm resigned to another gruelling shift when one of the androgynous beings informs me my job has changed. Apparently, I no longer have to write everything down. I just need to slough off the sick person in my bed, and then I can finally get some sleep. I sit up and carefully brush her dusty remains from my body. The next morning, I awake feeling quiet and refreshed. A nurse checking my blood pressure looks into my eyes. "Are you having delusions?" she asks. "Yes," I say, feeling like it's finally time to admit this. She unplugs me from the painkillers, but even before the drugs are out of my system, I know the beings are gone. Their work is finished — the foundation for my new immune system is in place.

When I get home from Ward 14C, it takes me six months to get back on my feet: to build up my stamina, to grow a bit of hair, to put on some weight. Finally, I'm healthy enough to rejoin the world, excited to start filling my diary with entries about regular life again. Getting ready for my first post-transplant date, I bite at my fingernails and try to decide if I should maybe change into a different shirt — one that doesn't reveal a glimpse of the scars on my décolletage. I wonder what I'll say if my date asks about them — when the right time might be to talk about what happened. I still don't know which side of the fifty percent statistic I'm going to fall on, and that's not an easy thing to tell someone. Five years from now, if I'm still well, I'll be able to say that I'm cured, but that day is a long way off. I decide not to change shirts, and later that evening my date reaches over and lightly brushes one of the scars he's been eyeing: the thin biopsy scar I wear like a necklace. "What's this?" he asks. It's the first time anyone has made contact with the raised line of still-sensitive skin and it's as if he's pressed a button. I find myself telling him a story about how I was once taken hostage in a bank robbery, a knife pressed to my throat. My date senses this is just a metaphor, but he plays along and I continue my tale, describing what a relief it was to be released — how my knees were trembling as I walked out of the bank and took my first big breath of safe, outdoor air. "I'm glad you survived," he says. "Me too." Confirming this outcome for him, I feel a little more certain that things will be okay. And right then, I make a decision. Until I'm ready to tell people the real details of my reboot, there will be only one rule when explaining my scars: each story must end with an escape.

It turns out this protective revisionism is only necessary for a few months. After that, I can pass as healthy again. My scars fade a bit, and I cover them more often, trying to put my illness out of mind. But it will not be quiet. In fact, for the whole first year, the experience only increases in volume. During treatment, there'd been little time to think about what was going on. Now that I'm in recovery, there's too much time to think, playing and replaying what happened to my body. Wait. *Too much time*? I scold myself for this poorly-worded thought. I've become superstitious — worried that wrong thinking of this sort might signal to some universal force that I'm uncommitted to the idea of survival. Did I believe in this force before my illness? Yes, I think so, but it was much more benevolent. Now, it's like a slumbering beast I have to tiptoe past many times a day. I need Ativan to sleep. More and more frequently, it doesn't work.

An early draft of a first novel has been patiently awaiting my return to health. When I finally sit down to read it again, it doesn't feel the same — the engine of grieving at its core has rusted. I begin a new draft anyway, and in doing so, discover that many words have been stolen from me by chemo. In their place are long pauses like ellipses with extra dots. What is the word for...that thing? I often wonder, miming the object in the air. I play many losing rounds of charades with myself each day. Soon, I start to worry that the edits I'm making to the novel are not of the same quality as my pre-illness writing. I trust my close writer friends to help me judge: is my writing the same? They assure me it is, but soon I realize that what I really want to know is something much harder to assess: Am I the same? Do I seem different? My friends and family are the collective oracle I frequently consult on this unanswerable question.

※ ※ ※

When I've been well for a year, I begin investigating some of the potential "cures" emailed to me by well-meaning people while I was sick. Could macrobiotics prevent me from relapsing? What about colonics? Supplements? Cleanses? Infrared saunas? Weed? In addition to exploring these options, I make two appointments: one with a cancer naturopath, and one with a psychic energy healer who comes highly recommended by a friend. The psychic tells me it's unfortunate I had to suffer through cancer treatment when baking soda would have cured me. The naturopath asks what happened two years prior to my illness, and when I tell her about a painful breakup and my resulting distress, she reprimands me for giving my body the message that I wanted to die. The anger I feel after these appointments generates an idea for a new novel, but I put the thought on hold. For now, I just need to focus on the current book I'm writing. It's the project I have the most chance of finishing should I get sick again.

If I get sick again there's no chance of a cure. This nerve-wracking reality is hard to live with, but my doctor offers some comfort at my two-year check-up; apparently, the rate of recurrence decreases dramatically after the second year. "It's like a hockey stick," he says, tracing a confusing L-shape in the air. I try to picture this line superimposed onto a graph, but fail. Was the hockey stick hanging on a wall? Was the player left-handed? My doctor also tells me that from now on I will only need to have a CT scan every six months, instead of every three. This is a huge relief. Waiting for the scan results each time is a multi-week cycle of catastrophic imaginings and little sleep. The rooms at the hospital have also begun to trigger me — the traumatic details of my cancer journey unfreezing at inopportune times and returning in bursts of sudden, vivid detail. Along with these flashbacks comes a new desire to describe them. "Do you know those Hieronymus Bosch paintings of hell?" I sometimes begin. "That's what 'The Procedures Room' at the hospital is like. People screaming, bottles of black bile, bloody gauze." The Distress Assessment questionnaire I complete at my next few check-ups shows a consistently untenable amount of worry, so my doctor refers me to the hospital's psychosocial department. Soon after, I get a letter in the mail saying I've been finished chemo for too long to qualify for a visit. I stuff the letter in the trash. What kind of psychiatrists don't understand how long it takes for memories to thaw?

One year. Two years. Three years. Each June post-transplant, I place a brass number into a blue dish that sits on my dresser: a reminder of my successful accumulation of healthy days. As the new drafts of my novel also pile up, I notice the book has become less melancholy. The pre-illness draft is now just a faint pentimento beneath the new version which is more about the birth of an artist, rather than about a woman destroyed by grief. People who've read both versions tend to link this change to the fact that I'm now a survivor, and they're right. But the reason for my burgeoning optimism isn't what they imagine. It's not a new "life-is-short, seize-the-day" attitude that's reshaping my words; it's actually a fear of expressing anything that smacks of annihilation. Terrified still of the slumbering beast who may only be pretending to sleep, I try to stay relentlessly positive, just in case my body's wellness depends on me explicitly affirming over and over my desire to live. Recognizing this self-censoring behaviour makes me feel like a coward — like there's a bully I need to stand up to. Midway through my third year of wellness, I try to infuse the final draft of my novel with some of its original darkness, but it doesn't work. That version is gone. I have to find a way to love this strange hybrid book that has been altered by my illness as much as I have.

In February 2018, I travel to Barcelona in early celebration of my five-year birthday, hoping as I board the plane that I'm not jinxing myself by jumping the gun. Within days, I've come down with acute bronchitis and end up in the hospital. The little cast-iron donkey I brought to Europe as a good-luck talisman has lost two of its legs. I try not to freak out about either of these things. I am so close to the five-year finish line, but lying in a hospital bed with an IV in my arm again, all I can think of is the time someone told me, "My cousin made it to five years, and then two months later she got sick." People say dumb things, and this was one of the dumbest. Even so, this woman was right: five years is an arbitrary line in the sand; my uncertainty won't ever really be gone. But at least my novel is finished. It's coming out next year, and after that, no matter what happens to me, my book will continue to exist in the world. The novel, now titled *Proof I Was Here*, begins with a day when everything changes for the protagonist and ends with her fervently hoping her luck will hold. My second novel, which I've just begun, will use everything I've learned about oncologists and psychics, and give me an opportunity to explore the boundaries of the mind-body connection so I can figure out what I believe. Is the quality of my writing the same? Maybe. But I'm not the same — I'm certain of that now — and neither is what I'm writing about.

Lifelines: Of Heart, Lungs, Blood, and Ghazals

Kateri Lanthier

I was cutting out hearts. Paper hearts. The stiff Bristol board sheets in arterial red and fever pink had to be turned into Valentine hearts, twenty of them, for my youngest kid's afternoon kindergarten class. William would attempt to write the names of each classmate on the hearts and to sign his own. The task, ordinarily a simple one for me (his was the greater challenge), seemed strangely difficult. It could have been because of lack of sleep — I'd been up since 4:30 AM, sending some anxiety-ridden emails to my siblings and father — or the effects of a lingering cold that everyone in the family had experienced over the past week. Or...I struggled to breathe.

I remembered stopping on the stairs a few days back, looking up at my husband on the landing and asking, "Why is this so hard?" Usually, I would barely consider the demands of a flight of stairs. But something was wrong. I'd started shovelling snow from the front path and felt winded after a few minutes.

I'd taken Will for a walk in a ravine nearby and found it hard to climb back up to the street. In the email, I asked my dad how it actually felt — did it hurt? — when he had a pulmonary embolism in his forties. I checked my messages. Dad: "No pain. It was just very hard to breathe. Go to the hospital!" I moved slowly, found my wallet with my health card, and asked my husband, Greg, to give me a lift to Sunnybrook Hospital after we took Will to school. Greg had a long-awaited meeting with an artistic director that afternoon. He would just make it to the theatre in time if we drove uptown immediately.

Before we left, I peeked online. It was up! A poem of mine had been scheduled to appear on February 14 on the Canadian Poetries website, edited by Shawna Lemay and Kimmy Doane. Shawna had told me she was thrilled at the serendipity of the title, "Valentine's Day." I posted it on my Facebook page, turned off the computer, and grabbed my coat. We crossed the city, Greg dropped me off at emergency and I walked in, carrying a copy of Johnson's *Lives of the Poets*. I expected a long wait.

Poetry was my preoccupation that day in 2013, as it had been since I had started writing again in 2010, after a nearly fifteen-year hiatus. My first published poems appeared in *Quarry* when I was thirteen, and before that, I'd won some prizes in a Northern Ontario poetry contest when my family lived in Sudbury. People asked me, "Did you stop because you had kids?" The answer is murkier. I stopped long before I had kids, just after I turned thirty. When I got married, I focussed on earning a living through writing about design and decorating for magazines and TV. There's no easy explanation for why I abandoned something I loved. Eventually, I couldn't bear to read poetry. It was a world lost to me.

Only after giving birth to my third child did the words start to emerge again from the haze, phrases and lines coming to me while I pushed the stroller. It could have been the near-madness of sleep deprivation. Maybe it was the word-welter in the spill of alphabet building blocks and picture books across the floor where small word-learners collided around me, asking questions about the universe. I started to write down what they said because it struck me as intuitive poetry. It still does. Their kid-speak became one of the sources for my first book, *Reporting from Night*, which an editor-acquaintance-turned-publisher brought out through his new press, Iguana, in 2011. I was immersed in child raising. When I started attending readings or giving them, my family had to adjust — they were so accustomed to my near-continuous presence. "Mummy, are you going to a *poetry reading*?" Nic, my oldest, would ask in a doleful tone. He would share the bad news with his siblings. I laughed, but also felt like a minor criminal as I strode along Dundas West in Toronto to a Pivot reading at the old Press Club, already overstimulated by the transit rides and the storefront lights, the weird sensation of walking on my own, before I stepped nervously into the hothouse of (typically) much younger poets and editors.

Valentine's Day

Cherry-bled mittens:
two halves of a heart.

Each holds your pulse.
Hug me in stereo.

The import of the rose
to a hostile climate.

Without reservations,
tables turned.

La fée verte?
I'm seeing stardust.

The Widow's emerald?
Trouble bath.

Nipples hard, forthright.
The sucker's punch.

Feathers plucked. Freeze frame.
"Going, going swan."

They told us: if it bleeds, it leads.
We're all hearts here.

I sat for hours in emerg, waiting for test results, hunched over *Lives of the Poets* while finding it harder and harder to breathe. I didn't know that people were posting kind notes about the poem because I had no cellphone with me. My old flip phone had died. I don't think the account was even extant. I was always running around with my kids in my own neighbourhood — I was scarcely even freelancing — why did I need a phone? To take photos, I'd carry our big Canon camera with me, sometimes, but more often I was just playing with the kids, chasing after them on the boardwalk or in the park.

After close to eight hours, the head of emergency came in to tell me that my guess had been correct: a test showed clots in my blood. They were sending me for a CT scan. He walked out to arrange for it. A woman sitting beside me asked me why this might be. I started to tell her that my dad had survived a pulmonary embolism in his forties and so maybe that's why I — I collapsed. The doctor later told my husband, "Your wife came in with her diagnosis."

Late that night, my husband brought our frightened kids to see me in emerg where I was hooked up to an arterial line (the "art" line in hospital parlance) and wearing an oxygen mask. I worried about how I must look to them. I felt submerged, half-drowned. "Massive bilateral pulmonary embolism," I tried to say, through the mask. I held their hands and then Greg brought them home. The gurney trip up to a dimly-lit ICU room was otherworldly. I spent several days there, where the older man in a bed next to me went into a sudden decline and died. Although I hadn't felt pain in the crisis itself, I was weaker than after twenty-four hours of labour with my first kid. A shaky trip on my own to the washroom, pulling my IV pole, was a triumph.

If I hadn't used the line "I'm already living an afterlife" in my first collection, I would have used it in my second, *Siren*. The line referred to having been something of a Queen St. West club kid who grew up and settled down in a conventional marriage. Now that I was in a bed on a ward, "edginess" seemed redefined. Days and nights blurred. The clots broke down slowly and, as they did, I felt pain. The lungs have very few pain receptors: this new aching in my back and chest was, paradoxically, a sign of recovery.

Days before I ended up at Sunnybrook, I'd been reading ghazals by Ghalib (1797-1869) in translations by Aijaz Ahmad, Adrienne Rich, and William Stafford, published in 1971. His lines were the first I remembered when I started to gain strength. His often-ferocious engagement with death-in-life was what I needed, now. I felt voracious: I craved the tremendous, startling leaps between couplets, the impassioned drive of the poetry. For several years, I'd been reading mainly contemporary poetry, trying to catch up with what I'd missed in my poetry hiatus, so these earlier poems were a surge from the centuries-old river of poetry, the continuum.

A portable heart monitor became my little companion. When

I felt strong enough to move on my own, I carried it on my walker down the hospital corridor. The first time I did this, I was nearly breathless. But the act of walking triggered poetry. This line appeared: "Sport with me. I am the coin under the leftmost sliding cup." I was thinking of the bright, winking, flashing imagery of Ghalib, the sudden illuminations and the self-castigating. The slyness and rapture. I had to run it over in my mind — no paper, both hands on the walker — until I got back to the room. This became my new practice, even after I left the hospital — walking, thinking, looking, writing lines in my head. I'd done it when pushing the stroller. Now I was doing it while trying to walk again. I have extended this practice into reciting the poems at readings. When working on the poems in *Siren*, I would lie in bed at night, running the lines over in my head, working out kinks, committing the unexpected to heart.

What strikes me now about my Valentine's Day poem are the clipped, short lines. I was holding so much close to my chest, to my heart. I connect this to my trepidation on returning to writing poetry. I was trying to make the poems into tiny gems, but in retrospect I think I was trying to make them hard and deflecting. I feared revealing too much. Ghazals, traditional and unrhymed, beckoned. Into the first of my longer-lined, more all-encompassing ghazals, I worked some of the things I loved best: the image of new leaves illuminated by a streetlight, a retro cartoon my kids found hilarious, a painting of a suspension bridge by Toronto artist Douglas Walker in which he somehow gave an actual glow to the lights along the looping structure. The poem is rhapsodic with the elation of recovery. And it also included my fears — the image of the gun as a fire set in a palm. It was light-dark, sad-happy, an unstable register that seemed the new reality for me.

The Coin Under the Leftmost Sliding Cup

Did you feel the Earth move? That was our Tectonic Dance
  Party.
The world is a crowded club with all the exits blocked.

I might sound like a goose in an opera gown, but I say again,
  I love you.
I'm tired of all this thinking at the very top of my lungs.

If only my fingers could keep up! Then the dialogue in my
  head
wouldn't unscroll like a thirties screwball in underwater
  slo-mo.

What if the truth of desire lies in Aesop upside down?
Where the fox's teeth are the Unattainable and the grapes
  full of rationalizations...

I'm not too cool to care, though. Nature and I have a lovers'
  quarrel.
I adopted the strut of the peacock and the nightingale's night-
  gown.

After 15,000 texts, can we say we have a past?
My love for you is e-phemeral, elliptical, ekphrastic.

Love to me was cotton candy: spangle, collapse, tongue grit.
With you, it's sadness scissored out. Lights on a suspension
  bridge.

Sport with me. I am the coin under the leftmost sliding cup.
Right, left, double-crossing. There. Now you're in *my* pocket.

Cellphone, psalter, cigarette, gun: we like to set fire to our
palms.
Rome burns as I photograph flowers or wear them as a bra.

Call it playing with fire. Call it connect-the-dots lightning.
Whenever we run down to the lake, the lake ascends sky
mountain.

Streetlight's an earthbound lunatic, courting June's
too-perfect leaves.
These gardens are a *plein-air* perfume factory, drunk on their
own power.

The Spaceman loved the Gumball Machine — *beautiful,
beautiful.*
But each time he took her by the arm, she lost another sweet
eye.

It's curtains for you, day. Stars eye us from the stage.
Ars longa, vita brevis, kid. Long walk, short pier.

The after-effects of the embolism were both profound and
invisible, on my life and in my writing. Invisible because it was
an internal medical crisis that presented few outward signs, profound because my writing took a sharp turn in a new direction.
I had given birth three times, had a miscarriage between the
first and second full-term pregnancies — a "missed miscarriage," which was a strangely prolonged upset of its own (and
might have been connected to my blood clotting tendency). I
lost my powerhouse mother to cancer when she was sixty-three.
Birth and death: I'd been up close with them. I'd been the home
and conduit for new life as well as the daughter tracing the veins
on her mother's hand and crying at the last sight of her small

pretty feet with their longer second toes, the sort of toes you
see on classical statuary. My five-month-old daughter, kicking
her bare feet in her stroller in a corner of my mother's room in
Princess Margaret's palliative care unit, had inherited that physical trait. But not until I was hooked up to the "art line" in emergency, with my kids by my side, looking scared, and my husband
looking helpless, did I feel close to my own inevitable death.

I've written only two narrative poems about my brush-with-
death. The first has ekphrastic elements. Although I declined
my specialist doctor's offer to attend support group sessions for
survivors of embolisms, I do think often about the sensations of
the experience. It was very cold in the shared hospital room that
February. One evening, a nurse piled our puffy winter jackets on
our beds to help us stay warm. I made notes while huddled
under the rough hospital sheets.

Heart Monitor

My blood is in a palace coup against my lungs,
Racing through the heart's hallways
The corridors of the powerless.

Oh, I contain multitudes, yes,
A throng of the mutinous. Ruby-throated
Clots in the bloodstream stole my breath.

Here I lie, untitled. Unfinished work.
Pale, bruise-eyed, nothing to see,
But an "art line" fireworks my veins

Blue, yellow, red! to the pretty screen.
That's my last duchess, over my shoulder,
Live-streaming spots of crimson joy.

It's cold in the gallery. Mint walls, peach "art"
(eternal still life: the uprooted undead
drinking water through their veins)

That no one sees. All eyes on screen
The resonance of emerald, the rush…
Remote heart monitor, cat on my lap,

Purrs to the nurse on another floor.
There, they never sleep, so I dream for them.
Their installation piece: The Scribbler.

Across the hall's The Scream. He has the view:
Ravine, icewater, the distaff drive
Where Trauma arrives.

Or perhaps I have the view: the lit-all-night
Stairwell, brick, snowflakes flying upwards.
Bent over my notes, what am I really?

The Lacemaker. My heart's apace.
I'll write to you until I lose
My sight, the thread and the current's flow.

On a check-up with my specialist at Sunnybrook, I mentioned
that I'd written a poem that touched on the experience. He
exclaimed, "I'd like to hear it!" Mindful of his time, I demurred
but he insisted, so I found myself reciting a few lines from
"Heart Monitor" in his small drab office, a few floors away from
where I had collapsed. A poem delivered by the heart, lungs,
and brain that made it through.

The second poem, its title a nod to Elizabeth Bishop, is as
much about eco-anxiety as it is about my own near-death expe-

rience, although it does convey, I think, the fog of recovery. (It
was a month before I could make it down the block to my kids'
school to pick them up.) And…there is a cat. I've just realized
that both of these second/nine lives poems from this Kat have
a cat.

A Colder Spring

Crocuses, you're down there somewhere,
but, sorry to say, I forgot you existed.
The New Ferocity gave me brain-freeze;
the continent a crystal skull of ice.
Across a gyre of debris-field waves,
your imperial purple has been dredged from floods.
Resolved into a dew, soaked earth overheats.

So it was with last spring with the cat. What cat?
I spent a week in and out of bed with death,
playing nurse or doctor in a backless gown,
hooked to a slow-drip icicle IV.
My sister brought crocuses to block the snow
of over-bleached sheets, the view, my mirrored blank.
Name snipped off my wrist, I was free to walk.
At home, my kids swooped, captive songbirds.
Funeral or wedding march? I climbed stair-stop-stair.
And there on the bed was the cat. We have a cat?
I'd forgotten she existed. Only then could I melt.

Minor and major changes entered my life after that Valentine's
Day. I take blood thinner medication every day and will do so for
the rest of my life. I carry a working cellphone, so I'm rarely out
of touch (double-edged, that). I'm a more assertive advocate for
myself within the health care system. I'd lost my sense of self,

to some extent. I was vigilant on behalf of my children but, like many people, I was reticent when it came to my own needs. When I hear of people dying from a pulmonary embolism, I'm cast back to my own crisis. Many people think of blood clot formation as a risk to older adults, but younger ones can be susceptible, too. I followed closely the stories about tennis champion Serena Williams's near-death experience with a post-partum pulmonary embolism and related complications — and her request for a CT scan, indeed, her need to insist on it, when the hospital was simply going to schedule an ultrasound. Young, healthy people who take birth control pills have experienced sudden breathlessness and died from blood clots in the lungs or heart. I escaped that for years, I can see in retrospect. One of the young interns told me in ICU: "But you look so young! And the notes said you have your period...." I wasn't young, really, but younger than she thought possible, it seemed, for a patient with blood clots. She went on: "You are lucky, you know. Some people don't get through a pulmonary embolism."

I got through three pregnancies without realizing I had inherited factor V Leiden from my father, which means that my blood tends to form abnormal clots — and clots are a risk both during pregnancy and postpartum. Given the genetic inheri-tance, I do worry about what the future could hold for my children, especially for my daughter, Julia. It might be that a small leg injury I sustained a month after Will was born started the vein damage that led to my embolism. At the time, it was examined at a downtown hospital and then dismissed as super-ficial thrombophlebitis. I gave my newborn to my husband to hold, while I was given a shot of blood thinner in the stomach. Then I was sent home. But I wonder if the serpent was sleeping in the vein.

The beloved American poet C.D. Wright died in her sleep of a blood clot that formed after a long plane flight. I had asked her for a Facebook connection a few months before. One day, some months after her death, she accepted. I was startled until I realized that it must have come through her grieving husband, the poet Forrest Gander. I felt grateful, oddly pleased, and then burst into tears. But I try not to dwell on my risks. The intern was right: I am lucky. I'd rather immerse myself in photographing the sky, the lake, the massive trees in my neighbourhood with my ever-present phone. To cheer on my kids as they develop apps, pass the deep-end swimming test, audition for the National Ballet School. To wander around art galleries, to read and reread, hungrily, as many books as I can, to write. Life jolts, sings, horrifies, and hums, as always. The difference is that now I feel as if I can pass a hand through a haze into the void. The line always seems close. I glance to the side and there it is. What's between us, in the best moments, is poetry — a shield, a connection, a page, a breath. We're all hearts here.

Full Belly, Empty Sky: Death and Parenthood

Ben Gallagher

> Why did you vanish
> into the empty sky?
> Even the fragile snow,
> when it falls,
> falls in this world
> — Izumi Shikibu
> (trans. Jane Hirshfield and Mariko Aratani)

Finding an answer years before the question. I was in the Halifax Central Library, lost in the non-fiction stacks when I pulled *The Ink Dark Moon* off the shelf and found Izumi Shikibu. Found this question about grief, the sudden death of her daughter, long before death found its way into my life.

Three years later I was in Halifax again with my partner Zoë when her mother was diagnosed with lung cancer, and we spent all those months watching her thin and angry and accepting, doing our own versions of the same process, only without the vanishing, without the final exhale. Being Buddhists, we spent three days meditating with her mother's body, staying with our breath, marking the departure. And in one of those arcs that only appear looking backwards, invisible connection suddenly visible, three years later Zoë was killed by a drunk driver.

I wanted to say to her I get it now, your grief through these years, how there is no returning, but I was left only with the wanting to say, and no one to say it to. Death is letting go of the many futures you believed in. Alongside the absence of your desires, you are given a presence of nothing being guaranteed.

I hated the idea of healing, as if grief was a temporary sickness. Despite a kind of floating fog that made the whole world looser, a trembling at the edges like paper in wind, the clarity I experienced was the absurdity of time as a straight line, of an inevitable story, of destiny or fate. There was only this emptiness of the present moment, and even that was hard to believe in. Any mention of healing felt like an attempt to hide from a basic truth.

It is very hard to live without a future though. Eventually I began to notice myself dreaming or planning things to do tomorrow, next week. It was a surprise to me to feel the ceiling of my joy rising. I caught myself noticing a finch in the bushes, orange rust on a door hinge, warmth in the breeze, and these images didn't evaporate from my consciousness immediately. Small joys continued, and I began to feel that I could loan my eyes to Zoë, that somehow my experience of the world was a way for her to experience it, too. Which also became a kind of responsibility towards myself. I kept saying no one will help you with your feelings but you, since Zoë wasn't there to know me intimately and keep me honest. She had a gift for asking questions it was impossible to hide from, and I was worried I would somehow avoid myself for the rest of my life, unable to see the origins of my actions, a crab lashing out at the tide.

When I asked myself in all seriousness if I could sense her spirit or presence, the answer was no. Shikibu sees a difference between the vanishing of her daughter and the vanishing snow, but I also picture the water cycle, falling snow melting, evaporating, returning as snow again. Death as an emptiness, an evaporation that returns as another fragile emptiness. Can we ever see the invisible?

> *Sometimes joy multiplies itself dangerously. Children are the infamous example. Isn't it bad enough that the beloved, with whom you have experienced genuine joy, will eventually be lost to you? Why add to this nightmare the child, whose loss, if it ever happened, would mean nothing less than your total annihilation?*
>
> — Zadie Smith, "Joy"

I am driving down the highway, past Exit 8, where Brinleigh and I stopped to buy two pregnancy tests from the dollar store. Both tests, taken outside of our trailer under the light of a full August moon, were positive. Every time I drive I think I can die at any moment because I know it to be true. My sister, racing to the hospital in Hamilton where Zoë lay four years ago, brain dead in the ICU, said she knew she could have died in a car accident that night too. There is no cosmic balance, one tragedy does not prevent another. But it doesn't have to mean that no joy will come.

I'm thinking about being a father, which I never expected would happen, some part of me believing death had ruined me for love. Pressed up against emptiness, against the absurdity of a future, who would want me? Who would believe my love for them? Yet here I am, four years later, vulnerable and tainted and almost a parent.

I worried Brinleigh would feel she was a proxy for Zoë. I tell her again and again I am having this child with YOU. I'm grateful for being loved, for being given a chance to find my way to

loving again. I also don't know how to separate my desires with
Brinleigh from my desires with Zoë, my future dreams, my
habits. I still cook eggs the way Zoë taught me, which was the
way she had been taught in turn by her mother. Now the eggs
are a legacy, another way I can remember both those fierce
women — but to Brinleigh they're just the way I cook eggs. My
dreams about having children, my fears about having children,
which were so active when Zoë and I were together, still circulate through me. I sometimes wonder if we'd had kids, whether
she would feel closer to me or further away. Although that
thought is also a kind of torture.

Yet it speaks to this desire in me for children, and did that
desire exist before Zoë? Did she make it possible for desire to
blossom, somehow distinct from her own existence? Did her
death push me past my fears even as it gave me new ones? I ask
myself these questions while dreaming of baby names with
Brinleigh, going through bags of hand-me-down onesies, worrying about our finances. Pressed against death for so long, I
have lost the ability to have a pure feeling — death is the thorn
in my joy, in worry, in love, in wonder. I do not want the thorn
removed, although I sometimes wish for it. I do not think it can
ever be removed, not by Brinleigh's love or by our child. I also
think, when I really sit with my empty truth, that death is what
makes those other feelings possible.

The connection between impermanence and worth is what
sits at the heart of Zadie Smith's essay on joy and pleasure.
Pleasure, she maintains, is something you can "have" distinct
from yourself. It can be replaced with a pleasure of equal
worth, a delicious meal one night becoming a beautiful concert
another night, and neither of them mourned once over. But joy,
she maintains, obliterates the self for a time and is a thing you
are. With joy, finitude is at the heart of the experience, the pain
of its loss being in some way a measure of its worth. Which

makes her wonder why anyone would choose the multiplying joys and risks of parenthood. Yet here I am, the next in a long line of humanity taking that perilous step.

> *'Fuck the human'…is to refuse that which has*
> *been refused to you.*
> — Fred Moten and Saidiya Hartman,
> *The Black Outdoors*

Grief sharpened my sense of an underlying suffering; everywhere I looked I saw loss and love tangled together. As I breathed into the particulars of my loss, I also felt compelled to think about the people whose deaths and sorrows go uncounted, unacknowledged. I feel that same compulsion whenever I talk about being a parent. I can't forget that every child is not equally valued. The precious nature of birth is immediately inflected by the disparities of history.

Stuart Hall talks about how we come to see who we are, the origin of our identity, as a kind of suture. We are being stitched together, always in an incomplete, temporary way, the discomfort of a stitch not yet become a scar. Our psychic sense of selfhood (conscious and unconscious) and the ways we are seen by society always contain a gap. For Hall, this was a way of talking about racism, how the social creation of "race" as a category pressed against his internal sense of self, his inherent worth, within a culture that on a structural level devalued him.

I'm not trying to make an analogy between structural racism and personal grief, as if they can explain each other, or are in any way equivalent. Only that eventually my sorrow required me to expand my feelings outward, so that comments like everyone grieves differently, or there is no wrong way to grieve, while true, felt inadequate in the face of an "emotional colour line" (as Cornel West called it). No matter how individual and precise my experience of sorrow is, it cannot be separated from history, from the history of my whiteness, from the history of race. This is what Fred Moten is responding to when he says "fuck the human." After being shut out of the category of "human" for so long, the term itself cannot be recuperated. Better to make new categories, or step away from categorizing altogether.

> *I am alive today because of medical technology.*
> *Otherwise my mother and I would have been dead*
> *long before my first breath, dead as the ovarian cyst*
> *that grew beside me. It was as big as a grapefruit*
> *before the doctors told her it had to be removed.*
> *Her grief, guilt, bitterness twined through that*
> *crisis called my birth. She was the first who wanted*
> *a cure for the havoc wreaked when the doctors*
> *pulled that cyst away.*
>
> — Eli Clare, *Ideology of Cure*

I leave Brinleigh at home for a week during her second trimester while I accompany my friend Loree to visit her mother in a long-term care facility in Virginia. Her mother has mostly stopped talking, caught in a cycle of infections and neglect that seems common within the US healthcare system. Loree herself uses a wheelchair, and we're both surprised at how quick people assume she also lives at the facility, despite her vibrant leopard-print tights, hot-pink lipstick, and general alertness when compared with the slow-moving elderly residents. Not to mention that we're both at least thirty years younger than anyone living there.

We go to her mother's room to offer her a sip of water. I lift the straw to her lips, holding the styrofoam cup for her as she locks her eyes on mine. When I think about Zoë's death, it feels sudden and cruel, but that cruelty is different than the long,

silent hallways in Virginia. Here, the cruelty comes from lives
prolonged medically, but stripped of pleasure. They have been
"cured" of death, within a system that makes loving contact as
brief as a rare bird. Loree uses her intimate knowledge of the
medical system to advocate for her own mother, knowing on a
deep level how much neglect is built into the system itself. She
coaches me through the best way to lift her mother's hips, and
analyses the various dismissals and excuses of the doctors that
come through the rooms during rushed visits. I recall my conversations with the organ donation team in the ICU, trying to
decide which of Zoë's organs might be used to help others live.
In the hospital, when they say "live" they must be imagining
someone smiling, surrounded by family. Do they also imagine
these long, anguished, not-quite-deaths much later, the other
side of their technology?

Reading Eli Clare engage with his own origins and life with
cerebral palsy, the complications of terms like "cure" and "healing" that immediately vilify disabilities instead of celebrating
them, I think again about our unborn child. I must admit I am
imagining our child will be born naturally, will be born perfect.
But as Loree and Clare have both shown me, there is a poison
in those terms, and so much to be celebrated in the vibrant disabilities that are equally full of potential in this birth moment.

> though all experience
>
> is through the body   I did not feel
>
> my hands pull   white sheets my legs shake when
>   two nurses cooed
>
> lean back   honey you are   bleeding more than expected.
> — Layli Long Soldier, "Dilate"

※ ※ ※

After my sister's labour, her placenta did not fully detach. She continued to bleed, more than a litre, and drifted back towards some elsewhere as the medical team leapt into action. Those of us waiting sat by telephones as hours extended impossibly in long, low shadows. Less than a year after Zoë's death, I sat in the dark of my room and wondered if I could handle another loss. Unsure what grief piled on grief looks like, I was certain that nothing was guaranteed.

As Brinleigh's labour approaches I contemplate her mortality as well, the possible death of our child we have yet to meet. We have spent so long studying the movements, Brinleigh full of an intimate knowledge that is purely physical, the feel of tiny feet rubbing against her ribs. I keep my death thoughts to myself; nobody wants them. Although they press themselves against me anyway, they are no longer at the front of my mind. They intrude mostly after visits with our midwives, or late at night when I curl myself around her as she sleeps. I think again and again about the falling of Shikibu's fragile snow. The tenuous, vital anchors to this world.

※ ※ ※

that is the center of life, that moment when the
juiced bluish sphere of the baby is
sliding between the two worlds,
wet, like sex, it is sex,
it is my life opening back and back
      — Sharon Olds, "The Moment the Two Worlds Meet"

※ ※ ※

Brinleigh and I sit on the couch watching what must be legs slide against the taut undersurface of her belly. We spend hours talking about our baby, imagining how we'll treat it, how we'll be changed. The invisible not what-is-gone but what-is-coming. I wonder about this going and coming, treated like they're two separate things — but I no longer believe in the straight line of time. I see emptiness everywhere still, an emptiness outside of time and bound inextricably with love. Not knowing, uncertainty, the opening to whatever might happen intimately pressed against the potential of the present. Which might be an experience of loss (my grief says it will be), but just as equally the centre of life. I watch it stir from my place on the other side. Helpless, eager, afraid.

The Story

Aislinn Hunter

We are on the road and my husband is driving. It's early evening, the sky turning to dusk. What do we have with us? Everything the heart can carry: happiness, health, love, a PhD studentship, a cosmopolitan life in a foreign city — Edinburgh lit up nightly below our flat on the Royal Mile. And we have whimsy: a road trip to the Borders where my ancestors worked sheep. A valley so rainy and miserable most Scots frown when I mention the village's name. This is my third, or fourth, attempt at Ettrick. Before moving to Scotland, we'd tried to squeeze the valley into packed vacation itineraries, but there were no direct buses from Edinburgh and hitching seemed like a bad strategy as so few people had cause to go there. But now we have a rental car — a compact Hyundai with skinny, low-tread wheels — and we're heading down the motorway toward the familial dead, singing along to the music on the CD player.

Just before the curve a sign on the left-hand side of the road says "Reduce Speed." My husband slows down from sixty miles per hour — the posted speed limit — and we take the curve going no more than forty. Halfway around the bend, one of the back tires catches some loose roadside gravel and before we know it we're spinning across the road and into a farmer's fence post, the passenger side window shattering on impact.

This is where time divides us. When the window shatters, I look away, but my husband looks toward me. Glass shards hit his face and he closes his eyes. For him the accident is over in seconds. But for me, eyes wide open, the accident goes on and on like a slow motion dream. We hit the post, there's a rain of glass, and then we're upside down — airborne — and I'm looking at a landscape gone wrong and thinking very clearly and angrily: We. Do. Not. Die. Like. This. But there's no power in the thought, no strength or certainty — just outrage. Upside down, the car careening through the air, I understand that we might die, and more than anything, I am really angry about the unexpected turn in our narrative.

A few seconds later the car rights itself, but then it rolls upside down again. We hit the ground so hard we come up a second time. I remember thinking: I'm okay, and feeling amazed by it. But then I look over at my husband who is gasping for air and I think, in that hanging time: he has internal injuries. And then we are upside down again and the impact from the ground makes the front windscreen and the sunroof shatter, glass raining over us like the bits of a kaleidoscope. I close my eyes then and we roll one last time and when I open my eyes the car has stopped and we are dangling upside down in our seat belts, my husband's head swaying just an inch above the crumpled car roof below.

※ ※ ※

It will take me years, a decade even, to allow myself to think about what happened after the accident as a kind of post-traumatic stress disorder. First, and most noticeably, there was the bodily effect of loud or unexpected noises, especially when walk-

ing alongside traffic. I'd flinch or tense at the sound of squeal-
ing brakes, car horns, even clangs from delivery trucks dropping
their gates. Months after our accident, we rented a car in Italy
and I found myself clenching the door handle and pushing both
feet to the floor as we rounded mountainsides and skimmed
along the terraced roads in Tuscany. I remember feeling
ashamed, neurotic. That one accident aside, my husband is —
and always has been — the best driver I know. In the ambulance
after the accident, one of the police officers who'd arrived on the
scene said that we'd crashed on the most dangerous, accident-
ridden highway in all of the UK. We were lucky, he said, and we
knew it. We'd had a terrible car accident, the car was totalled, but
we'd both walked away from it. We had cuts from the glass, aches
and pains for a week, but that was it. Lucky.

My anxieties around loud noises, around being a passenger,
faded with time. I was busy with my PhD, my writing, my life.
My husband had started a new career in the wine and spirits in-
dustry and he was doing incredibly well. We moved back to
Canada and got caught up in the excitement of grounding ourselves again. The accident became so remote in time, and in
our personal mythology, that when I went to see a local doctor
about some shoulder problems I was having I said "no" when he
asked if I'd been in a car accident. "Are you sure?" he asked. I
said "Yes, I haven't." He had to ask me a third time, and then I
said "Oh, yeah, like years ago, a big one: we rolled three times,
ended up upside down in some farmer's field, I dragged my husband out through my window because I thought the car was
going to explode." "Thought so," he said. "The problems you're
presenting with are typical of that sort of injury."

So there I was, years after the fact, with a body that was still
working out the trauma. What I didn't know then — what I
don't think I allowed myself to know — was that the real injury,
the most abiding aspect of the trauma of our accident was that

I'd become terribly afraid of dying. I felt certain — and mostly still feel certain — that I will die in a car accident. Because of this, it's not uncommon for solo car trips of over twenty minutes to feel something like a game of chicken: nights when I come home from teaching over the bridge deeply aware that I could nudge the steering wheel the slightest bit, hit the guardrail and be gone. I became so subconsciously certain of this death that I wrote poems about it. I wrote a love poem to my husband that included the lines:

> One day, my love, I'll be gone —
> and you will think *This was her hair,*
>
> *this was her mouth, this was the body*
> *she lived in.*

And so, without really being aware of it I go about my life — my fairly incredible, fortunate life — living in the shadow of this narrative: a story I am writing about who we are, and how I will die; and I reel out my future death and my husband's survival in footage the accident has given me.

※　※　※

This changes in February of 2017 when my husband is diagnosed with an inoperable and malignant brain tumour. He's fifty-three. When he's still under the anaesthetic of his biopsy surgery — a biopsy that occurs at a point when we're still holding onto the hope that the tumour might be benign — his neurosurgeon comes out to tell me that he probably only has a year to a year and a half to live. I go home and scream and scream and scream into the walls of the house and my screaming is a sound I have never heard before. Then I go back to the hospital where he is waking up and I say nothing, say he did great in the surgery and that I love him. As the weeks and months go by — weeks and months that are bad and then better, that involve dressing him, picking him up after falls, watching him go bravely (and humorously) through whole brain radiation and chemo; that involve wheeling him around on a wildly impulsive trip to France and Spain — we both agree on one thing: I would be better at dying and he would be a better caretaker. The disease has mis-struck, it got our competencies, our strengths, backwards.

We are almost a year in now, a year from the first slow sets of symptoms — a leg drag that was attributed to his back problems from work, a few issues of left sided weakness that led to a CT scan and then an emergency MRI. He's doing great — even if "great" is not who he once was, even if "great" needs naps, has a whole different head of hair, even if "great" has a hard time with food and loses his balance. The last MRI he had showed that his tumour — which was once the size of a lemon — is gone. Every week, his physiotherapist says he's getting stronger. This is cause for joy — deep and resonant, chest-filling joy. But as we, and many other brain tumour patients with his type of tumour know, tumours can come back. Which makes our joy fragile — like a paper lantern going up into a crosswind.

※　※　※

What interests me most about death is that it's the absence of life: that it is the black marker of erasure. When my own fear of death was at its peak, I took a workshop in London, England called "How Not To Be Afraid of Dying." In it, I learned that I was one of the rare few who is (illogically) more afraid of being dead than I am of actually dying. I have loved, and still love, my life so much. I am grateful for what fills it. My fear has to do with the absence of love and wonder: no more spooning in bed, French-toast breakfasts, the dogs' coats gleaming as they run out of the stream, no more great books, beautiful art, foreign cities, food that brings your mouth alive, wine made from grapes in a village you once stood in. No more fingers tracing your eyebrow, cheekbone, lips, no more laughter, dumb TV, creative struggle, no more history-in-things, no more resonant objects, classical music, twelve-year-old singers who can bring an aubade to life. No resurrection, retries, second chances.

There are people in our brain tumour support group who have lived a long time, have lived a decade or more, with equally dire diagnoses. My husband and I hope he will be one of them. But unlike some members of the group we do not see his tumour as a gift, as a game changer, or a great awakener. Years ago on a walk with our two Border collies, we stood in a clearing in the woods and said out loud how grateful we were just then for our health, the dogs' health, for the health of everyone we loved. We knew — in our fourth, almost fifth, decade — how rare it was to be surrounded by such pervasive luck. So this tumour is not a boon in any way except that it — in the form of mortality — is a deep and daily reminder of what a gift being in the world — and being together — is. As my girlfriend said after her breast cancer diagnosis: "This is it, we don't get a practice life."

※ ※ ※

Yesterday I was driving through Stanley Park. The trees were turning with autumn, the sun was out, and I wasn't in as much of a hurry as usual. I was thinking about the car accident in Scotland and I was thinking that what I've learned from the bridge that spans then and now — that spans "we don't die like this" (which was really me saying we don't die) to the awareness that my husband might die from his disease — is that I don't control the narrative. The narrative is a survival mechanism I've used in order to live with uncertainty. It was a response I used to quell my anger when the car flipped over, and a set of thoughts I used to mollify my fear every time I got into a car by myself and covered a long distance. Well, fear and grief are everywhere now. They're with me when I wake up and when I go to sleep next to the man I love. Some days I think he'll live a decade and some days I think we're going down the dark road again. But that's just the narrative asking me to make predictions. The best piece of advice we were given in our early days of his diagnosis? "If you can afford not to guess, don't." On the drive through Stanley Park, I tried to sit with only what I could know for sure: I love him, he loves me, the trees are lit with autumn, the sky is a wide and bracing blue. One day each of us will die. And on every other day we won't.

Autopsy

C. M. Faulkner

I. (2002)

I am taking the statement of a residential school survivor at a legal clinic.

I am a law student and I have been taught to interview with compassion and empathy. How to smile encouragingly, but not eagerly. How to look her in the eyes, but not so intensely that she will be uncomfortable. How to take notes, but rely on the recorder to capture it, how to be there for her.

Later, I will take my notes and the recording and I will write a letter, demanding money or an apology or both from the church and assailant. Sometimes, when the letter comes back, there is a cheque inside it. If there is a cheque and an apology, the client is happy and usually hugs and thanks me. If there is just a cheque, sometimes they're happy, sometimes they just leave. I am twenty-three, and I don't understand what causes the difference.

This woman, skin like origami, mouth folded in, pauses. "My parents were dead. My dad died of a stroke, my mom died because she froze to death while she was drunk. So when they said they were sending my sister to the hospital but that she would be OK, I believed them. She never came back and they never told me what happened. He called me into the office and told me she died. Then I cried and he cuddled me and that's when he took my clothes off that time."

I do not cry in front of her. I don't cry at all. A cheque comes, months later, but there is no apology, no acknowledgement, just the usual waiver. She signs it and thanks me for letting her tell someone what happened.

I lose my grandmother two months later when her brain bleed finally damages her brain enough that it doesn't work anymore. My laughing, bold, Camaro-driving, Piña Colada drinking grandmother, the person most like me in the world, hated me at the end, hated everyone at the end.

"We'd like to do an autopsy," her doctor says. "We just don't know what went wrong".

I don't cry then, either. An autopsy doesn't change anything.

II. (2006)

I am eating lunch and leafing through the autopsy photos. We are a week to trial and I am comparing the pathology report in front of me to the photos, to see if there is any difference, any possibility of changing the angle of the wound, the stab from behind. If the pathologist agrees the stab could have come from the angle my client said, it might mean not having to risk putting the client on the stand, not risk cross-examination. Of course, I think she is a liar.

Alison, the office manager, walks in holding files and message slips. "This is the Smith file," she says, and looks at me, fork halfway to my mouth, photos open to layers of skin peeled back showing pleura. She drops the file next to me, turns, and takes big strides out of my office.

"I'm quitting," she says. Twelve hours into my day, two weeks into her job, and she has decided to leave. "This isn't what I thought it was going to be like. I thought it would be like *Law and Order* and instead it's all sad people."

"It gets better," I say. "You wanted the job so badly; why are you quitting now?"

"I don't want to be like you," she says.

"I'm sorry?"

"You were eating lunch and you could look at those horrible pictures. That isn't normal."

"In the middle of a twelve-hour — soon to be fourteen-hour — day, I ate lunch. What's the problem?"

"Lasagne. You were eating lasagne." She has already packed up the photos of her husband and six-year-old daughter, some of my good desk pens, and the orchid that a client gave me months ago that hasn't bloomed since. She is too upset, she says, to give two weeks notice.

III. (2011)

He is slight, even for thirteen, and he sits in my office, knees folded to his chest. Like someone might hit him, I think, like someone might attack and this way he can defend his head and chest. I want to protect him, but not like I usually want to protect my adult clients from the state, but in a more immediate way, more like I would one of my nephews, or a weakened animal.

I get out of my chair, walk around my big desk. This child has talked to enough adults behind desks. He doesn't need anyone else to fear, I figure. I kneel down in front of him.

"Why did you throw the rock, Santiago? Were you trying to hurt someone?"

Kids in my office usually try to look tough. The legion of youth criminal justice act clients I've had before him stared fixedly at me, or are inattentive, or radiate hatred. I've come to expect that empty look and so when he finally looks up at me, his eyes the same shade of brown as mine, I am shocked. His eyes are wide and seeking, tears collecting in the corners.

"He called me a faggot. He called me a faggot, and when people call you a faggot, they usually hit you after. And he was so much bigger than me."

The police charged Santiago because the mother of the other kid called the school and the police. The police charged him because the other kid was bleeding when they saw him. The police charged him because they'd been called to the school before, because Santiago always seemed to be at the centre of a fight, because there was a weapon, because of the blood.

They charged him even though he was smaller and scared, and they took him to the police station and left him in a cell for an hour to teach him a lesson. I can't do anything about that last part, but I can do something about the rest of it even though the last part makes me so angry I want these cops fired. I never feel this way; being a cop is a job. Today, I feel as though I could go into the cop shop and start screaming and not stop.

"You're allowed to defend yourself, but it has to be fair," I say. "The problem is the rock, and…"

"Am I going to jail, then?" Small, quiet, terrified. Something in his tone so completely alone, it strikes my deepest lonely place.

"Oh, baby, no," I say, "No, that's not even a possibility, no. No, absolutely not."

He started to sob then, and reached forward, opening up his little body to me, his arms around my neck, sobbing like someone who has spoken their worst fear aloud. I have never held a client before, but this is a child so used to being called names and hit, he just needs me to care about him. I let him hang on, because I am not able to be the authority, the lawyer, the logical, reasoning adult; I carry the same loneliness and for a few minutes I am thirteen. I let him hang on because days at a time, it's all I'm doing too.

The Crown dropped the charges a month later when he saw the size difference between the two boys. I saw Santiago at that appearance, and as he was led out of the courtroom by his father, he looked back and at me. I smiled at him and watched until the oak door closed behind him. I waited a few minutes and then I walked to my car, and sat in the driver's seat, and sobbed for everything still ahead of him.

IV. (2014)

I propped the autopsy pictures open on the podium while I was cross-examining the pathologist. For every hour that I cross-examine witnesses, I put in at least ten hours of work. This choking case was particularly terrible; one of the few cases I have done where the attacker was a stranger. The deceased was a beautiful girl walking home from a party who crossed paths with the wrong man. Her family was in the gallery: decent, loving people who had never encountered the legal system.

"You have exhibit two open in front of you?"

"I do, yes."

"And for the benefit of the jury, those are the pictures in the blue Duo-Tang?"

"Yes."

"And these were pictures that you took during the autopsy?"

"They are, yes."

"And you performed the autopsy?"

"I did."

"And one of your tasks was to dissect the throat structures?"

"Yes."

"And the purpose of that was to look at the structures underlying the marks you identified as manual strangulation?"

"It was."

"And you found 'minimal crushing' is that correct?"

"Yes. What I meant by that remark — and I assume you're looking at my report — is that the underlying structures were not as damaged as I would expect to see if the cause of death was strangulation."

"Yes. In fact, the hyoid bone was intact?"

"It was, yes."

"And that's a common injury in strangulation deaths?"

"Not necessarily, especially not in strangulation cases where the victim" — he pronounced "victim" with a flourish, trying to help the Crown — "is a teenager or late adolescent, early adult."

I knew he would try and twist the knife in my back from earlier confrontations in other courtrooms. Some pathologists like defence lawyers and some hate defence lawyers, and he was the latter kind, with a particular dislike, as he once put it, for "girls who think they know what I do."

However, the jury in the F. murder case was about to see the best of me. The textbook he had written phrased it, "a hyoid bone fracture is a common injury in strangulation deaths, even where the hyoid bone is flexible, as may be the case in adolescent or young adult women." I could feel the fatigue behind my eyes, the weeks of preparation, the exhaustion about to give way to the moment where I could prove an expert, a witness, a victim wrong: the one exhilarating adrenaline rush that if we could bottle, no one would ever use cocaine. These are the moments I feel most alive. In the midst of death, I am in life.

I left the podium. My junior held up the textbook to me from where she was sitting at counsel table and I walked over ten steps to grab the textbook, and walked ten steps back; I made sure the jury was following my movements. I heard gasps and murmurs from the gallery. I paid no attention to the gallery. I never do. In the moment, I not thinking about the cause of any commotion; I am mid-cross-examination and if a bomb detonated, I would still ask my next question.

I finished cross-examination. The jury looked suitably impressed, except for juror number ten, who kept his head down, muttering, as was his habit. They filed out in a line, the judge left the bench.

My junior and I walked out of the courtroom. We were both exhilarated; she high-fived me. The prosecution must show the intent to kill for murder; if the pressure was not enough to crush the internal neck structures, how could they prove he intended to kill her? All the nights of strategy and preparation had just paid off. We were celebratory as we walked past the deceased's family in the hallway.

I used the upstairs bathroom, two floors and a corridor away from the family. As I washed my hands the deceased's aunt came near. "Look at me!" she demanded, and I did.

"How could you?" She was, unexpectedly, livid.

"How could I...?"

"The photos! Hasn't my sister been through enough? Isn't what you do enough pain for you? Dealing in pain, dealing in death, isn't it enough for you?"

She was looking at me. I looked back at her. I had absolutely no idea what she was talking about. I tried to be gentle; she was hurting, she was angry. I was also afraid. Very, very afraid. I was two floors and a corridor from the sheriffs, from my junior, the court clerk, the sheriffs, and she was between me and the door. I started to inch toward her, toward the door, toward safety. "I'm sorry, but I really don't know..."

She looked at me and I knew she hated me then. "You left the photos open on the stand. When you went to get whatever it was you were doing, you left the photos of my niece's naked body so that my sister could see them. So that my sister saw her neck cut up, and her bruised body, and her dead. You did that. Hasn't she been through enough?"

I had. I had done that. I hadn't meant to. But I had known they were sitting behind me, and I didn't think. What I had done was thoughtless, but I didn't mean to hurt them. I left the autopsy photos open behind me because I was in the middle of doing my job. The mother would have seen the pinpoint bright red star pattern of the petechiae in her open, staring eyes. I had looked at that picture more than I had wanted to — her big, fawn eyes, her sharp collar bones.

I shocked both of us: I burst into tears. I sat down on the industrial, brown-tile floor with my back to the sink, and I sobbed. Adrenaline drained out of me, left a vacuum that late nights, exhaustion, grief about my crumbling relationship, and the picture of her eighteen-year-old niece rushed in to fill.

She got down on the floor with me, this woman I'd never met, would never have met, but for the fact that Legal Aid assigned me to this case, this client, this place. She put her arm around my shoulders, held me through wracking sobs. "I'm sorry, I'm sorry," she said, "You're just doing your job. Your parents must be so proud of you. You're doing a good job. It isn't your fault she died. I don't blame you. You can't change the fact she's dead. I know, I know."

V. (2013)

We are talking about his case, about the gun, about whether they could prove it was him on the videotape, whether the 7-Eleven clerk he'd robbed would show up to court, when he says it:

"You'd make such a pretty corpse." He says, "You're my lawyer because I like thinking how beautiful you'd be when you were dead, blood pooling from your neck. And the smell of your hair. I would smell your hair for hours."

There is no glass between us, just the table. I've sat with murderers and sex offenders and never been worried for myself; now I'm talking to a man accused of robbery and I want to run, scream, hide, because looking in his eyes, I know he means it. I know I'm in danger, like I haven't been before. I end the interview, leave the lockup, call Legal Aid, and tell them it's a "lawyer-initiated change of counsel." I take my name off the intercom at my apartment, start sending all my mail to the office. I change shampoos. The smell of jasmine nauseates me now.

There is nothing to report, and I know as a female lawyer, I would be ridiculed or thought of as soft; male lawyers would try and steal my clients if I reported the threat to anyone, but when the police show up at my door a year later, I'm not surprised. They are not in uniform, so I refuse to open the door until they give me their badge numbers and I call 911, my heart pounding in my chest. I know who they're here about. The dispatch puts my call through to the grey-haired officer's cell phone; I hear it ring in the hall, he answers it, and I let them in.

"It's called Duty to Warn," the older one says, while the younger one looks everywhere but my face, and I can't tell if he's figuring out how secure my apartment is, or just won't look at me. "He got paroled to a halfway house and left there two days ago."

"Why are you telling me?" I ask, and now the younger one moves away from the conversation, is overly interested in the view from the window. "He did a lot of writing," the older one says. "He left a lot behind at the halfway house."

"Like what?"

"You don't want to know," the grey-haired one answers calmly, "but we do reasonably think you might be at risk." The younger one looks at me then, a look of distaste, and I can see he thinks I deserve whatever the former client has said he'll do to me.

"Drive someone else's car for a couple of days, OK? And you have priority 911 response, so make sure your phone has caller ID enabled on it." The older officer leans forward, his face softens, and he says, "You're one of us, just like if you were Crown; we'll protect you." But I can see the younger one doesn't agree, is restless, wants to be gone.

At the door, the younger one turns back, and I can see he can't help himself. "You were counsel on the F. murder case." It isn't a question.

"Yeah, I was."

"Well, then, be careful what happened to that girl doesn't happen to you. This guy said he'd rape you to death."

The older one is far enough down the hall that I'm sure he doesn't hear his partner. If I reported the police officer for saying it, I would never be taken seriously again; he knows it, and I know it too. I stare, close the door, turn both locks. It's August, but I go and lock all the windows, the sliding glass door, turn the chair to the window and try and figure out if someone could get into my sixth-floor apartment. My mind is preoccupied with escape strategies and if I should put a lock on my bedroom door so that there would be two doors to get through before he could hurt me, slide his hands around my neck.

That night that I don't sleep at all. I wonder if I should have called my parents to tell them I love them, or gone on vacation or had a kid. I think of Santiago, how I would have been a good mother to him.

They catch the former client five weeks later in Saskatchewan. He was caught in the act of slashing a woman's neck. They don't return him to my province, and the parole board now notifies me when he comes up for release, although he won't be released for a long time.

I don't sleep a full night again, except for one in the arms of a man in Berlin; he is gentle, tender, kind. Even then, I'm the first to wake up; even then, on swinging my legs over the side of the bed, I wonder what I was thinking, the recklessness of going home with a man who could have cut my throat. Any man can cut your throat, but when I looked at this man, I didn't see blankness in his eyes, only warmth, and I had to take the chance. I am so very tired and all I want is one night where I don't dream.

VI. (2017)

My business manager has been with me now ten years, hired to replace the feckless Alison. She is my friend; I didn't expect that we would be when I hired her — she was stern, hard on me about expenses, and my sometimes endless spending. Over time, she's become my greatest support; she runs the business, I run the practice. Together, we face everything.

Today, she meets me at the door. We have developed a series of codes — glances, shrugs, an upturned smile, a grimace — for dealing with files and clients. This is the first time in a decade I couldn't read her face.

"I need a few minutes," she says. "I know it's the end of the day, but I stayed."

Fear — a reasonable fear, as she's in her sixties — shoots through me. She seems so serious, I wonder if she's decided to retire. I have no backup plan, no alternative. My mind races ahead to all the reasonable things I will say. I know I won't be able to be reasonable later, alone in my apartment with the door locked and the deadbolt on.

She takes me into the spare office and closes the door. She sits down across the desk from me and she reaches out and grasps both my hands, and I know whatever it is she's about to tell me, I will never be able to unhear it.

"Honey, they found Santiago," she says. "He died. We don't have all the details. He'd been living on the street because his dad kicked him out and his friends say they'd seen him on Church Street and then they couldn't contact him. They found his body in Cobourg."

Santiago has been missing for a month. The police "missing persons" fliers showed a man in platform shoes, and eyeliner, called him an "up-and-coming member of the LGBTQ community." His friends are interviewed in the local gay newspaper, *Xtra*, and they all say the same thing: loud, proud, beautiful, artistic, loving, kind.

I think of his brown hair, his gap tooth, his arms around me. I think of the million times that I'd wondered if he was OK. I didn't know he was on the street, or I would have broken all the rules about professionalism and distance; I would have taken him home, to my home. I would have bought another apartment, one with two bedrooms, and I would have made him go to art school, or aesthetician school or dance school or whatever he wanted.

"I didn't tell him I loved him because that wasn't professional," I confess to her.

"You did the best you could, love. You always do."

"I would have been his mother. He's the kid I wanted and didn't have." I am crying, like I haven't cried since the day in the bathroom with the aunt, and my business manager is holding my hands across the desk, a tether, a lifeline. "He was what, nineteen? He doesn't get to be an adult, he died alone, and I could have been his mother, and I loved him and I didn't tell him. How did he die?"

"They're going to do an autopsy. I'm sure he knew you loved him."

An autopsy doesn't change anything. I tell my people I love them every time I finish a conversation now. I still don't sleep through the night. Sometimes when I wake up, I think Santiago is in the next room, on my couch, because I've found him in my dreams and brought him home.

The Golden Circles

Maureen Medved

When she was five, my daughter realized she will die. She looked at me with stark betrayal as if I'd slapped her. I told her, "It won't happen for a long time, and by then you will become part of the flowers and the trees."

She cried, "I don't want to become part of the flowers and the trees!"

I could hardly tolerate the cut of her pain.

Years ago, I had seen a tiny black lamb leap across an open field. My daughter was once like the lamb, but now the inevitability of death had diminished her joy.

"Maybe when you are older, they will discover a cure for death."

Her face brightened as the power of this lie seeped in.

But was it a lie? Science was making progress.

I have experienced many near deaths, complicated, varied, and innumerable. By threatening me all my life, these deaths have taught me how to live. I now view death as a benevolent circle, tightening, glistening, deepening, and sucking me into a golden point inside myself I hadn't wanted to acknowledge.

※　※　※

When I was a child, I got the usual ailments: tonsillitis, bronchitis, mumps, earaches. Then in my early teens, the first circle caught me. I woke up unable to walk. Pain and exhaustion covered the world in a greasy membrane. My legs became weak, swollen. Then the hospital, pin pricks, electrodes. Over the year, I recovered. The doctors arrived at no conclusions. *Maybe a virus*, they said. I didn't want to consider anything more serious. During those pre-internet years, I believed death came only for the old, stupid, and unlucky. Death: what is that?!

Magazine rock stars glittered in our otherwise sterile, suburban imaginations. Girls hitchhiked. Smoke curled in movie theatres and on buses, airplanes, and campuses. Sex and death both enticed and confused us. Those were paradoxically repressive times: Sunday store closures, God Save the Queen, and the Lord's Prayer. I hated this world and applied myself with a Girl Guide's focus to studying tiny knots where individuality could be picked open and unravelled. For years after my illness mysteriously disappeared, I kept getting sick and avoided thinking about it, allowing more intense experiences to fill the space between this circle and the next. I wanted to taste every part of the world. To throw myself against the light and burn.

※　※　※

Ten years later, living in Montreal, the second circle caught me. Early to mid-twenties, all-nighters, Les Foufounes Électriques, jaunts to NYC, hanging out at The Pyramid Club, the Cat Club, CBGB, Tunnel, and playing Flipper super loud in the Montreal office where I assembled packages for a company that promoted performing artists. Words and warnings surfaced inside me like a Magic 8-Ball, but I pushed them down. I never felt well, but it took decades for me to know this. I lived hard and fast, and the future burned far away off the edges of the horizon.

154 | AGAINST DEATH

I wrote reviews for a magazine. For reasons I didn't yet understand, I needed to pound and twist the incongruities of my life into something meaningful in the form of little stories. The manual typewriter weighed ten pounds and came in a metal case. I laced the black ribbon through the front mechanism. Carted around this newborn, one I could leave alone for hours. I couldn't tolerate a greater responsibility. *What is that?* people remarked, looking at my little case. Since I didn't know why I had to write, I couldn't explain it to them.

The mid-eighties. I'd just returned from London, visiting a man who'd twice broken my heart. I wouldn't allow it to happen again. My motto: no love, no people, no commitments.

That Christmas I flew home to Winnipeg. Walked from one winter into another. Snowbanks. Ice speared from awnings. With every step, my heart strained to pump the blood through my body, and rushed hard inside my head. I stared at the stark prairie sky, blue against the white landscape. *That's strange*, I thought, *I can hear the ocean.*

I hadn't yet called my family to let them know I had arrived. That night at a friend's house, my head sagged into the turkey and gravy. I took a cab to the hospital. They shoved me on a gurney and moved me from the ER up many floors where they parked me in an isolation room where robots attended to me, I realize now, in what were probably hazmat suits. *We don't know if you're a threat to us or if we are a threat to you*, they said. *Your hemoglobin is plummeting. You're lucky you got here on time. If you'd waited one more day, you'd probably be dead.*

The idea of dying within a day struck me as dramatic. The hospital called my parents. I hadn't seen them in six months, and now they hovered at my bedside. I occupied the little white room through Christmas to New Year's and just beyond. Friends delivered mix tapes and tiny packages. I had a new, little portable cassette player and listened to Flipper and Black Flag repeatedly and chose to believe everything was normal. One day a doctor popped in. "There is a new disease. It's called AIDS." The doctor was perfunctory, solemn. "We'll give you a test."

I wondered if it was even possible that I could get a disease I'd only read about in newspapers. This was like a science fiction movie.

Then I thought, *Shit. Whatever I did to get this totally wasn't worth it.*

The doctors explained to my parents and me the ways I could have contracted such a disease. I'd grown up in the suburbs. A new house. Bay windows. My father sold insurance. I'd dated a high school football player. I'd once had a perm. As my parents stared in stunned silence, I knew this wasn't what they'd had in mind when they'd conceived me.

The hospital stabilized my hemoglobin with prednisone, an oral steroid, then discharged me early in the new year. *You probably won't be going back to Montreal*, they said.

Each day I'd return to the cancer clinic where they'd reduce the prednisone, and watch as my hemoglobin plummeted to dangerous levels.

For three weeks, as I went back and forth to the cancer clinic, I waited for the result of my AIDS test. I sat on the tweed sofa in my parents' rec room, watching bad television movies about men who got AIDS as a punishment for cheating on their wives. I made promises to God, but as I didn't believe in a god who could understand the English language, I knew this was not the time to become a hypocrite.

I rarely went outside except to go to the hospital and pharmacy to pick up my prednisone. Now the steroids made my joints ache and my cheeks pulse with tiny red veins and swell so big that my eyeglasses broke when I tried to put them on. People I'd known for years stopped to ask if I knew myself. *You look like Maureen Medved. Are you her sister?* I said, *I am Maureen Medved* until they gathered their shock and crept away.

Then one day the doctors said, *We can't keep you on this high dose of prednisone.*

Well, what happens if I can't come off it?

Let's cross that bridge when we come to it, they said.

The terror sank in. This could actually happen. Was happening. An urgency pedalled fast inside me.

I didn't want to die, but life wasn't fair. The world and its suffering. Even children. Babies. Why should I be an exception? There might be an average life span, but that was for actuaries. Life made no promises.

The Jell-O shivered in its bowl. *Your favourite,* my mother said. Jell-O was my favourite, but writing had now become my reason for living. I knew I needed to do this one thing before I die even if I didn't know why I did it and even if nobody read my stories.

Three weeks later I got the call. *You don't have AIDS,* they told me. I held the phone to my ear, and my knees buckled, even though I knew it was a cliché.

You're not out of the woods yet. We diagnosed you with a rare blood disease: autoimmune hemolytic anemia.

The way we understand it, they explained to me, *the spleen is malfunctioning and causing all your problems. The spleen will have to go.*

Well, what is a spleen anyway?

Well, it's an organ, they said.

Don't worry. It's just a little operation, they told me. I focussed on the word little. Then they vaccinated me, so I didn't develop something called OPSI (or overwhelming post-splenectomy infection), but I strategically chose to avoid the details. *Football players get splenectomies all the time. And you can travel, but you'll need to get more vaccinations.*

After the surgery, I lifted my blanket to look down at the little scar. But the scar ran across my entire body and they had stapled my flesh together, so I looked like Frankenstein's monster and could no longer wear tiny shirts without freaking everybody out. Then they told me if I survived the next few years, I would probably be cured. I retracted like a snail. I was twenty-five.

I didn't want to think about any of this, so I applied myself more deeply to the writing, and the writing allowed me to commit to others. Even though I refused to acknowledge how sick I'd been, something about the process of almost dying made me take tiny risks. I did an MFA, wrote a book, articles, was invited to teach, and got an academic position.

By my late thirties, I'd allowed myself to fall in love, but a baby would be impossible as the psychological trajectory of my life had not prepared me for pregnancy. *Don't worry,* they told me. *You probably won't get pregnant anyway because of your age.*

Great, I thought to myself, *almost off the hook!*

Then by my mid-forties, and after many losses, a little girl surfaced within me. Stunned by fear, wonder, amazement, I became intensely protective of that tiny pulsing life. I lay shaking and strapped to the gurney like a crucifixion when they presented her to me. I could never have imagined love. Commitment. People. A daughter! She stared at me with trust, curled her fist around my finger, and held on until I cracked open and feelings I didn't know existed seeped out in strange ways, making me the target of those uncomfortable with their own fragility.

The circles deepened. Tightened. Signs that things weren't all right. I needed to believe I was like the others. Baffling illnesses persisted — pneumonia, shingles, sinus infections, cellulitis, strange cells that multiplied in threatening ways, surgery, and various painful procedures. The indignities accumulated. My body disintegrated. *What do you expect?* the doctors told me. *You have a young child. Every new parent feels that way.* Coffee and sugar galvanized my resources.

A movie adaptation of my first novel had come out. Now I was working on *Black Star*, a novel on ethical philosophy. I had never studied ethics. It would require research. Focus. I expected, as with my first novel, that this would take only a few years. But it had already been years. Every time I sat down to write, my brain, no longer available to me for this highly complex and intense creative work, snapped shut as perfunctorily as a doctor's file.

I could teach, perform my duties, write articles, but no novel would come. My characters reached out to me in the dark, but I was too weakened by disease to grab hold of them.

※　※　※

The third circle arrived when my daughter was two. Spring. Flowers. Sunshine. My husband, Isidore, had come home from the doctor to tell me that he needed open heart surgery within the next few months. As he delivered this information, my back seized and my head seared with pain. I shook on the floor and our daughter clung and wept for me as Isidore pulled her away. My daughter and I were once intrinsically linked, but now my illness separated us.

When I arrived at the ER, a nurse shouted at me, *Where do you live?*

Up the street, I said.

She screwed her face at me, then shouted back over her shoulder at another nurse, *I think she said she lives on the street.*

I have a baby, I said.

You're very brave, the nurse said. Then I heard her call back to the other nurse, *She's a mom who lives on the street with her baby.* Then to me, *What drugs are you on?*

I don't use drugs.

Okay. She sounded angry like she didn't believe me.

They pumped pain medication through my veins, took my

blood, then wheeled me to the door. *Please, don't send me away,* I begged. I nodded off in the wheelchair until a taxi carried me home. I heaved myself into the house as my daughter wept for me.

Within hours, I was shipped back to ER, a defective parcel, too sick and in too much pain to be afraid. *Septic shock,* the doctor said. *Your organs are shutting down.* He flashed a tiny light into my eyes and asked me difficult questions like, *What year is it?*

I slanted on the gurney as they pumped me full of water. *We are doing this to increase your blood pressure. You're going into organ failure. Your husband will be here as soon as he finds a sitter.* Far away, a voice argued with someone on the phone I knew was probably Isidore.

The idea that I was dying flashed repeatedly inside me as I stared at a computer screen that instructed on proper hand-washing protocol. Even with my daughter, even knowing that she may not remember me if I die. The doctor infused me with morphine. I guess that's it, I thought, and I held my daughter's face in my heart as I floated away.

Isidore arrived. His eyes blasted open as he steadied himself. I had blown up like someone in a fat suit with the infusion of water they had pumped into me.

Then several weeks later they announced, *Your vitals are finally stable. Good news, you're going home. Bad news, your veins are scarred from all the medication.*

Then they threaded an IV from a vein in my arm up close to my heart in a PICC line to deliver high dose antibiotics. My daughter! After two weeks, I'd finally gone home. Where my daughter and I had once been intrinsically linked, the machine they'd inserted into my heart had now replaced her. My daughter stood in the living room and turned to me without recognition.

Every day a nurse came to the apartment to clean the site surrounding my PICC. Now mothers pushed their children away from me as I sweated and dragged my IV pole down the street. After weeks of receiving the antibiotics, the PICC line came out. The doctor said, *Well, that should take care of things. None of the usual bugs would survive the blast we just gave you.*

Then came the fourth circle. Two weeks after they removed the PICC, my doctor gave Isidore the green light to prepare for his heart surgery. Again, I started shaking. Septic. Hospital.

Well, I guess that didn't work, I told the doctor.

Well, it worked for a while, he said, shaking his head. *This is the same bacteria.*

That's kind of weird, right? I said.

He looked perplexed. *Well, it doesn't usually happen.*

Again Isidore had to postpone his heart surgery as I slid into organ failure, and once again suffered septic shock, another PICC line, and strange tests involving radioactive blood tracers to find the bacteria that made its way inside me.

The city sent a social worker to our apartment. She advised us to consider who would take our daughter if we both died. *Trust me,* she said, *you don't want to put her in public care.*

Isidore's mother flew in to help us. As soon as I became stronger, the doctors took out the PICC, and Isidore flew to meet his parents in Toronto for his heart surgery.

Only four months had passed since my first septic episode. Now it was fall and, as Isidore recovered, I returned to work. My symptoms persisted. Old newspaper clotted my brain. The novel. I couldn't dredge up the strength. Even speech required stores of energy I couldn't find. I wandered the halls of the university where I worked. A ghost. Maybe I already was dead. I tried to write, work. Specialist upon specialist. The pain, the exhaustion. A daughter. Husband. Stories. Here they were, and soon would be taken from me.

Over the next few years, periods of incapacity and trips to the ER punctuated my life. After one intense infection, the infectious disease specialist sent me to the immunologist.

The specialist did his tests and called us in. *You don't have a spleen, which limits your ability to control certain types of bacterial infection. In addition, you are not producing adequate levels of antibodies, which further compromises your immune system. You've also got this abnormal antibody (monoclonal protein) circulating in your blood at a relatively high level, and you need to be checked every year to see if you develop multiple myeloma, a form of bone marrow cancer. But don't worry, we've made strides. I mean, you don't want it, but if you get it it's no longer an automatic death sentence.* Then he told me that they could now tell by certain characteristics in my T-cells that I was either born this way or had taken a certain chemotherapy drug that I'd never taken. Then that specialist sent me to another specialist.

Wow! said the hematologist. *Thirty years ago you were diagnosed with hemolytic anemia. It was a mystery then, but now we know it's all part of the same condition you have now.*

With the progress of science, they could finally piece together this constellation of symptoms. The infectious disease doctor, the immunologist, the hematologist, and a number of specialists with their minor roles. Maybe a cure for death was around the corner.

The Boy in the Plastic Bubble was a movie in the seventies starring John Travolta based on the lives of David Vetter and Ted DeVita who had SCID (severe combined immune deficiency). I had a milder subset of primary immunodeficiency called hypogammaglobulinemia. I don't live in a bubble, but my condition is incurable and infections could be life-threatening.

Every two weeks for the first few years, the hospital infused me with intravenous antibodies (immunoglobulins) culled from the plasma cells from the blood of strangers. Then because the hospital itself could make me sick, I have learned to infuse myself at home once a week, something I will need to do for the rest of my life. Just as I will need to take antibiotics at least twice a day every day, and sometimes more, depending on whatever bacteria I am fighting. I carry a letter explaining emergency protocol that I present to the ER if I suspect an infection and additional wide-spectrum antibiotics that buy me two hours to make it to the hospital.

※　※　※

Now with this new world and its baroque protocols, Isidore and I were too stunned and exhausted to be relieved by my diagnosis. Isidore was still recovering from his heart surgery, and had gone through a series of TIAs, transient ischemic attacks, or baby-strokes, and had gone temporarily blind in his right eye. We lived separate lives as we tried to survive, tending to our own medical crises. My daughter wandered past me like a stranger.

We need to change it up, I told Isidore. *Maybe we could travel.*

In the context of our lives, the word travel seemed ludicrous. Maybe Mexico? But the doctors said they didn't recommend it as Isidore sagged with his noble stoicism.

The doctors told me to avoid travelling to places where I'd be more likely to develop an infection. Though my risk would be reduced with the antibody infusions, and possibly also with the vaccinations given to people who don't have a spleen, I would likely not generate a normal antibody response to vaccinations, anyway. And as I have no spleen and minimal antibodies, I would have to stay in major cities with a high level of critical care, state-of-the-art medicine, clean water, sanitation, and few infectious diseases, and, for the rest of my life, stay within two hours of a hospital in case I developed an infection, which could quickly become septic. Most flights are more than two hours, but life, I've learned, is about calculated risk.

I tested my limits, but without weekly immunoglobulins, I deteriorated fast and the fog descended. As I carried my supply home from the hospital in little boxes containing vials of clear sticky liquid, I became grateful and angry in a childish way. I wanted a normal life. I had bought into the concept of unlimited options like a high-end credit card, an illusion propagated by a consumerist fantasy machine. But I was alive. We were alive. I had to accept my limitations and had a choice to make. Then deep inside myself, and within the tiny scope of my life, I found joy.

Today, I have a job. I write, research, study. As I continue the medical protocol, my body and brain grow stronger. I've never had true health, but with my treatments, the fog that has sur-rounded me all my life has finally lifted. Ideas loop in intricate ways. My little stories come more easily. They are bigger, denser, and more complex. This renewed clarity and energy enabled me to finish my novel, *Black Star*. But the daily antibiotics. The weekly infusions. The sanitizers. The bags of pills and medical documents. The vials of immunoglobulins. The diagnosis brings its indignities. My two-hour window to make it to the hospital before it's too late.

As each circle embraces me, I need the world less. By reduc-ing the world, I have learned to commit to writing, and an interior life that makes me happy.

The circles live inside me. We are part of the same organic fabric. The same fabric that made my daughter, and the one that makes the flowers and the trees.

Isidore, my daughter, and I still live together, but walk around unusually alert as we take each step and wonder if it will be our last.

My daughter and I have found a new way to be close. At ten years old, she still asks, *Have they found the cure for death yet?*

And I say, *They are still working on it.*

I wait for the next circle. The one that will finally take me when I can no longer fight. Just as the oryx is lifted to be licked, evaluated, and devoured by the lion. But I am not yet the oryx. I want to be the little black lamb, racing through that open field.

Just as with each near death, I circle closer to the final. The next time may be my last. I am prepared just as I have prepared my whole life.

Someday these words may be here, but I may not.

I don't wish to live any life other than one on the verge of death.

As for my daughter, the inevitability sinks in with each turn, each step and breath. Each time she asks, the spaces between grow longer, and I know soon, she won't need to ask anymore.

Let This Be Familiar

Emma Smith-Stevens

A neurobiologist might explain my psych ward stay at age thirteen, the first of twelve or so, by pointing to the thorns on the branches jutting from my family tree — the drunks and junkies, the impulsives and insomniacs, the mood-disordered and anxious. My DNA would be twin vines wound tightly around not only that first hospitalization, but also the addictions I commenced in rapid succession: I harmed my body with blades and flames — then cigarettes, sex, drugs, starvation.

The neurobiologist would likely assert that, like all people, I'm better represented by a double helix than past trauma or whether I'd been breastfed. My first locked unit and all that followed was decided by rogue neurons and receptors that pre-date my first breath; and, like most parties involved in dysfunctional relationships, those neurons and receptors know what they know, which is only how to do what they do, whatever the cost, and when presented with alternatives — peaceful coexistence, harmony, balance — they cannot be persuaded of a single goddamn thing.

Yet frank logic may suffice to understand that first hospitalization. A glance at cause and effect would point to a night in seventh grade as the toppling of the first in a trail of dominos.

Already on antidepressants, I was taught by the most popular girl in my grade how to give oral sex to another girl. "This is what lesbians do," she said, pushing my head down between her soccer-player thighs. It was fine. Another weekend, we did it again. And again.

At the start of eighth grade, I mentioned the relationship to the girl's best friend, whom I thought knew everything but actually knew nothing. Both girls declared war. They told everyone that I was liar. I received the silent treatment from all our classmates. "Molester," "pervert," and "dyke" followed me down the hallways, whispered loudly by passersby into my ears. One day, everyone in my homeroom formed a line and hawked loogies into my locker. Another day in the bathroom, the girl I'd been having sex with and her best friend rammed my back against the stall doors, and punched me in the stomach until I was curled on the tiled floor, sucking air like a guppy.

I received a letter penned by my ex-lover, folded into the smallest possible triangle and shoved through a slit in my locker. Everybody hated me, it said. Everyone at our school knew I was on psycho pills, and since I was so depressed I should just kill myself. The world would be a better place. I should do it today.

Below were the signatures of almost every student in my grade.

Late that night, I tied one end of a short bungee cord around a closet doorknob in my bedroom and wrapped a loop around my neck. There I was, staring through a swiftly disappearing pinhole into the star-spangled beyond — and then I yanked the cord up, off, so I was free and gasping. Thanks to primitive instincts I didn't lose my life. What I did lose after I made a shaky confession to my parents was my freedom to a lockdown psych ward.

※　※　※

Doesn't it seem intuitive, though, to describe my first hospitalization as a result of being sexually abused when I was so young that I don't remember any age? At thirteen, all I had were a handful of images and snapshots that would suddenly appear, and sensations: my throat closing up, nearly vomiting, death standing right behind me. All men seemed to be looking at me *that way*. I could never say no to a boy or man's thirst for my body lest things get dangerous. My only chance for safety in the world was to become solely a brain, floating like a ghost above my body. Looking down from dizzying heights, my physical self — the glut of a heinous crime — was somehow abstracted. In fact, everything was like that. Nothing seemed real.

In my secret self, I was breaking. I was — I knew — what I most feared: weak. I had nightmares. I was trembling inside, perpetually nauseated. I panicked at my nakedness reflected in a mirror or the eyes of a boyfriend or girlfriend. My flesh was the site of unspeakable shame. Where more suitable for such grotesquery — such menace — than a place for those who, as the law for involuntary commitment to psychiatric wards reads, "pose a danger to self or others?"

※　※　※

My first hospitalization can also be credited to my parents' savvy. They said, "Would you like to go somewhere where they can help you feel better?" And I said, "Yes."

Then I was on the ward with my parents. Up and down the main hall, patients were screeching, demented, pacing, muttering, wandering, slumped in a wheelchair. I was down on the floor. My arms were wrapped around my parents' legs. "Don't leave me here," I said. "I made a mistake. This isn't good for me. I need to go home. I won't do anything bad. I can't stay."

Strong arms gripped around my waist and slid me backwards

across the floor, away from my parents' backs, which were turned to me and got further and further away. The arms — a strange man's arms — were suffocating me. The arms released me into a dingy white-ceilinged room with scuffed, beige padding on the walls. I froze. Then I leapt forward, pressed my forehead against the Plexiglas window in the door that had already shut and locked me in, and watched my parents, who stiffened at my screams and banging fists, but did not turn around, as they were let into the clear-walled waiting partition between the unit and the elevator, until finally they stepped aboard and the sliding metal doors swallowed them down.

※　※　※

I stopped frequenting psych wards through acts of grace: kindnesses I never earned, but finally could appreciate and build on. I went from homeless with no prospects to living in a halfway house overnight, placed there by the helping hand of a stranger — a sober biker down in a fucked up little Florida city where cocaine and pills had spat me out.

Over the next few years, I became increasingly empowered — first, by the right diagnosis and medications, and then by working with a smart, compassionate therapist. I no longer keep secrets, the kinds that weigh a person down. I've begun to acknowledge my traumas and their effects on me, enough so that I've enjoyed some degree of freedom from shame, and I'm willing to work for more. I no longer view life as a story that unfolds outside and far away. Living has cultivated in me a hunger to experience what it means to have agency, to chase my desires and confront my aversions, to cultivate my talents and curiosities, to appreciate that resilience has been with me and carries me still.

Today, my heart breaks for my younger self and for the shattered woman I sometimes sense beside me, who yearns to merge with me but never completely succeeds. I fight, and fail to shove back the memories and moods that once skinned me, seared me. I wear a coat of armor. I continually hone its design, compelled to discover how lightweight and agile I can make the plates of steel, welded by flames so bright as to blind and hinged for freedom of motion. My armour allows what I want and need inside, yet is strong enough to hold me safe and upright.

※　※　※

Today I am sick as ever — less in the mind, much more in the body. I often feel closer to death than back when I wanted to kill myself. My muscles are weak, my joints in terrible pain. I am exhausted. My heartbeat is much too rapid, the movements of my gastrointestinal system far too slow. When I attempt to board an escalator, the metal steps may as well be moving at twenty miles per hour. When I stand on one foot to put a sock on the other, I fall over. I sweat profusely without provocation. My muscles ache and spasm. Until I began medication for nerve pain, my skin felt like glass shards were continually being sprayed against it. This physical malady began when I was most joyful: I had just gotten married, had many newfound friends, and had recently finished graduate school. I was writing and writing, anticipating the publication of my first novel.

While I have diagnoses for various symptoms, my doctors have not yet rendered one for their underlying cause. However, I am about to start an intensive treatment — infusions of immunoglobulin four hours a day, once a week, in my home. I am submitting to this remedy because it helps some people with autoimmune diseases with symptoms similar to my own. I want to get better. I don't want this illness to be the answer to the question of my life's trajectory. What I want is not to die — not yet. I have learned some of what life beyond survival is like and I want more.

※　※　※

I must correct myself: I have a very real diagnosis for these physical symptoms. There is a massive correlation between autoimmune diseases, which women suffer eight times more often than men, and trauma. My diagnosis is being molested. My diagnosis is having been raped, my breast palmed and twisted on the subway, assaulted in my sleep, having a man's hand thrust up my skirt and into my underwear at a bar, hollered at in the streets, demeaned, my claims ignored or silenced. My diagnosis is being locked up in too many psych wards to count, strip-searched, called "crazy" and "psycho" and "slut" and "cunt," getting force-fed pills and injected against my will — receiving medications that made me unable to have a say in who I was or what I thought or what happened to me, drugs that made me drool, my own words suddenly choking hazards. My diagnosis is: I lost much of my childhood, my teens, my early adulthood to the whims of men, the will of doctors, my brain's malfunctions, and thoughts instilled in me by countless horrors.

These facts inhabit my body. They set my joints aflame, and I cry out for water. My peripheral and autonomic nervous systems scream for help. I scream along with them — and am heard.

※　※　※

Now instead of yearning for pain — to feel alive or to hide from some even worse pain — I wish instead for honest emotion and safe opportunities for compassionate communion with others. What has awakened in me is a devotion to love. Is that familiar? Let it be. Let love be as instinctual as the body's simple breath.

Waves

Fiona Tinwei Lam

When we were growing up, my mother often wished out
loud that she were dead, right in front of us. She said
this many times both before and after my father died of liver
cancer when I was eleven, the eldest of three kids. She said it
coming home, exasperated after a hard day at her general medical practice, dealing with mostly immigrant women and kids
lined up out of the door of her tiny office, or after dealing with
piles of bills. Perhaps one of her patients had miscarried, or a
birth had gone wrong at the hospital. Perhaps there'd been too
many patients, too many closed faces, condescending and dis-
missive male colleagues, and smirking bureaucracies. Perhaps
I had broken the proverbial camel's back by forgetting her
birthday, not making dinner, or neglecting to wash a sink full
of food-encrusted dishes sitting in scummy water — somehow
making her too-hard life even harder.

Sometimes she said it while she was driving, ranting
about mortgages and work and being alone without any help. The
three of us would sit numbly not sure what to say or do as she
would go on and on. Then she would become enraged by our lack
of reaction — our lack of sympathy, compassion, advice, whatever it was that she wanted. We were blank walls hemming her

in, isolating her further, and she needed more. "I wish we were all dead!" she'd shout, stepping on the accelerator, until we'd jolt to a halt just before the intersection. Perhaps these incidents taught me that wishing for death was a normal way to express an urgent desire to escape — from troubles, uncertainty, grief.

My paternal (and only living) grandparents had always disapproved of my mother as being profoundly unworthy of their son, disapproving of what they considered her substandard origins, and pronouncing her unattractive, too old, and deficient as a wife in every way. Their constant criticism extended to us kids as well. If a relative ever suggested that I looked like my father, my paternal grandmother would retort sourly with pursed lips, "She looks just like her mother." Although they were wealthy, they refused to help her out financially during the difficult six years following my dad's death.

I remember a bus trip my family took to the Grand Canyon. The canyon was vast and unreal, a slight haze veiling and muting its depths. When I looked down, I imagined myself jumping in, or simply letting myself fall. I could feel the dizziness in the pit of my belly, imagining falling and falling. Would it go fast or in slow motion? Would it hurt, would I feel my bones breaking, my head caving in? I thought of the coyote on the reruns of *The Road Runner* cartoons that I watched after school — that scrawny brown coyote's long, long fall, beside an anvil, under an anvil, on top of an anvil, his scraggly ears waggling, eyes widening into white circles with the realization. Of course, he'd never die, just get squished into an accordion or a compressed puck, arise in a whorl of dust, his weaving steps and spinning head orbited by stars. His shattered, crumpled, crumbled body would somehow resuscitate, rehabilitate, reincarnate for a second, tenth, hundredth resurrection. I knew I was no Wile E. Coyote. Would I eventually hit bottom, or just crash and rebound against the craggy ridges and land somewhere, scraped, broken, before falling again to land on a precarious ledge? I imagined screwing it up, waiting hours in agony while rescue crews would arrive with ropes and harnesses. More trouble for my harassed, over-whelmed mother, more trouble for my hapless younger siblings. A burden to everyone.

I fantasized about death through high school and university, wrote poems about death and to Death, sometimes obscured by metaphor, sometimes not. Every time there was a rejection, a failure or setback — and there were many — I'd mull over how to do it. A bridge? Stepping out in front of traffic? But a deep-seated terror of pain, of disabling myself and of hurting my family always stopped the fantasies mid-track.

I first saw Jimmy Stewart in the black-and-white movie, *It's a Wonderful Life* on TV when I was a teenager. I wondered if my existence had made an impact in anyone's life without my knowing it. I'd led a very sheltered middle-class life. I'd made few friends, being a severe introvert who had always been at the bottom of the social pecking order. A boring, unremarkable average student. Clumsy and uncoordinated in gym class. Unfashionable, plain, dumpy. I was highly forgettable. I excelled in nothing. I hadn't made a difference to anyone.

I sometimes wondered if my mother's life could have been happier and better if she had had a son instead of me. She would have vindicated herself as a wife, making my father happy and his parents more accepting. My father wouldn't then have had to deal with my mother's constant harangues about his parents. Maybe he wouldn't have internalized the domestic tension, which would have possibly meant that he wouldn't have gotten cancer or maybe it would have been caught earlier and he wouldn't have died, and my mother wouldn't have had the stress of trying to return to work as a doctor after an eight-year absence from practice, and then the family wouldn't have struggled financially, and my mother wouldn't have become so exhausted, depressed, and stressed and then she wouldn't have gotten macular degeneration and then Alzheimer's, and she wouldn't have depended so heavily on my siblings, whose lives wouldn't have been distorted around caring for her since they were kids. I couldn't imagine a world that was worse without me — just the opposite: "It's a Wonderful Life — Without You."

I continued to feel this way into adulthood, through my thirties, after relationships dissolved, after having a kid as a single mother, and after re-partnering in my forties. Nothing made a difference. Oddly, my mother's death even deepened my wish. Despite our conflict-ridden history and the ten years of her deepening dementia, I missed her presence and for about six months was submerged in thoughts of being with her and my deceased father wherever they were. When I did emerge from the fog of grief, I still couldn't shake off the feeling that living my life was merely a joyless duty I owed to my family, to keep living until my body gave out in some way.

But then I arranged a holiday to Maui during the holidays with my partner, Ted, and my son, Robbie. Robbie was eager to go snorkelling, so I booked an excursion. Our boat was one of three stationed at Molokini Crater. About sixty tourists were jam-packed into the small zone of calm, warm waters trying to spot fish. It was hard not to collide into another tourist. The boat then took our group to another location, this time with open water far from any shore and other boats. By then the sky had clouded over and the wind had started up. Having felt so safe at the crater earlier with the crew keeping close scrutiny over everyone, I decided I didn't need the flotation belt I'd worn earlier.

All of us descended into the water and quickly dispersed. I swam looking downwards, following the volcanic seam underwater where there was more marine flora and fauna. When I finally came to the surface, I realized I was gurgling—my mask wasn't on quite right. There was a lot of water inside. I took it off, but couldn't get it back on properly. The waves were getting choppier. I was far from the boat and the other snorkelers. I attempted again to fix my mask. It didn't work. I tried to inflate the flimsy, uninflated life vest I was wearing. It didn't do anything and I had barely any breath to inhale into it anyway. The waves were getting higher, slapping me in the face each time I was trying to take a breath. Water filled my nose and mouth. I looked around. No one.

My stomach clenched, all senses suddenly on high alert with hyperclarity. Urgency sang through my limbs and brain. No one could see me. No one knew that I was struggling. Things were getting worse fast. For a long moment I imagined just giving up and letting myself drown. I wondered how that would feel, but then had the proverbial flash of an imminent possible future: no one discovering that I was missing until a head count was taken after everyone else had returned to ship, my son and spouse going nuts on realizing I was not on board. Then the crew looking out over the water and finding my body, trying in vain to resuscitate me. Or not finding my body until hours or even days later. A crisis for everyone aboard. Robbie in extreme shock, with years ahead of therapy and self-destructive behaviour. Robbie blaming both Ted and himself. Ted also blaming himself and even turning to drugs again. My sister and brother having to fly out. Trauma upon trauma. A huge nasty tangled mess.

I tried to bob up and wave my arms back and forth to the boat which looked like a toy from far off. The captain was looking out over the water, but somehow never looked in my direction. I swam forward a bit more, swallowed more water, and tried again. He still couldn't see me. I could feel panic closing in. But I knew enough to push it back with all my willpower. Not to waste any energy flailing. Pure rationality and clarity clamped down on my nerves. Do not panic. Find someone. Swim forward. Try to breathe between the waves. But the timing of the waves was un-

predictable. Some came long and slow; all of them came one
after the other, relentlessly. I saw a young fellow swim past me
underwater — too fast for me to stop him to get his attention.
Then I saw an American passenger I recognized — an athletic,
grey-headed father of a family.

"Excuse me," I said loudly. He didn't hear me. "Excuse me!"
I said even louder.

He looked up, surprised.

"I need help," I said flatly, looking him in the eye. I couldn't
say anything more due to the waves.

There was a moment's pause as he assessed the situation.
"Take my arm," he said.

I did and he tried to swim with me toward the boat. For what
seemed like forever, I tried to kick along, spluttering, swallowing water, gasping. He stopped and tried to signal the crew on
the boat in vain. Eventually, we were close enough to get their
attention. The captain on board started yelling and gesticulat-
ing at the crew member in the water who was supposed to be
looking out for us, but he was too far away. By the time he came
over on his paddleboard, I was about four or five feet away from
the boat, holding onto a big, clear inflatable ring with cartoon
figures that belonged to a young kid and his mom. I waved him
away. "I'm okay."

I swam over to the ramp and climbed onto the boat myself,
declining the captain's offer of assistance. I sat for a while,
panting and blowing my nose and coughing up the salt water I'd
swallowed. I threw off the uninflated, completely useless vinyl
life vest and threw it onto the pile. After everyone had returned
onboard, I calmly told Robbie and Ted what had happened, and
thanked the man who had helped me. He and his family kept
looking at me for a reaction, but I remained stoic. I sat in the
hold of the boat by myself, not wanting to talk to anyone. The
young crew member who had been in the water to supposedly

watch over us, came and sat a few feet away. Perhaps his boss had chastised him. Perhaps he felt guilty even though it hadn't been his fault — it had been mine for having the hubris to go out into the open ocean without watching out where I was in relation to the boat, for not wearing the foam flotation device around my waist.

"Anything you need?" he finally asked.

"No," I said. I was still digesting the experience — or recovering from it.

That night we returned to our small hotel room. I couldn't sleep. Thoughts kept circling. I was still on the boat or in the water. The panic I had suppressed was now surfacing now that I was safe. I couldn't concentrate on reading or on preparing for next day's trip to the aquarium.

"You know, I could have died." Ted and Robbie stopped what they were doing and looked at me.

"You're safe now," Ted reassured me. "Everything's fine." Robbie agreed. "Just stop thinking about it."

But I couldn't. I kept reliving those waves smacking me in the face, and not being able to breathe. I couldn't sleep. I started to write in my journal. And as I wrote, I realized that beyond the release of suppressed terror, something profound had shifted within me.

I tried to identify this change. It seemed that I no longer wanted to "unexist." Out there in the water, I had not wanted to be dead. I had wanted to live. It was my very own "it's a wonderful life" Jimmy Stewart moment without any visitations by angels-in-training. I suddenly knew the necessity of my existence as part of the fabric that sustained the lives of others around me in some way, as if we were all part of a massive unseen tapestry. Everyone had a part, and held space for one other in a network. My death would have created a rupture — unexpected, unplanned.

Of course I knew that I could not and would not ever hurt my son. My absence would have marked his life indelibly, however irrelevant I thought I was becoming in his life. I also knew my partner would be scarred, perhaps irreparably. For the other passengers, my drowning would have ruined their vacations. For the crew and the company: disciplinary action, a lawsuit, firing, demotion, damage to their company's reputation, insurance company litigation, financial consequences for the crew's families. For my siblings: all that paperwork of dealing with consular officials, the difficulty and expense of transporting a body. I'd be on the news in Hawaii and BC: the stupid, drowned Canadian.

But beyond anticipating the scope of potential harm that might be caused by my death, I realized that my mere presence on the planet had import and significance and meaning. No need to prove anything to anyone. All my accumulated flaws, mistakes, and failures that I'd brooded over for decades with microscopic intensity didn't matter. Even if I never wrote, let alone published another poem or essay or book, never got a prize or an award for anything, never taught another class or workshop, never stumbled through another piano piece, or cooked another meal, or coordinated another extracurricular activity, just being alive, being able to listen and communicate — love, caring, sympathy, empathy — had meaning and purpose. I had a role. I wanted to witness my son's life stages, both the big ones and those minor transitions to adulthood. Being present was sufficient. I was sufficient.

This realization didn't make me elated or exuberant. For the rest of the trip, I had a furrowed brow, whether it was visible or not. Somehow, I'd jumped out of a deep, lifelong worn-out groove. This new way of seeing myself felt unnatural, unfamiliar. No one else could see it or feel it or know it except me. It took a few months to sink in. I was suspicious of happiness like an animal that is so conditioned to the leash that it can't venture outside the fence.

But slowly I started to recall all those glimpses of momentary joy and pleasure — a bowl of tiny, sweet garden raspberries, a tarte Tatin, a surprise birthday cake brought my friends in the hallway in grade ten, watching Robbie as an infant fall asleep in his crib or gurgle with joy, necking like a teenager as a crazy middle-aged woman with crazy middle-aged Ted at Pearson airport next to the yogurt stand that never seemed to be open, those belly laughs that brought tears to my eyes while playing silly board games with my family, watching Robbie in his latest school play, Ted's irreverent jokes (e.g. "PETA stands for people eating tasty animals"). For an Eeyore like myself, those moments came infrequently, but they did not *not* come — a double negative that suddenly made sense. That lid of a death wish came off permanently. I had forgotten its presence over the decades as it had become imbedded in my worldview.

※   ※   ※

For the past few years, I have tentatively ventured forth without that greyness that had subtly infiltrated every thought and deed before. People talk about the zest for life that brings flavour and tang to experiences, relationships, and events — maybe I always had it but couldn't name it with that shadow over my senses. I know now that wonder and delight come from both expected and unexpected places: a few lines of a poem, a snowdrop on the boulevard, the abundance of arugula in the backyard, Ted's toes tapping on my leg in the morning, listening to my son's arpeggios on the piano. I have started to be able to receive and perceive it all. True, I am pessimistic about the state of the world. Sure, I continue to experience setbacks and make galling mistakes. But a line from Mary Oliver's poem, "The Summer

Day" comes to mind: "Tell me, what is it you plan to do/with your one wild and precious life?" No more shutting down and hiding in fantasies of nonexistence. Time to face life with a yes.

The Stars Are Strangers

Harry Langen

I don't have a map. The stars are strangers. Differently con-figured. Sometimes I'm standing barefoot on a platform drifting across my personal sea, its pulse and heave lulling me. Other moments on a soft earth, I walk and am nearly stupefied by the intensity of the flower beds, their delicate petals trem-bling at the slightest breeze; the colours of the leaves on grand trees have shown me greens of such variety that any attempt to describe them would mortify the personality of the infinite for its shallowness. Can one fail spectacularly? I take heart in the presence of a forgiving host.

In the last week, my world of the mundane ceased to exist. One caring professional after another informed me that my brain was bleeding and a mass on my liver is cancerous and inoperable. Separate hoe-downs. And the lung specialists explained that they couldn't use blood thinners on the embolisms embedded in my lungs because such treatment would exacerbate the brain bleed. A weird dilemma. Who was to know Limbo has a wicked sense of humour? Hence, the trek across my personal sea of mortality. My death may not be imminent but it will be a surprise for its suddenness, and the mystery of its timing is the existential tease.

So I witness a riotous upheaval of nature and hear words

with a micro-observational power. I see more clearly what my mentor meant when he stated "words are organic." And now I contemplate that if words are indeed biological, so is meaning. Now I receive affirmations from nature that my body has been invaded, intervened upon, at a time when the planet is suffering a similar crisis. Poetic happenstance? Is it egotistical to imagine that the state of my physical health is a true reflection of the state of the macrocosm? That amusement works for me at the moment and, actually, I wouldn't be surprised that this timing is all entirely relevant to me. Each of us are tied into the machinations of the universe and our bodies reflect intimately all this divine commingling. Humankind may participate with this godly creation, no matter what stage we may be witnessing. Runners and dancers know this. They have stepped into that rarefied atmos of being suspended in continuity of joy.

I have used the terms "moment" and "time" occasionally here so I need to make myself clear: I believe simply that there is no time. There never was. Just a relationship to the truth and perhaps the extreme and intense peace of knowing. Jesua ben Yusef said, "The very hairs on your head are all numbered." Well, that works the other way, too. Through micro-observation and a heightened state of awareness, and an attention span longer than that of a hummingbird's singular wing-bat, each of us may witness the intensity of nature's multidimensional outbursts. And I spy now not only the stunning beauty of it all, but also the mathematics, geometry, the symmetry and balance inherent, and the intent of the drive of nature.

I keep interlopers at bay now. Cycles of anxiety are dissembling, and fears dissolving. Self-persecutions and judgements are all dissipating like the fog on my sea. The anger and turbulence relents. Now when I move my lips and emit sound, I am more careful to reach out to sense — not prattle but incur the affection of the listener, not express contempt but convey meaning relevant to that listener. The cacophony, the noise of humankind is what is overwhelming; not the challenge of my current predicament. It is with words of substance that I will find resolutions. I will find silence. I say, turn off your gadgets. I say, extend your humanity. Rediscover conversation. Compliment strangers. I seek out that other, precious silence now. I need time for prayer — now there's a reason for time! I have been invited into the House of the Creator. I must, at least, wash up! I want to fit in. And if I think I've become lost en route to that holy abode, I will persevere. That's what I'm doing now under this new sky. I was not a trivial being. We may, each of us, be champions if we find the meaning. Find the words.

On Work and Terminal Illness

Susan Briscoe

Sure sign of an over-developed work ethic: one of my first thoughts upon receiving a terminal diagnosis was to wonder what special work was waiting for me on the other side. So much for resting in peace!

I was about to be wheeled into surgery to remove an undiagnosed tumour growing faster than an alien in my uterus when the surgeon I'd never met before told me I had an aggressively terminal sarcoma that likely wouldn't respond to treatment. It was a death sentence, but with no firm date. With chemo I'd have maybe a year at most, she said later.

At that first moment, along with an enormous sadness at leaving my dearly loved ones and this exquisitely beautiful life, I really did immediately wonder what mission I might be assigned post-death, even though I've never believed in that sort of afterlife. It was somehow impossible for me to fathom that there wasn't some reason for this loss — for me, the loss of everything; for my loved ones, the loss of mother, daughter, lover, sister, friend. For society, it meant the loss of any good work I had hoped to do. As I had just turned fifty and my children had moved out on their own, I now had the time and energy and motivation to do a lot: in the past year I had earned my college a nearly quarter-million-dollar federal grant for a research project on Indigenous post-secondary students' stories, and I'd won a small arts grant to write a book of poetry about mothering a teen through his addiction. I was finally ready to fearlessly change the world.

While I unexpectedly felt the need for direct meaning in this loss, as if it were a purposeful though involuntary sacrifice, my very rational intellect knows that there cannot possibly be meaning in all the senseless suffering in this world. War and genocide and starvation and violence are so very horrible because they are so senseless — and avoidable, if we could only all learn to be decent. I know this. I know people who have faced the deaths of innocent loved ones with no consolation that there was a purpose to their loss. And yet, the human compulsion to seek meaning is powerful. For the moment, I decided to accept my need for meaning and see where it took me.

Because I always have big projects on the go, that was the direction my thoughts took: there must be a really big, important afterlife project ready for me — a behind-the-scenes kind of mission. These were the days just after Trump's inauguration, so I thought maybe my new assignment was to help take down an evil president! Or find a new strategy to help stop climate change. Or end violence against women! It had to be something pretty darned huge if I was to give up everything I love for it.

In the weeks after my surgery and diagnosis, I fell into doing what had occupied me before I got sick: some research, some reading, some thinking, and some writing about topics that interested me. That was how I worked in my jobs as a teacher, researcher, and writer. Only now the topic was death. I started posting my writing about my new experience with dying on

Facebook, simply to reassure friends that I was not, in fact, experiencing it as they feared — from the many kind notes I received, it seemed most were imagining that I was suffering terribly, that I was perhaps even in anguish and despair. This wasn't the case, and I wanted my friends to know that dying, if you weren't afraid of it (I wasn't, and you needn't be either), was not actually that bad. I wanted them to know I was okay.

Very soon, the writing I was posting on Facebook was too extensive for that venue. It needed its own blog. Without too much thought, I called it "The Death Project." I was excited about this new writing and soon surprised by the positive response to the blog. I already knew we needed a new and positive conversation about death in our death-phobic society, but as hundreds of strangers began following the blog, I saw how urgent this need really is. That's when I realized, my new job wasn't waiting until after my death: it had already started. My new job was to write about dying. This was how to make my death worthwhile.

Realizing this has allowed me to take on my new occupation in the way I have gone about most of my work in recent years. Because I have been blessed in this last decade of my life with work that I enjoyed and found deeply meaningful, work has been how I like to spend much of my time. It's what I did/do (tenses do get confusing when you're dying!) with my life, regardless of time of day or week. Enjoying my work means I go about it cheerfully, with curiosity, energy, and interest. So taking this death project on (it goes beyond the blog to other associated projects) as my new job means that I can, to a considerable degree while my health permits, go about my life as usual, being myself, doing my work, all in generally good spirits — though I do hope the deadline gets extended!

I do, nevertheless, take plenty of time for visits with family and friends when they are available. Knowing I am occupied with my work allows them to go ahead with their own full lives and work without guilt. And while I have a strong work ethic, I'm not really a workaholic — I'm more than happy to take time for fun or relaxation when I can. Since going on sick leave I have, in fact, been enjoying an easier — and more balanced — routine, with time to read and visit and take up creative projects.

I see from all this that dying, in its best terms, really means living. My work requires that I keep living in the way I have always found meaningful until I simply run out of time. If I am already living my right life — doing good work, loving the people I am supposed to love, being kind, staying organized, nurturing my spiritual connection to all life, having some fun — there's not much to do in the face of death but keep on until the end.

Tears: Grief Ritual

angela rawlings

We stand with arms outstretched
and in our upturned palms

tears
dewdrops sea spray
human egg diamonds icicles
jellyfish...

> — Mette Moestrup, "Lacrimosa"[1]

WETTER

The small arctic fishing village of Henningsvær in the Lofoten archipelago provides the temporary home for the multi-arts festival Kvinner på kanten, translating from Norwegian to English as "Women on the Edge." It is November 2013 — my first international trip and second public performance after my mastectomy and during chemotherapy treatment. A recent conversation with a retiring onco-psychiatrist introduced me to the realization that I'd entered a period of mourning, rather than depression — mourning the body that was, mourning excised body parts, mourning the life I'd had and the imagined life I might have lived had I not cancered. Deep inside

the Arctic Circle, an edge cuts through conversations and inter-
actions of women gathered for the festival.

On this edge where rocks are lapped by the Norwegian Sea. An
edge difficult to discern due to little daylight and near-constant
blizzarding. This edge where fishbodies and humanbodies are im-
pacted, interpacted through deaths and lives. On this festival's
kanten, I meet with Danish musician Miriam Karpantschof and
poet Mette Moestrup who partner their work within the queer
feminist music-and-poetry duo She's a Show.

Disclosure, at times, becomes a necessity to alleviate a sense
of other-than. Soon after arriving in Henningsvær, Miriam and
I disclose our health situations to each other. Years earlier,
Miriam and Mette had been in a car accident, which shifted
personal body relationship through injury and the types of work
they would be capable of producing together in future. To elu-
cidate the differently alive shifted through death's threat to our
bodies, we disclose.

With every encounter, Miriam and I attend water or water
attends to us. "What might becoming a body of water — ebbing,
fluvial, dripping, coursing, traversing time and space, pooling as
both matter and meaning — give to feminism, its theories, and its
practices?", writes Astrida Neimanis in her essay "Hyrdofemi-
nism: Or, On Becoming a Body of Water." We walk Henningsvær's
harbour during the two hours of daily twilight, taking photo-
graphs as close to the pier's edge as we dare step. We creep
through a late-night blizzard in Svolvær to find vegetarian fare.
Frozen water, interior melt, salty sea, boil. We make each other hot
chocolate and tea during festival interludes, honouring the water
inside us. Our new-formed friendship moves swiftly to the intimate
gesture and eye contact of those who know, and more so of those
who mourn physiological limitation. We form ritual in our com-
ing-together, in an unfamiliar Arctic terrain that tests the habit-
ability of our bodies through its ice and snow.

Fig. 1, a triangular mountain seen from Henningsvær, Lofoten during two hours of sunlight and a break in the blizzard, November 2013. Credit: angela rawlings.

WELLS

Iceland has been a home for me since 2009, and I wrote my year-long cancer treatment throughout the country's languages and lands. During cancer treatment in 2013, between each round of chemotherapy, I circled the foreign-familiar subarctic terrain documenting death with my camera and audio recorder. Glaciers trickled and waterfalled. Jellyfish and whales washed ashore. I stripped off my shirt in December 2012 near winter solstice beside the hot springs of Kleifarvatn (vatn translates as both lake and water in Icelandic). In January, I bared my recent surgery scars by the decaying body of an Arctic fox. February, glacial lagoon. In March, I moved half-naked between icebergs standing as tall as me, washed ashore black sand after they'd begun journey from the ice cap Vatnajökull into the North Atlantic. My body was haunted by death, hunting for lifewater.

Mette and I first met in Iceland in 2009, when we were invited to perform at the Nýhil International Poetry Festival. At the time, we travelled as a caravan of poets to visit the waterfalls Seljalandsfoss and Skógafoss, hiked back to the hot spring Seljavallalaug, and touched the glacial tongue Sólheimajökull. Hot water, falling water, frozen water. Mette and I reunited in Oslo's Gardermoen airport in 2013 en route to Kvinner på kanten, where we skipped small talk and went straight to death and cancer. Surprise and urgency in our conversations, like jökulhlaup — a flood caused by volcanic eruption underneath a glacier. Mette's dear friend had been diagnosed with cancer — I had been diagnosed with cancer — her friend had recently died — "But you," Mette urged, wide-eyed, "you live! You are alive!"

It is now July 2014, a few months beyond my final chemotherapy injection, removal of a port-a-cath, surgery to reconstruct a nipple. Mette has brought her son Villads and godson Leo, both fourteen years old, on a family trip to Iceland — a way to build their family connection after her friend's death, who was also Leo's mother. I meet them to explore the countryside for a week. The boys' English-language skills are impressive, and we trade translations of Danish and Icelandic throughout our road trip.

The boys sing the chorus of Crazy Town's "Butterfly" in the backseat as I drive. "Come my lady, come come my lady, you're my butterfly, sugar, baby." This throwback to another place and time — late nineties, before the boys were born and as Mette and I navigated our early adult years in separate continents — brings cascades of laughter from the front seat each time they sing the chorus. It's an unexpected lightness in a trip marked by mourning. Since his mother's passing, Leo has begun the graduation process of living with Mette and Villads. The boys — so different in character, both processing their grief in different ways — join their voices for the bemusement of Mette and me.

Water is everywhere here, and we come into contact with ocean, waterfall, hot spring, lagoon, steam, rain. The boys climb a NATO oil tank, ascend a ruining farm silo, and hike to the top of a waterfall to capture unusual perspectives of land and water. Near an active whale slaughterhouse in the depths of rural Hvalfjörður, Leo pulls himself horizontally along a boat rope that anchors a once-sunk whaling vessel to land.

The Iceland we explore collectively is not the Iceland of my cancer rituals. In this new known and unknown land, we navigate our grief in parallel. Signs of life cling to the ruining silo as graffiti and the vessel as barnacles. The boys name our quartet of travellers "De Vilde Vandaler" (The Wild Vandals). A different life feels possible as we crawl from the cradles of our traumas. We're wild, we sing, and our hearts swell as we traverse an unexpected summer of chosen family.

Fig. 2, Leo scales a rope attached to a docked whaling ship in Hvalfjörður, Iceland in July 2014. Credit: angela rawlings.

Wash Ashore

In July 2017, Miriam and Mette wear starched burlap ankle-length capes, the spines adorned with sparkling and translucent objects. On Copenhagen's Amager Beach, they take turns striding through white sand to wade into the salt-water strait of Øresund. In the water, they pause, bow from the waist, and then walk backwards to restart their ritual approach once more.

When Mette and Miriam wrote commissioning video work from me for She's a Show, they proposed environmental engagement as the particular nexus through which we'd meet. I proposed geo-sensuality. Intimacy. Ritual. They gifted me an in-progress "Vandcomposition" (vand — Danish for water), where Miriam had sutured multiple sounds of lapping waves and water droplets amidst a slowed-down piano quote from a Messiaen composition. Now, we film their repeated entries to Øresund as the central ritual-work for the video. This is the grief ritual.

While attending to her best friend's cancer diagnosis in 2013, Mette wrote the Danish poem "Lacrimosa," embedding within it "tumours, silicone implants" in the list of semi-transparent objects that may be cradled in an upturned palm. "Lacrimosa" partners Miriam's "Vandcomposition" to provide lyrics for the She's a Show track for which I'll film our grief ritual. As part of our ritual work — mourning across languages and experiences — Mette, Miriam, and I work collectively on a Danish-to-English translation of the lyrics. We care for each word, considering how best to translate while inhabiting the vocabulary with stories of our own brushes with grief. Once translated to English, the chorus of "Lacrimosa" refrains: "We stand here with arms outstretched / and in our upturned palms // tears." Each word in Danish and in English we also hold in our upturned palms.

After this refrain in "Lacrimosa," Mette extends the number

of objects held within palms through a triangular numeric system (1, 3, 6, 10, 15, 21, 28, 36, 45). Each subsequent stanza grows in length by the number of objects stated within it. The first stanza has one item (tears). The second stanza has three items (tears, dewdrops, sea spray). The third stanza has six items (tears, dewdrops, sea spray, human egg, diamonds, icicles). The stanzas build upon the object list, adding more transparent objects as each subsequent stanza is introduced.

tårer

dugdråber skumsprøjt

menneskeæg diamanter istapper

gopler bobleplastik sæbebobler krystalregnbuer

snegleslim lim glaskugler hårbolde fra parykker pailletter[2]

Mette's triangular stanzas mirror a body standing with legs spread apart, with head at the top and feet at each bottom corner. These triangles shape tears. Mountains. Breasts. Glaciers in melt. The slope of sand dune to foreshore.

We use the list of transparent objects as a starting point to develop further our grief ritual, gathering nail polish and pickled onions, balloons and bouncy balls to adorn grief capes Miriam and Mette sew. I film their hands sewing, gluing, and taping translucency to the stiff burlap. The next day, we cycle to Amager Beach. Mette and Miriam strip to black tights and tank tops, wrap the grief capes around their bodies. They approach the Baltic Sea, wading deeper with each renewed approach. I film their repeated entries. Sailboats bob in the Øresund's depths along the horizon, while sea swimmers pass laps at closer distance. Grieving is a public and private spectacle, the burden weighing into the glittering burlap as they wade up to their shoulders.

The translucent objects of Mette's lyrics transmute grief and light. Cancer lurks in the subtext of She's a Show's final track, called "Tears: A Grief Ritual." Sounds of water and piano lurch at the utterance of "tumours, silicone implants." I edit three videos to accompany the song — one displaying the preparatory sewing of the grief capes, the second their repeated entries into the water, and a final video with the hands of collaborators cradling transparent objects in their upturned palms. Grief as private and public, as individuated yet collective. At the video's end, an upturned palm transforms its calm to grip a smoky, oversized marble. Tumours. Silicone implants. Grief as murk in the grip of the body. We play a role in the processing of each other's embodied grieving, and in how we witness and enact rite.

Fig. 3, Still from "Tears: Grief Ritual," where Miriam and Mette are depicted in their grief capes standing in the Øresund. Credit: angela rawlings and She's a Show.

After the Flood

After the accident. After the cancer. After disclosure. After translation. After the ritual. After the video. After the blizzard. After Kvinner på kanten. After winter's dark. During grief. Before winter's dark. Before diagnosis. Before clarity. Before glacial floods. Before tears. Before the rituals. Before I finish writing this.

Icelandic writer Andri Snær Magnason and I drink coffee and water as we discuss the breathing patterns of glaciers, how they inhale over the land to the shore and exhale, retreating up the mountains and into the atmosphere, over millennia. Our human circulation is brief by comparison — temporary circles drawn on a metaphoric shoreline of land exposed by glacial retreat. With so much discussion of climate breakdown, is apocalyptic speculation of human non-existence a spectre that keeps us from embracing our momentary peak happiness? The threat of rising oceans fills our coffee and water glasses.

I ask if Andri ever returned to visit Kárahnjúkar Dam, a site in East Iceland over which he fought to stop development given how the dam would flood acres of sensitive volcanic desert. No, he never returned after the dam was built. What would there be to see, and how could a person grieve what was now subsumed by water? The flood transmogrified the land, rendering it other than what it was before, insisting and instituting new ecosystems of difference. How to grieve what is underwater?

Our affects triangulate our relationships to time, place, ritual. We rite a place into our bodies, or a place rites its body through emotional impact. We grieve in a place. We grieve a place. A place no longer exists. We were place. We become grief. We carry our grief into a different place, house this grief within an archive of geographic memory.

Trauma, then grief. Geophysical force. A flood from a dam. And whales wash ashore.

---

1. Excerpt from Mette Moestrup's "Lacrimosa," written in Danish. Tårer translates to English as tears, with the subsequent lines illuminating transparent objects, including "dewdrops sea spray / human egg diamonds icicles / etc."

2. Ibid.

When Earth is Unveiled

Jane Mellor

What do I know of the love that ate you alive?
I have not felt that
— yet
your eyes.

The flurry of living surrounds me. I notice it and don't. I am here and not. They say when a person loses a limb, they feel it, as if it's still attached to their body. It itches or hurts or aches. It's a sadness, that loss of limb. You can't get rid of it.

Will I one day unload the weight of grief, or do I want to? Holding on might be my only piece of he who was a piece of me.

※ ※ ※

I know something else. Sometimes happiness smothers me. I stand in a haze, surrounded by a din of voices, a blare of laughter, hugs, chatter. It's love, really. It protects me from falling. Apart. Even though I'm responsive and present, I'm only half there because loss is responsive and present too. My closest companion. It's a damn nuisance. It will always be.

❋ ❋ ❋

I remember exactly.

Two pings. The impatient phone glow.
                                        Outside
a woodpecker messaged in morse.
Unable to decode,
                I lay looking
                at the rising sun
perplexed at the speed at which earth travelled.
                Too early,
I thought,
        yet there it was.

I didn't need to answer, didn't want to hear.
The murmur of empathy,
        the matter-of-fact tone.

I remember exactly. Deep moan
ascending to   Wail.
        — to bear the unconscionable —
How guttural.
A mother's anguish.
Is it possible the world stopped?

While secretly,

                behind my back,
the rustle of life went on and on and on.
Don't. Answer. The Call.

We can't bear to hear appropriate words
at inappropriate times.
There is no right time.
To die. To call. To tell.

I remember exactly.

※　※　※

Rewind:

We lived in the outback of rural British Columbia. A cabin in
the woods. Our home we constructed ourselves: two-by-six,
squared-off timber beams, tongue and grooved to fit together
like Lego logs. We lived like settlers, no electricity, no running
water, a wood stove for heat. But the house was unfinished, a
work in progress, loft still open on all sides to the floor below.

The smell of birch and cedar and pitch wood. The smell of
wretch and pain and fear. My eighteen-month-old son had fallen
from the upstairs loft. Hit his head on the carved wood arm of
the overstuffed, living room chair. He was dead. Then he sput-
tered, coughed and his breathing, though shallow, was audible.

The rest played out as a slow motion nightmare. Jostling him
so life would continue. Carrying him to the car, my husband
driving like a madman the twenty-five miles to town. Racing by
ambulance to a larger town. Puke permeating. Tears streaming.
Carsick. Heartsick. Sick.

※　※　※

It was a depressed skull fracture.

"A child's head is like a ping pong ball," the neurosurgeon said matter-of-factly. "We have to go in and pop it back out, but we must move quickly before more pressure is put on the brain."

The surgery was a success. There would be no repercussions from the accident. He had survived. He had lived.

My son couldn't lift his head for weeks. When he did, it bounced up and down. A pitiful bobble-head. Ten days in hospital as he gradually improved. We watched the limbless, scarred, and hopeless wheel the hall past us, stop by to talk. Day after day. It was a rural area. Farm accidents were common.

I slept beside my son. Night after night. Then one day we went home.

※　※　※

Limber legs over fences,
river rocks as puzzle pieces
where deft feet landed
solid as sound.

Brave hunter, stick as spear.
Only the dog,
in wakeful slumber,
kept watch the doorstep
of your wild kingdom
while you
presided over creek,
hayfield, stands of birch,
even through glints of frost.

Seasons turn hard
and harder through years,
the acreage bereft of child's play.
When summer comes,
I   will   cartwheel   again   with   you.

❊ ❊ ❊

Was it premonition? How does one survive a twelve-foot head-
first fall?
He did.
Children are pliable, bendy, resilient. From the get-go
he was the likeable kind.
Engaging. Amusing. Clever. Thoughtful. Fragile. Fated.

Near death changes you, You.

❊ ❊ ❊

Fast Forward:

Can't remember when I morphed
into a drifter.
Was it after loss or
an afterthought that one moonless night
you'd let go?

Sometimes I can't breathe. The nearness
of it all.   I saw a red balloon
drift skyward until swallowed
in the tongue of a jet stream.

Sometimes images
encourage another step forward, toward
forgiveness or regret, or is there
another way to mourn?

Unload the burden;
a pile of laundry, misplaced socks,
a smudge of colour on whites.
Drifting inward — toward comfort,
until swallowed into helium.

※　※　※

Only thirty-five. Thirty-five years old.
A good kid. A fine young man. Troubled.
Inside, his warm heart simmered. We didn't know.

Depression.　Depressed Skull Fracture.

Depression is like visiting a foreign country. If you don't speak
the language it's a challenge to get along. You can try using a
phrase book. Refine your accent. Use simple speech, choice
words.

I discovered
    words do not forge the threshold of
pain.

Angry words. Frightened words. Confused words. Sorrowful
words. Aching words. Try to be helpful words. Remorseful
words. There are no words to penetrate that wall.

What? Do? I? Do? With? That?
His torment is now mine. It resides in the deepest depths of me.
His death = my death.

※ ※ ※

Those who don't know. Those who keep secrets. Those who are
cowards. Those who fear.
Those who love too hard? Yes, that's it. That was him. My son
loved so hard.

※ ※ ※

We were sitting around the table
being angry and sad and pitiful
and she said,
What we need to find here is some light.
So,

I've been searching,
and there's something electric
in wintertime's lean toward spring,
when the rains begin,
earth is unveiled
and you see a worm or caterpillar or moss-covered stones,
and sometimes people sing.
It's an opening,
and you take it.

It's difficult to mourn when outside
is alive and well.

Birds shuttle from branch to branch,
though greenery has yet to feed the wintry day.
Breath is grey.
Yet air's crispness flushes skin
and a voice inside says to look skyward,
up, toward.

It's difficult to feel alive and well
when loss is a dark pit,
where the smell of frost no longer lingers,
the taste of a crocus gone.
When you remember all is nothing now,
when you want to throw it in the air,
scream: "Catch!"

❋ ❋ ❋

He was thirty-five. Self-medicating. Surviving on his terms.
   OxyContin. I'd never heard of it — then. So naive. Where
had I been?

   But he'd slipped out of our reach. Unable to surface. For too
long. The future was cast, a tattoo of loss forever imprinted, ink
seeping under skin, into veins, colouring what would come and
be forever.

❋ ❋ ❋

The celebration of life was...
                              ...it was.

※　※　※

Empty living room.
Deluge of cards stacked beside
wilted dahlias.
Quiet.
Unbearably.

Why you?
You were no more marked than others.
My mind spins
around unanswered phone calls,
night sweats,
fear of, (what next?).

I think of that spring you shot up like vine.

Nothing remains as it was.
That would be dull,
yet I long for a repeat,
another look.

Remembering you is like smelling sweet peas,
that noon in the church-like space.
    There was blue.
What ran beneath smouldered but we could do nothing.

Now it is time to move on.

Yet my feet are planted
right where I left you still growing,
that crooked smile holding on to
stamen, leaf, petal.

Goodnight Stars, Goodnight Air

Jessica Michalofsky

We are packed and in the car by 8:15 AM, me and S, my nineteen-year-old son, who is withdrawing from meth and heroin.

It's a thirty-minute drive to the Schwartz Bay ferry terminal to catch a ferry that takes us from Vancouver Island across to the mainland, and then a ten-hour drive over several mountain ranges to reach the interior of the province and S's dad at a derelict cabin in a remote valley in the Kootenays. I am taking S there not because I think it's a good idea, or because his hermit father who has suffered a brain injury and smokes pot like other people breathe air will capably care for him, but because I don't know what else to do, and there is no other place to take him. I imagine him unbreathing on the bathroom floor of a 7-Eleven — beyond Naxalone, far beyond CPR — a vision that implants itself in the cells of my thinking and refuses to be unthought.

I stay in the passing lane the entire trip to the ferry terminal. If we miss the nine o'clock ferry, we'll have to wait until the next ferry at eleven, which will mean that because it's November, a good portion of our trip will be in the dark. Plus, though it seems increasingly unlikely now that we're actually in the moving car, there's always the possibility that S will change his mind. We've been here before — him showing up at my house sick and disheveled, wanting to get clean, booking appointments at detox, and then just a matter of days later, disappearing back into the abyss of drugs and lies, again. Getting off the Island seems imperative.

I start to be hopeful. Maybe everything is going to be okay. Maybe this is even an ordinary car trip. My mind plays the game that S is going to be all right. Without the drugs, the recovery can begin. The clock will restart. The withered plant watered just before it dies of neglect. He'll go from a scab-faced, emaciated zombie, exhausted but compelled by a frenetic call to mindless motion, back to being the funny, smart-talking teenager he'd been just a year previous. Handsome, with wavy hair and gentle hands. Wholesome food, clean clothes — and everything can begin new — all we have to do is get off the Island, far from downtown Victoria, Pandora Street, the addicts and their lighters huddled up against the building out of the rain; just last week as I'd walked back to my car along Quadra Street, a young man S's age, face picked raw, shoeless, arms outstretched, mouth agape, turning in a slow gyre.

Perhaps there was something wrong with S, the way I had raised him. It was my fault. I had not said no enough, or in the right way. A lack of healthy boundaries, the literature described it. Or, I'd said it too much. There was a school that professed this, too. Had produced in the small and tender S too much anxiety. Was too impatient, focused on my own needs rather than his. Went to school, had lovers, needed time alone, demanded time alone, though as a single parent, hardly ever got any.

I think back to the hundreds of times where I lost my patience. Once, when he was about five and I was wild and ragged with frustration, I threatened that he'd have to go and live with his dad if he didn't go to bed.

I come up behind a slow vehicle in the passing lane, a Toyota pickup with ladders strapped to the top and buckets in the truck bed. I decelerate, shifting from sixth to fifth, but not braking, and sit right on the bumper of the little truck. The spray from the tires hitting the windshield. I can see through the back window a mop of grey hair, probably an old guy, heading to a job site, listening to the news on the radio, thermos cup in his hand. My heart thuds as I sit on the truck's bumper, and finally, nearly bursting with rage, I toot the horn until the little truck jerks into the slow lane and I speed past, foot solidly pressing on the gas pedal. We make the ferry with five minutes remaining.

※　※　※

Outside is blustery, it's a rainy day, so once on the ferry, we climb the stairs to the top lounge and tuck into seats that look out onto the grey sky and greyer ocean. Once, a seagull hovers beside the boat, seeming to check us out. S looks grim in the harsh light of day. His fingers compulsively search out and pick at red welts on his face and neck. I ask: "You hungry?" He is. Apart from the toast and eggs at my house this morning, he hasn't eaten in four days. Maybe five. He says this to me like he himself is just now becoming aware of the fact. I buy him a hot chocolate and a muffin. The fact that he has an appetite is a positive sign. It's not eating that you want to watch out for. Not that I know this about heroin and meth withdrawal. It just seems intuitive to me. Like when he was little and woke up in the middle of the night vomiting, and I'd help him to the toilet and clean his face, or bring him a basin and empty it. Cool cloths. Sips of water once he was able. A little toast later in the afternoon.

※ ※ ※

We reach Hope at around noon. Pulling off the highway, I cruise down the main road of the small town, passing a string of motels and fast food places, and choose a gas station where we've stopped previously. We will get gas and eat some lunch. There is moment when I contemplate seeing how he could pass for someone with an illness, a skin condition — maybe we are normal people with hopeful lives — and we even smile at each other. It's the game again.

You can gas it up, I say to S, almost jocularly, as I lean into the open car.

I'll fuck it up, he says.

I ignore the swear word. Evidently, now that he is nineteen, and a drug addict, he can swear around his mother. I think to say something and then change my mind. There had been a decline in superficial niceties in the last few months. It is not wholly unwelcome.

No, you won't. I toss him the keys and turn and head into the gas station to use the washroom. I am the good mother. Strong, encouraging independence in her offspring. Standing at the sink, I look into the mirror. My cheeks are pink, and apart from a few lines around the eyes and mouth, I still have a look of youth about me. But as I turn, I catch a glimpse at my face and see that I am holding my mouth oddly. My lips are a little pursed — like I am expecting a kiss — a tension that pulls up the corners of my mouth that seem to fall automatically into an ugly frown. S had often remarked to me that I have a mirror-face, a specific face I put on when I look at myself in the mirror, and this had struck me in a deep way. Is it possible I keep one reflection for myself and show another to the world? Once, too, when he was very small he told me of a nightmare he'd had. In it, I was a witch with alphabet letters for teeth.

Still, the overall impression of myself is one of competence and vigour, and I feel I broadcast this supernatural wellness as I walk back through the convenience store at the gas station. I notice I have caught the eye of a man filling a to-go cup with coffee as I stand at the rack that holds the chips. And then I catch myself in that act of attention-seeking, for isn't that what it is? And proceed to the till and hand my debit card to a fat woman blotched with acne who is uncommonly polite to me, and feel within myself a lick of shame.

※　※　※

Outside, the air is damp and cold. Blue-grey clouds ring green peaks that hug the town in a kind of myopic embrace. If the mountains — granite cliffs from which melt water pours, spire after spire of spruce, hemlock, cedar, low clouds of rain and spray and fog — feel closer here, it is simply because we are higher up on earth's piled up crust. We are closer to the sky; some bulk of the continent has been ascended.

The city and its despair are behind us. Below us. Now, there will be only wilderness where you feel small. Small towns like this, with gas stations and plain decency.

※　※　※

The next stop is several hours away. A silence falls over the car as the real driving begins. S bunches up his coat against the window and sleeps, and I put in my ear buds and listen to music. Snow appears on the side of the road, and the sky is dark grey. I have some ominous moments when I realize that I am driving into the mountains in the middle of November with no snow tires, which strengthens as we climb into the white. But it only rains and threatens to snow. We're just on the cusp of winter.

※ ※ ※

It's only several hours later, when the sun is setting behind us and we've left the Okanagan Valley and begun the climb into the Kootenay Mountains that we begin to really speak. The weather is clear here, we've left the rain and the threat of snow behind us. The road practically empty, and the setting sun pouring over the rolling, treeless hills of sage and grass. I am focusing on trying to locate a single, forlorn cabin. A greying cabin on the side of a hill. Once I'd told my boyfriend W about it, and we'd agreed it was something we always looked out for on this part of the drive. I am angling my cell phone above the steering wheel, trying to catch the hills lit up orange and umber by the sun setting in the west behind us. But the phone's camera won't work for some reason. And it seems dangerous to keep fiddling with it while I am driving, and I need to pee. So, I pull over and squat in a ditch near a fence post. The air is cold. The temperature is dropping because of the clear sky. And then, perhaps because I have been in a small car all day, I experience a change in perception. I am neither of the car nor of the outside. Not S's mother pulling him from the clutches of death, nor anyone remotely capable of such a thing.

I am no one. The orange flanks of the mountain have no thoughts and belong to no one. This happens to me, to both experience myself and notice my thoughts. Like a voice-over in my thinking, or as if I'm writing it on a page for someone to read.

They'd go on being hills after the sun set, as the cold dark night set in. Animals would emerge and run with their wide eyes across the surface.

Back in the car, I start the engine and turn up the heat, pick up my phone and poke at it absorbedly. I have returned to the thought and the task of wanting to send W a photo, some sort of emblem of solitariness, a camaraderie in loneliness across the miles. Currently, W and I are in an "off" phase in our relationship. I am "giving him space." It's a tolerable torture. I suppose we have what some would call a dysfunctional relationship. But S now wants to talk. So I put the phone aside and listen to him. He is apologizing. It's hard to have ordinary problems when your kid's doing drugs. Any time spent thinking about other problems feels selfish. And people judge you as if all aspects of your kid's addiction are connected to other, unproductive parts of your life. The voice in my head: driving her addict son through the mountains, spends her time fantasizing about a man she sometimes shares a bed with.

Sorry for being such a fuck up is what he says. A sharp feeling of remorse draws me back into seeing him sitting beside me in the car. A small red car, with its engine running, little orange lights flashing, on the flank of an immense mountain. Fucking up seems beside the point. I say so, but the words come out too fast. It's himself he is hurting. This seems like a pointless thing to say. I tighten into my thinking, aiming for a balance of not too many words, but the right ones. A few words come out, but I wish I could reel them back in. I decide to say nothing. There is, for the moment, nothing to say. I put the car in gear and release the clutch so that we are moving, gearing up as we gain speed, and once again flying through the early evening, past the hills and fence posts and patchy pines. The wheel turns easily under my hands and the car careens at great speeds across the black road.

The things I say should be poised between providing comfort and guidance. They have to be the right words, or else they will ring hollow. Cynics and the desperate, I know, latch on especially to anything that sounds inauthentic, though of course, that is the problem with drugs: it takes away any genuineness so that everything is either tragic or cynical. Poor me or fuck you.

For a long while there is silence. I think about my own recovery from drugs and alcohol fifteen years earlier, when S was a toddler. For a few years after I quit, I craved it. The escape and the release. I sought out every form of support group and counselling, and whined and complained my way into a mostly tolerable sobriety. I put myself through school. I did well. Got lost in iambs-dactyls-post-structuralism-epistemology-To-the-Lighthouse and came out the other side in a respectable job in the English department at a small community college. I parented S in what felt like a mostly stable and loving home. I did my best. *Blueberries for Sal, Wind in the Willows, Goodnight Moon.* I made smoothies and pancakes and we went skating and sometimes I yelled. Once in a while, I threw stuff. Eventually, I stopped craving the kind of obliteration that alcohol and drugs provided. I began to find that I could experience the same thrill — sex, drugs, rock and roll — in more subtle maneuvers. I made fewer grand gestures. I became more sensitive. I cried — a dead raccoon, an ambulance, a piercing horn solo. I experienced a constellation of emotions — gutting shame, existential dread — and between these — a kind of tumultuous and euphoric gratitude that could lead back to tears. I became unconcerned with what I ought to do: if I wanted something, pursuing that — despite the moral or financial cost — as long as it didn't harm others — was the right thing to do. I felt different from other people — not better, just different. Changed, maybe. And I came to see I was leading an extraordinary life. Life had not become better; I had. This is what I want for S, but how can I explain fifteen years of recovery to him?

※　※　※

I think about when my mom was dying in the hospice during the winter, how I went out running and repeated a scene in my mind as I ran through the snowy streets. In the fantasy, I would feed my emaciated mother the kinds of things athletes eat and drink, filled with carbohydrates and electrolytes, and my mother would revive, be pulled back from the brink of death. There was an actual line between life and death. And some miraculous thing would happen to the cancer. It would disappear. Like Superman turning the world backward on its axis and making time reverse, and rescuing Lois Lane from where she'd fallen into a crack in the ground because of the earthquake. The ground reopening as if birthing Lois, not crushing her. Or how I'd heard about a thing to do with children: have them observe what happens when a plant is not watered. At what point can the plant be revived? When is it too late? And then the only task would be to re-energize my mother. Fill her with the stuff of life. Sugar and salt and potassium. And then, in a day or two, she'd try a little scrambled egg, and her life would begin to renew. Like a green plant, she'd become firm again. It was so ridiculous that it was comforting. So ridiculous, that it was imaginable.

※　※　※

We have ascended high enough in the hills so that we can see the sun above the horizon of the surrounding mountains, and as we head down the other side, lose the last rays of light, and the hills ahead are cast in blue shadow. That will be the end of daylight on our drive, and only darkness and mountains lie ahead. The indigo light of the road coming down and only the approach of occasional cars. Headlights, first, luminous points on the horizon, then imminent upon us, the blinding glare, the windshield lit up, the passing car rushing past us within a few inches of the line. It seems I take our lives in my hands every minute of the drive.

※ ※ ※

Sometimes he thinks of killing himself, he says. About which I am not surprised, but how should I respond? We have come down out of the high hills and are following a river as it winds its way through the trees. I take a few seconds to think about what I want to say.

What I do say: it is okay. He mustn't be afraid of his thoughts. But he didn't necessarily have to obey them either. He could do whatever he wanted, whatever brought him joy. I had absolutely no agenda for him other than to live his life.

It was his life. And he could do with it what he wanted. Want. Foremost, one must want: this was the trick. A curiosity to know what happens next. And next. What comes over the next hill, beyond the next curve. It's partly a lie. But it's a good lie because, like all good lies, it's also true.

We drive on like this in silence for a bit, and then talk about love, of all things. The break up with the girlfriend that seemed to precipitate the long binges with drugs. The girlfriend who is now living with her dealer.

Isn't he glad that he'd loved her, even though that had been painful, not worked out as he had planned? But my words strike me as perverse. Empty and romantic. I want to impart something of my learning. How I'd followed W to the very lowest places of love — the grovelling and begging, the constant reframing that allowed me to turn the other cheek, not out of selfishness but out of compassion, or perhaps it had been a sort of selfishness — but it had been the right thing to do. The decision to love instead of being loved. I would do it again and again. There could be no embarrassment or rancour in love. One had to come to it willingly and be harmed by it or be forever uninitiated.

My words echo in my ears. I give him what I know, even if it is too little. And yet, I know he is hearing at least that I am try-ing to say something. We are two people who are alive, driving on a dark highway. Who knew how long life would be. It could stop at any moment. But wasn't it okay just this minute?

I say that: *Is it okay just right now?*

And S says, *Yes, it is.*

※ ※ ※

We continue on in the dark. Up high, the sullen shapes of dark mountains. We eat potato chips from the bag. Silence falls over the car again.

My mind turns back on itself. I say I make fewer grand ges-tures, but when I observe myself, isn't it also true to say that I have a propensity to hyperbole. Romanticism. Overstatement. Hysterics.

What I don't say: I have already decided — if S doesn't make it, I can kill myself.

That ever since my mother died earlier in the spring, ever since W had left me, ever since S had been using drugs, I'd been sitting in my attic suite listening to the same song on auto-repeat for months on end, turning over tarot cards and crying. That I'd let practically everything go: the garden, the house, my job. I mean, I did these things, but they didn't mean anything. That most of the time I focused on simply not thinking about S dying. I thought thinking about it could increase its chance of happening. So I'd listen to the same song for several hours, or swim three kilometres, or run twenty kilometres, anything to create a painful sort of hypnotic sensation. And this was my only attachment to life.

That I had played the game of: if not S, W. Who would I be if S died and W took me back? Would I be the ghost lover, perennially fragile? The woman with the dead heart. Pitifully loved by W, who would take my body in his strong arms and fuck me without ever knowing me — because I'd be unknowable. She lost her son to drugs, people would whisper. An empty husk of a woman — missing some integral piece of herself. Or, what if it was W I would lose and S would make it? Would S be enough to fill my life? How long before I'd be turning my eye? After all, how many times had my mind veered from the catastrophe at hand to the imaginary romantic notion of W? What kind of mother was I? Had I ever really loved S adequately? How many times when he was a child had I wished he'd just leave me alone for a bit, go play, so I could sit and think in silence? His need for me seemed boundless. It might be impossible to be a woman and a mother at the same time.

That I had begged God, please don't take S from me, and that had brought tears up and over my eyes, down my face. A big gulping child, snot in my nose.

Is it a selfish thing then, this desire of mine? For S to live, for him to do well. Do I want it for him, or do I want him to live for me, to give my life meaning? Is that fair? Why else then would I want to die if he were not here?

Am I rescuing him so that I'll have a will to live?

Who am I saving: him or me?

Unlucky Luck

Jennifer Van Evra

I teetered in front of the police officer, who looked back at me
and blinked indifferently. The music from the stage thudded
in my chest as the thousands of Who fans screamed. It was one
of their several final tours. I felt like I was about to pass out. "I
think something is wrong," I yelled toward the officer's ear; he
nodded and half-smiled, then turned his head back toward the
stage.

Maybe he didn't hear what I said over the thundering noise.
Maybe he thought I was just another drunk teen. But just
moments before I had been sitting in my seat beside my
boyfriend Matt when my heart took off and my whole body
flushed. I began to sweat, and felt like I was going to throw up.
My throat began to constrict.

Humans share a trait with many other animals, and it's one
that could serve us well in the wild, but not in the modern
world: when we are in grave danger, our instinct is to retreat,
and find comfort in a quiet corner. It's what spells the end for
many, we are later warned.

"I'm fine. I'm fine," we protest.

I wasn't fine. So I had done what most eighteen-year-old girls
do: I beelined for the bathroom. Walking from the bottom of

the steep stadium stairs to the top was like climbing up a down-moving escalator, my goal seeming to recede with every step. At the top was that police officer, standing tall and official, arms crossed.

Suddenly a woman took my elbow and yelled in my ear, "I'm taking you to the first aid tent." I don't know who she was, or what moved her to step in, but that small act may have saved my life.

Rows of bunk beds lined the first aid bus, a makeshift hospital packed with teens learning tough lessons in alcohol consumption, or lost on bad drug trips. I wasn't on a bad trip; I wasn't on anything except a McDonald's apple pie and a bag of roasted peanuts. The ambulance attendant took one look at me and said we were going for a ride. There were no cell phones, so no way for me to tell my boyfriend. I felt like I was breathing through a straw.

What happened next was a blur of sirens blaring, doctors and nurses barking orders, IVs and beeping machines, tubes and injections. When it was all over, there was no thumping music, no screaming crowd. It was quiet, and everything was white. The doctor leaned into my field of vision, welcomed me back and asked, "So what did you eat?" It struck me as an odd question. Why did he care what I ate? He noticed my puzzlement. "You know what this is, don't you?"

I didn't — at least not yet. I'd had bruises and stitches, broken bones and asthma woes, flu bouts and nasty falls, but never had I come so close to dying. It was a life-threatening allergic reaction, to what exactly was unclear. A test later revealed it was peanuts — something I had eaten nearly every day since I was a young child. I was handed an EpiPen and told I would need to be vigilant about what I ate, likely for the rest of my life.

At first I didn't take the danger seriously, and neither did most of the people around me. I had always eaten whatever I wanted:

peanut butter and jam sandwiches were a mainstay; Oh Henry! bars and ice cream Drumsticks and Reese's Peanut Butter Cups left such an indelible impression that, almost three decades later, I still remember their exact taste and texture.

Allergies weren't nearly as common as they are now, and there was little awareness even in the medical community, let alone in the general public. Furor over the introduction of peanut-free classrooms was still more than a decade away, and foil packets of peanuts were still the norm on airlines. Friends jokingly tried to throw peanuts into my drinks at parties, and we all laughed. "Guys," I would plead half-heartedly, even though deep down I knew the consequences could be dire.

But when your immune system turns on you, denial and ignorance don't get you far. I continued to eat in restaurants, fast food places and friends' houses, often too embarrassed to ask more than a few broad questions about what might be in the food. I was blasé about reading ingredient labels; after all, I never had to before. I continued to work in restaurants, too, until the day I collapsed behind the bar at a high-end eatery that was offering a Thai special for lunch. The emergency room doctor warned that I would need to find a new line of work.

If a reaction surged in a social situation, I would try to calmly wish it away, smiling and nodding in countless conversations, looking for the quickest way out as my lungs grew taut and my tongue began to thicken in the back of my throat. I would struggle to focus, imagining what would happen if I keeled over right then and there. Sometimes it would peak and recede, like a shark swimming silently past; other times I wasn't so lucky.

Too often, the assumption that everything would magically "get back to normal" landed me back on a hospital gurney, sporting what I came to call my blue evening gown, as nurses and doctors rushed around, their eyes wide. "There are only three things that really scare me," one doctor said after bringing me back from the brink. "Heart attacks, strokes, and anaphylactic shock."

That fear gradually tightened its tentacles around me, too. As the allergies worsened into my late teens and early twenties, things I had always eaten began turning on me, landing me back in hospital. Shellfish, nuts, eggs, tomatoes, and soy were among the former allies that launched a full-blown rebellion. At first it was unclear what exactly I needed to avoid, and for a time, every meal felt like a game of Russian roulette — but one that I was forced to play.

Most people wake up every day believing they are not going to die; it's how we are able to function in the world. Sure, they buckle their seat belts and look both ways before crossing the street. They lock their doors and are careful with sharp objects. They steer clear of dangerous neighbourhoods, and keep combustibles away from fire. But death is a distant notion, something that exists only in a hazy, far-off future — not potentially right around the corner. If they truly believed their lives were at imminent risk, most would never make it out the door.

Because of my severe allergic reactions, the risks we take every day became viscerally apparent. I was barely into my twenties, but I recognized the potential for death at every turn — driving a car, flying in an airplane, walking too close to traffic on a narrow sidewalk, going hiking in the woods. When people said, "You have a better chance of dying in a bathtub than you do on an airplane," I didn't feel better about flying: I looked suspiciously at my bathtub, taking extra care as I stepped in or out. I no longer left my home assuming I would return — and some days I almost didn't.

Everything became about calculating risk.

※　※　※

The sun was beating and the wind was high, more than enough to fill the sails and heel the boat at a comfortable angle as we headed toward open water. The night before, I was bartending at a neighbourhood watering hole when a regular introduced me to two friends who were going sailing the next day and looking for crew.

When they cut the boat's engine, the only sound was the flickering of the sail and the water pressing against the hull. We set our tack and I stretched out on the warm deck, my arm resting on the gunwale. Everything was perfect.

When I felt the searing prick on my wrist, I couldn't place the sensation. My brain instantly offered options: maybe it was a loose wire, or an ember from a cigarette, or a piece of rigging that had gotten hot in the sun. When I looked down and saw the wasp fly away, I knew I was in serious trouble. We were too far out to get help in time. My first thought was, "I'm going to die." My second thought was, "I'm OK with that."

I explained to the two young sailors that I had been stung, and given how far we were from land, it could be bad. I told one to call the Coast Guard and turn the boat back toward shore; I told the other I was going to take an antihistamine and give myself a shot of epinephrine — which only buys you about twenty minutes — and that he should keep me alert and talking. I didn't panic; in fact I felt eerily serene.

As the Coast Guard hovercraft sped toward us, my face swelled, my lungs began to rattle and wheeze, and my heart raced to the point where I thought it would burst — an effect both of the blood pressure crash that comes with anaphylactic shock and the shot of adrenaline. I decided that if I was going to die, it was a good place to do it.

After myriad close scrapes, I learned that it's the less hazardous moments that tend to instil panic — a deep cut or a nasty burn or a badly broken bone. When there is life-and-death danger, things become perfectly still and the minutes slow, like particles in a suspension. It's after the emergencies that the nerves are allowed to jangle. When one of the sailors stopped by my hospital bed to see how I was doing hours after the immediate danger had passed, I trembled and choked back tears.

Chance was not on my side that summer. A few weeks later I narrowly made it out of a van fire, the ambulance attendants confessing that, from what witnesses had told them, they expected to be pulling bodies from the wreckage. Some friends and I had just left a nightclub and I shivered in my little dress and shoes; passers-by snapped photos as the flames lapped the underside of the overpass. The fire chief pulled a charred piece of metal from the wreckage, handed it to me and wryly joked, "Here is your fire extinguisher."

Days later, I was at home and pulled a pair of jeans off the clothesline. It had been a rough few weeks, but friends had convinced me to join them at an outdoor festival. "You need to get out," they said. Standing in my bedroom, I slid the jeans on, then felt a sharp prick in the side of my thigh. I dropped the pants, and there was a wasp, lying on the floor. It paused, stunned, then flew off. I paused, stunned, then swore loudly enough for my roommate to come running. When the firefighters arrived, my jeans were around my ankles, and I was watching my leg, expecting the swelling to begin.

The ambulance attendants soon followed. We all looked at my leg, and it was red, but fine. My breathing was normal. My heart wasn't racing. Somehow, I had been spared the wasp's venom. We were sighing with relief and cracking jokes when one firefighter recognized me: "Weren't you the one whose van exploded?" Without missing a beat, the ambulance attendant said, "Weren't you the one who got stung on the sailboat?" We all laughed. What were the chances?

It always came down to the chances.

I wish I could say I was thrilled by the averted disaster, that I felt alive and vowed to pursue my dreams. But really what I felt was to-the-bone exhaustion. I recognized my good fortune — I called it "my unlucky luck" — but all I wanted to do was crawl in bed and sleep.

That fall I was set to fulfil a dream — an internship at a high-profile magazine in San Francisco. I mustered the courage, or at least the brute will, and moved south — but found myself in a metropolis where I knew no one, where I couldn't afford a medical emergency, and where I couldn't assume that anyone would pick me up off the sidewalk if I went down. It should have been a career highlight, but it was darkened by the random blindsides that had come before. I wanted desperately to stay, and I wanted desperately to retreat to safety. Where safety could be found, however, was unclear.

※　※　※

Outside the medical world, there's an odd divide when it comes to allergies. Some people take them very seriously; in my early twenties, my close friend Lisa would scrub every pot and every dish to within an inch of its life before serving me anything, and would do everything short of walking ahead with a bullhorn demanding safe distance from all who crossed our path.

Women joked about how "lucky" I was that I had allergies because they made it easier for me to stay slim. One room-mate, after eating a Toblerone bar near a plate of my food, pointed out how easy I would be to kill. "How do you get any-one to date you?" he asked blithely. For others the mere mention of life-threatening allergies can induce jokes and eye rolls; one co-worker said she felt that conquering them was simply "mind over matter."

People with severe allergies all have these stories, and given the chance, we laugh darkly over our respective mishaps, close calls, and brushes with ignorance.

Some say you don't know how strong you are until you're forced to be strong, and friends who have been on hand for the scarier moments applaud my resilience. "I don't know how you do it," they say. But my answer is always the same: What alternative do I have? Being strong is not a choice. It's a demand. Granted, adversity has helped make me who I am, and at times I have surprised even myself, but given another option I would almost certainly take it.

I don't envy parents who have to raise kids with the same condition, patting their heads as they leave for school but quietly praying they don't become a statistic. My allergist told me about one mother who nearly lost her son to an allergic reaction and was so afraid it would happen again, she fed him nothing but lettuce and pears. One high-level government aide I spoke with was so traumatized by her first near-death reaction that she became afraid to eat, and shed twenty pounds in a month.

For a magazine article, I interviewed a mother who encouraged her young son to turn himself into police on a misdemeanour marijuana charge, only to lose him to an anaphylactic reaction to dairy during the one night he spent in prison. A video showed him begging for help as he died, the guards standing by doing nothing.

My heart broke — and I knew that, at least until then, only dumb luck had spared me the same fate.

※　※　※

Once you settle into the notion that death could arrive at any moment, it becomes more familiar and comfortable, like a hard leather chair that softens over time. The sense of immediate danger ebbs, and you control what you can, but loosen your grip on what you can't. And you try your best to live.

Don't get me wrong: I am not some Zen master who has conquered my fear of death. It's just no longer an abstract, far-off idea. I think about the day my partner and I will be separated one final time, or when I will last see a close friend. I wonder if I will outlive my dog. I cry at airports. I worry about unfinished business. I keep my will up to date. We all know that death could happen anytime, but sometimes I forget that not everybody knows it could happen tomorrow. Or today. Or this minute.

One day I was walking to a work meeting, like a thousand other meetings, and I cut across a grassy boulevard. Along the way I stepped on a buried ground nest, and soon had wasps stuck in my shoe, my waistband and my shirt, all of them punishing me for my misstep. I called my partner to hear his voice, wondering if this time would be the last, as the administrators sat uncomfortably waiting for the ambulance to arrive.

When the notion of death becomes a more constant companion, it brings with it an odd sense of calm, of not getting tangled in the hassles of everyday life. I find people's complaints charming — the way they rant about the rude cashier at the grocery store, or the pie crust that isn't flaky, or a co-worker who said the wrong thing. To me their anger is a remarkable luxury, just as mine would be to someone on a palliative care ward, or as theirs would be to someone in a war zone.

Of course, life demands at least some level of mundanity. The bills need to get paid, the laundry needs to get done, the driver's license needs to be renewed, the taxes need to be filed. People say we should live every day like it's our last — but if I did that I would weigh five hundred pounds and be broke within a month. We work jobs, some we like, some less so. We grocery shop. We sit on hold. We watch TV. We grumble, we bicker.

The farther the near-death moments recede, the more we fall into the comfortable notion that everything will be fine — and then we grumble and bicker more.

But what remains is a fundamental appreciation of the time we have, as worn as that sentiment may be. A walk in the woods with my dog, an honest conversation with a friend, plants poking up in my garden, a favourite song, the flavour of a ripe pear — any number of tiny moments can bring remarkable wonder. I don't need to go bungee jumping or deep-water diving; sometimes I just marvel at the fact that I can put one foot in front of the other — left, right, left, right.

One friend who survived a suicide attempt talks of the glass of orange juice someone set down beside her the next morning. She found the way it glinted in the sun achingly beautiful.

And while joys are more joyous, regrets cut deeper because of the acute awareness of the preciousness of life. Time wasted makes me antsy, and I avoid putting things off until later because I know later may never arrive.

The fact that I lived to forty in itself seems like a miracle; anything beyond that is a bonus. I have only recently started planning for retirement, although I confess it feels more like a contingency plan for an extreme long shot.

I also find myself driven to help reduce other people's pain. When you've been lying helpless in an emergency ward enough times, you come to understand the particular loneliness it brings, so when there's an emergency, I step in, not out.

I have called ambulances and held hands in crowded ERs; I have raised funds when financial hard times hit; I have cared for seniors left alone by time and chance; I have washed dishes and emptied attics; I have attended births; I have arranged funerals. I have baked. I have listened.

That's not to say the impulse is exceptional — but near-death experiences prepare you for actual death experiences. It has nothing to do with white lights at the end of long tunnels; it's an understanding that arrives with particular force when you come close to the end of the road, even if you wind up turning back. *How do you stay so calm?* they ask.

Tonight I'm going to a restaurant where all of my coworkers from another city, whom I have never met, are gathering for a social evening. I checked the menu and they serve bowls of warm nuts, the most miniscule fraction of which could do me in. There may be harm in going, or there may not. I may die or I may not.

Given the choice, what do I do? Sometimes I go, and sometimes I don't. Sometimes I pay a price, lying in a hospital bed struggling for breath, and sometimes I walk away invigorated. There are no crystal balls to consult, no dice to roll, no mathematical ways to calculate or predict. (How a wasp ended up on a sailboat miles from shore continues to confound.)

Of course the same holds true for all of us sitting around the table. Anything could happen to any of us at any moment; I just don't have the luxury of denying that fact. I'm just unlucky enough, or lucky enough, to see it.

On Writing and
Becoming a Reader

John Asfour

Ed. Note: Blinded by a grenade explosion in Lebanon as a teenager, John Asfour confronted the metaphysical ideas of "being" and "meaning" early in life. He came to Canada at age twenty-three as a speaker of Arabic, quickly learned French and English, and achieved a doctorate in literature. Equipped with James Joyce's words, "For the eyes, they bring us nothing. I have a hundred worlds to create and I am only losing one of them," John was busy. Throughout his career as a scholar, poet, editor, translator, and activist, John engaged with diverse communities; it was during his residency at Historic Joy Kogawa House in Vancouver that we met and became close friends and later, co-editors. He gave me permission to record and publish this relaxed, and at times giggly, interview when I visited him in Montreal during his illness. John's daughter, Mikaela Asfour, a wonderful writer and editor herself, edited our long conversation after his death in 2014 specifically for this book.

Elee: So, what year did it happen, that you picked up the thing?
John: Summer of fifty-eight. I was thirteen years old. A bunch

of kids were playing in the front yard. I can't remember whether we found the object in the front yard or somebody brought it in. All I remember is that we gathered in the front yard and we started playing with it.

E: What did it look like?

J: Just some object, about ten centimetres long. It had a lid on one of the sides. And the other side was round and flat, like a capsule. And that's where the gunpowder was — in the capsule. So, I took off the lid, and started banging on the other end. I guess the metal got hot, or God knows what happened, in that thing.

'Cause later on, someone explained it to me — that it must have been a little bomb left from the Second World War somewhere, in the village, or outside the village. And when it got hot in my hand, it exploded.

Part of my index finger of my left hand was blown, and some of the shrapnel went into my face and the rest of my body. And my eyes got some shrapnel.

E: Were your brothers with you?

J: My younger brother was standing next to me. He got some shrapnel in his legs. And I said it at the time: that I'm glad nobody else was affected, of the kids who were next to me. Two or three of my cousins. And I think there were other kids, too.

I think the major — major hit — was in my face and in my arm, my leg. I still have some shrapnel in my left arm and my left leg.

But the real effect was that the pressure of the explosion caused my retina in my right eye to become detached drastically. And it got detached, also, in the left eye. But in the left eye it lasted longer. So I could see, afterwards, for about three years, out of the left eye. And I lost my sight totally, in both eyes, after a major operation when I was sixteen.

E: So, what happened? You were knocked unconscious?

J: No, not really. The strange thing is that most of the people in the village heard the explosion. I didn't hear it.

My sister grabbed my arm and started pulling me and running me to the clinic in the village. And, luckily, there was a doctor on duty at that time. He put me on the table in a room on the second floor, at a school run by the nuns in the village. He bandaged all my wounds. And then my brother, Tony, came and carried me back home. The next day, it was decided by my parents and by the doctor to take me to Beirut, to the hospital, where they looked after my wounds. I must have spent a week there.

You have to remember that there was a war going on in Lebanon at the time. And transportation, and moving around, and finding a good eye clinic, or a doctor, was not so easy. And I think the eye doctor who was on duty at the hospital was not really professional; or was not good enough to realize what should be done for my eyes, or what was wrong…

But, you know, that's in hindsight. Another doctor told me later, had there been a good doctor at the time, I wouldn't have lost my eyesight. Or my eyesight wouldn't have deteriorated to the extent that it did.

E: And what does that do to you?

J: At this point, it doesn't do anything. It just happened. There is no use living in that past, or wishing that the result would have been different.

E: Let's talk about what your mental state was, when you were that young boy.

J: When I went back to the village, most people who would come to visit us — to see how I am — would want to look at my eyes. To see what happened to them. And, after the third or fourth visitor, I didn't want to see anybody. So I would go and hide in my room, and tell my mother to tell them that I'm either sleeping, or not here. Or tell them, "He doesn't want to see anybody." At that point, I did not want to be somebody that people would come and look at and make stupid or uncalled-for remarks.

After a while, I realized that I could still see, and I could still go outside and play with the other kids during the day. But suddenly I discovered that, at night, I couldn't see. I needed help all the time. And that fact was only known to my family. We didn't tell anybody.

And, for a while, I kept going back and forth to the same doctor who saw me first. And then, one time we went to see him, and he saw us coming. He told the secretary to tell us that he didn't want to see us.

I guess he knew that he'd botched the job, and there wasn't anything that he could do. That night, we went to stay overnight at my cousin's. And I remember sitting next to my dad, and [him] crying all night. And realizing that his own son will be blind for the rest of his life.

For the next two and a half years, we looked for other doctors. And we found one who says that we have fifty-fifty chance on my left eye. If we operate, I could either gain my sight back in my left eye — or, if the operation did not work, I would lose whatever sight I still had.

E: And they weren't going to operate on the right?

J: The right retina was damaged. And there was nothing to repair it.

E: Did you have input into the decision?

J: Probably, they would have consulted me. But it was up to my parents to decide whether we should take a chance and have the operation. And I went along with it. I did not object.

Three years after the explosion, I had that operation. And when I woke up, I couldn't see anymore. I went back home, and I stayed home. I refused to see anybody or go anywhere, or try anything. It was probably one of the most difficult times for my parents and my brothers and sister. They didn't know — although they were very supportive and helpful.

For instance, if, during the day, I refused to go outside or go for a walk with them, they'd say, "Okay, well, how about at night? We'll take you for a walk at night. Nobody will see you, and you won't see anybody." So that would work.

E: So, when the accident happened, you stopped going to school.

J: That's right.

E: And your brothers and sisters kept going to school?

J: Oh, yeah.

E: So then, you had the operation, at sixteen. You came back to the village. You didn't want to see anyone.

J: Mm-hm.

E: The whole village was curious, and dying to know what was going on with you?

J: Mm-hm.

E: And your family formed a wall around you?

J: Yeah. The real breakthrough came when — a relative of my mother's was living in Beirut. And one of his neighbours was a teacher in the school for the blind in Beirut. He knew that I became blind, and I was wasting my time. Not learning anything, not doing anything. Not going to school.

And he knew that I was the type of child who would do well in whatever circumstances afforded to him. So he asked my sister, "Why don't you take your brother to that school and see what benefits he can get out of there?" If she had to convince me, at the time, I did not need much convincing.

E: Were you feisty, as a kid?

J: Oh, yeah. I probably was a real terror at one point, when I was a child. I ran all over the place. I got into mischief. I remember coming home with my shirt torn, or my pants torn, and my mother would smack my bum. And she would have her favourite phrase: "I don't know what to do with this kid."

The type of life that kids live in a village is amazing. You're always in the open. There are always things for you to get into.

And I was very, very curious. It's probably part of my curiosity that got me into trying to find out what that stupid object was.

So, suddenly, this kid who was running ten-thousand miles a day in the little village — suddenly he's not able to run around. He's not able to run.

It took a lot of adjusting.

E: Do you remember any of the things that you thought, or that brought you comfort, or that changed your thinking in those first three years?

J: Not really. It doesn't happen overnight. And I don't buy the idea that suddenly you get this vision that would make you change, and would bring you comfort. I went through the same routine that anybody with any conflict would go through. That is, you get angry. You get upset. You get regretful. You get guilty.

And, also, you try to pray, and plead. I come from a Catholic family. And I would game with God, and I would game with religion, every night. I would say, "Okay. If you think you're a merciful God, and you love me — tomorrow morning I should get up, and I should be able to see."

You buy that logic for a while. And then you say, "Okay. Well. What am I doing? Am I trying to test God?" And if the accident happened by the will of God, I think the will of God also would change it. But...

E: So you didn't put away God?

J: Oh, no. No. No. I never put God away when I was a child, and I haven't till now. There are principles and rules and ideals in the New Testament that, to me, are amazing. Just the idea of love. The idea of forgiveness. The idea of Jesus saying, "Give God what is God's, and give Caesar what is Caesar's."

And the idea of salvation — even salvation — I do have a set of ideas that would govern that. And, in the end, if the God that I've formulated and have accepted in my life exists, I would like to sit down and have a conversation with Him at some point. Or Her.

E: Mm-hm. So, do you feel like you reached a point of acceptance, or forgiveness?

J: Forgiveness of what? There is nobody to forgive. Nobody.

E: Okay...

J: Acceptance? Of course I accepted it then. You know, it was my acceptance of what happened to me that made me go and try my damnedest to do what I've done throughout my life, and lead a full, and fulfilling life. And I think I've succeeded in doing that.

E: So, take me back to — Antoinette takes you to Beirut. To the school.

J: Yeah. That was a fascinating, incredible experience. My sister goes with me, with a cousin of ours. It was so hard for my mother, especially. She was crying her heart out. These are village folks. And they didn't know what was available in Beirut.

They thought what everybody else in the village thought: John is going to a place where they will feed him till he gets very fat [laughter], and John will be dependent on other people for the rest of his life. Little did they know, there are schools for the blind.

Anyway, my sister takes me there. And the director of the school takes me by the hand, and gives me a tour of the place. And, my God, was I ever surprised. There are books! There is music to learn! There are sports!

But the most fascinating thing was that there were two-hundred blind kids in that school. They were all running all over the place, shouting to each other, playing, going to classes! And I thought, what the hell is going on here?

And they would come and start wanting to play with me. Wanting to engage me in whatever they were doing. I would get with them for about three minutes at a time, then release myself and go stand by a wall somewhere, and look at them. Look at them, and listen to them, and look at them. And I'd say,

"What the hell? Don't they know that they are blind?" And I guess they didn't. Or, they knew that they were blind, and they convinced themselves that they could study, and learn, and do their damnedest to lead an acceptable and normal life...

E: So, at the school, what happened? When did you switch?

J: It took a few days.

E: That's it?

J: Maybe a few weeks. There was a girl there, and a guy, who really sort of befriended me. And they started showing me how to write in Braille. How to use things in the workshop. I started going to different classes. And the kids would depend on how much they memorized of what was read to them. They would also recall and retell each other what they remembered the next day. And the geography teacher, or the history teacher, would come and quiz them on what they'd studied the night before. So, I would sit with them. And I would start listening, and say, "Well, to hell with it. It is possible."

E: Despite the fact you hadn't been in school for so many years?

J: That's right. Of course, you're in a dilemma, you know? One minute you feel that there will be improvement. There will be a chance that you can do things with your life. Another minute you say, "Oh, no, it's not going to happen. All of this is a façade."

Mind you, at the time when I went to that school, there was only two months left of classes. So I did not get very much input. The following year, in September, when I went back to school, I'd made a few friends. And I sort of understood what the schedule, what the curriculum was. And I said, "What the hell." You know? "I will try."

And I kept trying. And after a while, I could see that there is a difference. And the difference is, is it better to be here, and be open to opportunities, in the school? Or is it better to stay at home, and not do very much?

E: So, is that when you sort of said, "Okay, that's my decision, and now I won't be embarrassed, or hiding"?

J: Right.

E: And then, within the space of a year of meeting other blind kids — you kind of voted for life?

J: Again, as I told you, it doesn't happen overnight. It takes time. And, along the way, you pick up defences. You pick up resolutions. You pick up reactions — or responses. How you deal with whatever happens to you at any given time. Yeah — I would say I'm lucky to have had a loving family and loving friends who I've met over the years. And lucky to have had a nature that is outgoing and positive, and sees the positive in a lot of things.

E: Do you hear people trying to define you by blindness?

J: Oh, yeah. You'll see "blind poet," "blind professor" — a blind this, a blind that. The blindness is so visible that you can't hide away from that. I will be going down the street, and I can hear a woman warning her children, "Please, please, stay away from the way of the blind man." These people don't know who I am. Don't know what I do. So, it's society that has these stigmas. But, if you let them bother you, you spend half your life being bitter and upset. I ignore stuff like this.

E: So, moments that define you, more than becoming blind — that seems like a tremendous shift in your psychology. Dealing with issues, as a sixteen-year-old, that people sometimes don't deal with until they're at an advanced age, and capable, psychologically, of handling them — you had to handle all that so early. So young. As you were still becoming a man.

J: It wasn't easy at all. I had to handle, also, the fact that — will I be able to find a job, one day? Will I be able to meet a girl and kiss her lips, one day? Will I be able to have a home and a family?

But the real breakthrough is this: do you keep thinking that you are blind, and because of blindness, you can't live life normally? Or, do you accept blindness and try to invent other ways and means to achieve things while you are blind?

E: Do you feel like you kind of dealt with the heavy lifting early on?

J: Early on, I had wanted to do a few things. And I thought I had the talent to do them. And I just ignored all the difficulties that would come with these things. Of course it was not easy to come to Canada and learn English and go to one of the best universities, in the English department, get a PhD from an English institution...

E: Before the internet...

J: Before the internet, before any technology. It wasn't easy. But I knew, if I afforded myself some tools, and if I managed to find enough people — loving people, and helpful people, and people who do things for others just for the love of it — I used to think that I could do it. And I did.

When I was doing my PhD, I almost had an army around me, doing things for me. My father read for me. In about four years, he read about two-thousand volumes of Arabic literature. And Mrs. Catherine Newman read for me for fourteen years, voluntarily. Not one penny. My brothers were helping me in Arabic. My mother was cooking for me, was taking care of my daily living. And my sister was helping me. A few friends were helping. I had a few professors who were towers of strength for me, and helped me along the way. So there was no reason for me not to do these things, and not to achieve what I set out to do.

E: Did you have to learn how to accept?

J: Of course. The first acceptance was looking at those two-hundred kids in the school for the blind, and finally deciding that they do know that they are blind. And they've accepted that fact. That's why they are running around, going to classes, playing music, acting in the theatre, working in the workshop, going for walks, playing football — on and on and on. So, that major acceptance, I guess was very instrumental in propelling my other acceptances.

E: Was that the death of [self-]pity?

J: You will be surprised if I tell you I never felt sorry for myself. Never.

E: What about when you wouldn't go outside?

J: I wouldn't go outside because I didn't want to hear other people commenting on who I am, and what I am. Because they hurt my people. They hurt my mother, my father, with their comments.

A woman meets my sister, the day she brought me to school — meets her in Beirut, downtown, and tells her, "I hear that you brought your brother to this institution. Is it true that you don't have enough bread anymore, in the house?"

So this is why I stayed away, and didn't want to go out. Simply, I did not want to expose people who cared for me to things like that. But, sorry [for myself]? No. No. And, you know, I've never felt sorry for other people, either. I feel sorry for what we human beings do to each other, and how we treat each other. That's the honest truth.

E: I know you spend a lot of your time helping, and volunteering, and doing activism. Do you have a concept of there being a wheel of that sort of thing?

J: When I got involved in social activism and human rights issues, and defending other people, and helping other people, wherever I could — I realized that there's a lot of fear in people. And a majority of us do not dare speak out. So, wherever I thought that I could speak out and be the voice of others, I got into being that, three-hundred percent. And I think I may have made a difference in a few people's lives.

E: This is my Barbara Walters question. If you could tell yourself, as a thirteen-, or sixteen-year-old, something, now — knowing everything that you know now — what would you offer to that young John?

J: Somehow, I envy that child. Because — the innocence that he lived in — and the beauty that he lived in, and the love that he knew — was later marred by what the adult John has seen. And what the adult John knows about life and existence, and humanity.

For instance, there was no need, in my mind, to start a war in Iraq. Or to start a war anywhere. And to kill so many people, anywhere. And humanity doesn't do very much about it, and doesn't make a little effort to change any of that.

In other words, I don't think that thirteen-year-old had a reason to be disappointed in what he saw, and what he knew. But later on, he saw a lot of regrettable things.

Would I have done things differently? Maybe I would have. I have a few regrets in my life. But I guess that's part of trying different things.

E: You know, what I think's really interesting is the way that you went from being out of school to being a scholar. I mean — who knows? Hindsight. But, would that have happened? You can't draw a causal relationship. But...

J: I don't know if that would have happened. But something close to it, probably, would have happened. I mean, I wouldn't have been contented in just staying in the village, or staying put — not that I don't have any respect or admiration for people who have stayed, and have lived their lives modestly and simply. But I think, most probably, I would have done something close to being a scholar.

E: Is there one of your works, or one of your efforts, that you're most amazed by? Or the ones that you thought might have been farthest from your grasp, when you were in your darkest moments?

J: It was not a simple task to get a PhD.

[Elee laughs]

J: It was not a simple task to publish a book of translation of

Arabic poetry, which still, twenty years later, is being taught at universities, and being used, and being sold, and bought, and [is] part of the Canadian literary canon. It was not easy to publish so many volumes of poetry, and quite a few anthologies, without working really diligently, and hard, to get these things done.

I'm quite proud of what I've done. I've been published by very reputable publishers. I've done work with bright, and brilliant, scholars, and organized conferences of a lot of skillful people. Served the community with a lot of diligent individuals. So, what can I tell you?

E: Take a bow.

J: Thank you.

[Elee laughs]

Eye of the Storm

Rachel Rose

"Be brave!" shouted my mother above the roar of the helicopter blades. "Sit still and don't touch anything!"

I was. I did. I was four years old and she had trained me well. I sat with my teeth vibrating in my head, as still as I could be, while she worked. I was brave as I watched her thrust needles into a patient's arm. I was brave as I watched her rummage inside a woman's body, bringing her hands back slick with blood.

I don't know how many times I flew with her in the helicopter. The roar is still in my pulse: the way she ran crouched with me in one arm, her black bag in the other. The alders whipped and danced backward on their spines around us. I was belted in and ignored as she worked over the body of the patient she was evacuating. I leaned, forehead to the window, both hands on my ear protectors, watching the world shrink below us.

We had a pact. My mother could trust me not to cry or make demands when she was doctoring. In return, she showed me things that I knew were off limits for ordinary children. She gave me knowledge, and I paid the price.

My mother could raise the dead. For years I watched from her shadow, but I never did learn her magic. Once when a woman was choking to death on a ferry to Nanaimo, they called for a doctor. My mother got up from her seat and asked a woman nearby to watch me. Then she disappeared. My mother saved the woman's life, and came back flushed with victory, her long amber hair falling around her cheeks, eyes bright.

Someone bought me an ice cream bar. Others brought my mother coffee, squares of cake, crowded around her, wanting to be in the presence of someone who had fought death and won. She was never just mine. I always knew I had to share her.

※　※　※

What does it cost to do the work that is almost unbearable to do?

I was brave picking lilies from our garden for the baby who died in the commune next to our house. I didn't know that baby; there were so many of them, but my mother took it hard. It was told to me like this: the baby had a bad cold, and he wailed and wailed in the cabin. At length, he fell asleep and his mother put him on the bed and went out to chop firewood. When she came back, he was dead. The lilies were tall and white and left traces of burnt orange pollen on my hands.

I was left alone in the house while my parents went to the funeral.

※　※　※

One morning I walked across the pasture with my friend. We were six and she already had pierced ears but my mom said I had to wait. Her hair was blown thistledown. She said, "I have to turn my earrings a hundred times a day. I'll let you turn them for me," and I twisted the gold studs while we counted.

Another morning, I watched my father coming out of the lake carrying my friend's body in his arms. The search had gone on all night. Water ran from her body and her hair, tangled with duckweed and silt. He passed her to her mother, who wrapped her in her shawl. The crowd of searchers stood around silently, hanging their heads. My father turned, walked away with his arms held out from his body, as though he had been burned.

But that's not true. In fact, I wasn't there. I was asleep in bed while he searched. But I remember it even though that's impossible. It was only told to me after the fact, one of those memories that stains.

We were six, but she never got any older.

My father taught me to swim right after. I learned to swim in the lake where she drowned. He was obsessed with making sure I couldn't pull the same disappearing act on him. Again and again, he drilled me across the brown waters. On my front, on my back, crawl, breast stroke, crawl. When he was satisfied, he'd let me chase frogs among the cattails while he swam laps, cutting through the murky water with fierce strokes.

※ ※ ※

The phone call, the pager, the ride, the lift, the sense of emergency in the air; all of these were the lullaby of my childhood. The ambulance lights, the speed, the helicopter lifting off, the stretcher, the blood, the patient being evacuated, screams or groans of pain from the stretcher, the urgent shouts, floodlights, scalpels, bandages, the feeling of being forgotten and thus at peace, floating in and out of sleep in the eye of the storm. In the hospital waiting rooms of my childhood I drifted, eating crackers and doughnut the nurses brought me, watching TV, the hours slipping by. Lullaby. I felt peaceful. I felt at home.

※ ※ ※

The proximity I had to birth and death from the time I was a baby does not distill itself to moral lessons, though it marked me. I learned younger than most how fragile is the membrane between animation and stillness. But it happens to everyone as we move through life: we lose people. We lose those we love and those we barely know. The blessing of a long life is coming to terms with loss after loss after loss.

Because I wanted to understand this passage more deeply, I became certified as a hospice volunteer. The other people who volunteered to do this work were some of the most extraordinary, compassionate people I've ever had the good fortune to meet. Each of them had been marked by deaths, and had already witnessed people as they left the world. Each of us was searching for a better way to move through this transition, for strangers, for loved ones, and for ourselves.

The most profound moment in this volunteer training was our homework exercise: to write our own obituary. The next day we read our death notices aloud to the entire group. It was the rare hospice volunteer who could read the summary of their own life with dry eyes, though our voices caught at different points: She read, *An environmental and spiritual activist, she was famous for her pies and her parties, and was predeceased by her sweet dog, Coco.* He read, *He was the beloved father of James and Jennifer, as well as a retired surgeon and a volunteer with Operation Smile.* She read, *Ordained as a Buddhist priest, she leaves behind many friends and her cherished community at Mountain Rain.*

Who were we actually, when it came to the end of our days? How could we distill our lives down to five or six sentences, to the essence of ourselves? Any way you ask this question, it becomes this deeper question: What did we do upon this earth that truly mattered? What legacy will we leave?

We were fortunate to be able to read our own obituaries in

generous and supportive company. No one mentioned the money they'd earned or hadn't earned. No one cared. All of us hoped to be remembered for what we had given to others, for the love offerings we left in our wake.

To speak of your legacy as if you had died while you are still alive, and to be witnessed doing it, provides a rare opportunity to reset the path of your life. The years we are allotted are fleeting; we are guaranteed moments of joy and of suffering, and we are guaranteed, each of us, to live until we die. But hospice workers know that we live right until the moment we live no longer. The process of dying can itself be a rich consolation, a chance to be loved, to grow, and to find peace. The process of dying can, for some, provide the opportunity to create a legacy. Even death can be a poem, a poem that ends on the exhalation.

What I took away from the deaths I observed as a child, and in particular those I knew who took their own lives, was a strong wish for my death to match the way I live. Each of us creates a death legacy, great or small, generous or hurtful. If I have learned something from sitting at the bedside of those who are close to leaving, it is to pay attention to how we leave and to what we leave behind. We all die, whether we live in awareness of that fact or in denial. To leave a legacy of pain and suffering for those who come after is, to me, the worst fate possible.

At sixteen, I sat with my best friend's grandmother as she took her last rattling breaths and died. She was a difficult woman, a Holocaust survivor, never happy with her family or the care she received. A few weeks before, I had rubbed lotion into her feet. I had tried to boil her an egg. It took three wasted eggs before I boiled one to her satisfaction. But as she lost the power of speech, some change manifested itself in her, and the bitterness fell away. As her son sat in vigil at her bedside, she blew him kisses; he kissed her back. So much hurt was healed in those last deathbed kisses. When she had died, he lowered her hospital bed so her body was at rest against the sheets. He rested too a while, his head on her stilled heart.

To be in the presence of the dying is to learn how many ways there are to meet death. When I get close to the end, I hope to have the opportunity to erase some of the hurts I will have caused. So, even though she lost everything, and saw the worst that humans can do to each other, I'd say my friend's grandmother was lucky. She escaped the Nazis and created a new life for herself in America. And though this knowledge left her traumatized, at the end she left a legacy of kisses light as soap bubbles.

Three Times

Rabi Qureshi

The very first time I was diagnosed with cancer, I was assured it was one of the most treatable kinds. That once they cut me open and sliced it out of me, and threw in a little radiation, that would be it. I was guaranteed with a hearty laugh that I wouldn't be worrying about this ever again, and that my life would be the same.

My body has never been the same again. For a fifteen-year-old who took her young, energetic body for granted, severe acne, fatigue, memory issues, focus issues, and gaining forty pounds within two months, were not small changes. I've been relearning my body, every single day since that cancer battle.

I focussed all my frustration on a small hormone pill that had suddenly become part of my daily morning routine. I kept trying to get by without it, until I was unable to function.

It's funny to watch these words string together as I try to communicate my experiences. Adapting to the new "normal" took five whole years. By age twenty, I was finally starting to level out. I lost the added weight and was getting into a routine. Sleep wasn't great but once in a blue moon I had one of those delicious nights where you close your eyes and in the blink of a second it's morning, and you're fully awake and ready for the day. I know those nights existed, but I can no longer recall what they felt like.

At twenty-one, I was ready to take my life back and attending art school. At the same time that I was starting to get disenchanted with the dream of becoming an animator, my body must have seen it as the perfect opportunity for another forced halt. Not a break, a halt.

I still have no clue how many tumours they removed, but that's another story altogether. Those surgeries changed my body in a way I've never been able to heal from. Post-op I had a leak, which inflated the skin on the left side of my neck and shoulder like a grotesque water balloon. After putting me on a liquid diet for eight days and realizing the leak wasn't going to heal itself (it was related to the metabolism of fat), doctors scheduled an emergency surgery to go back in and clamp it. I won't get into the details of what was leaking and all the medical jargon, just that I had a giant tube sticking out of me, draining into a big tub, spilling onto my bed and gown. It wasn't long before my skin was irritated by the constant dampness. They finally admit that they may have nicked something they weren't supposed to, and fixed it.

I force myself to skip a lot of detail here. During the next three years the pain from the damage made it impossible to sleep. Talking myself down from suicide became a daily chore.

Again, the words seem so simple when strung together. It's funny how much weight words gain. What's even funnier is that you could have the words, the experiences, the heavy weight of it in your chest, but until you get validation of some sort, you can't move forward. Because there's always doubt: What if I'm just lazy? What if I'm just weak? What if it really is about mind over matter? What if I'm just a very negative person, and the power of positivity is all it'll take? What if the cancer came and went and now I'm just being overly dramatic?

I took a scalpel to my life and dissected it in every which way I could, trying to dig my way out of depression and fear. What else are you supposed to do when you can't work, go to school, or have a social life because you don't know when those few precious hours of sleep will come? Sometimes I only had forty solid minutes in two days. Or two whole hours in three days. There are large chunks of my life I don't remember. Blurred days of crying and staring at the ceiling and just being numb. When someone asked me how I was dealing with it all, I remember saying, *What choice is there?* It's laid out in front of me and as long as I treat it as an unknown amount of time, all I can do is just keep getting through it. What else can you do when your own body becomes your battleground. Your prison. The most terrifying isolation cell. There's a Winston Churchill quote I came to appreciate in those days: "If you're going through hell, keep going."

So I kept going. I managed to arrive back at college at the age of twenty-four to study event management. That first year took everything I had, but I hadn't been happier in years. I struggled to get enough rest and missed a lot of deadlines, but I was a part of humanity again. I was in control again. I was getting my body back, and was once again losing the weight (this had become an indicator of my health for me). There was still no such thing as routine, but I was scraping by. The waves of suicidal tendencies were reduced from daily to weekly occurrences. I counted my blessings for that. So I ignored the lump that appeared under my skin, even though a part of me already knew what it was. It didn't appear to be growing very rapidly so I kept putting it off. Maybe I'd get it diagnosed in the winter break. Maybe the March break.

The semester ended, I got a summer job, I landed my dream internship, and I realized that if life really was getting better, maybe I had something to live for. So I went and I got diagnosed. What caught me off guard was that this time, it was an all new cancer, and completely unrelated to the first two occurrences. I believe one of my surgeons used the term "shit luck." My brain nearly imploded from the level of the understatement. But yeah, he said it right. That was really shit luck. Neither side of my family had a history of cancer, so that about sums it up.

All the while that all this was going on, I was trying to get away from a toxic home environment. Family, however well they mean and however deeply they love you, can inflict the most exquisite, thorough levels of damage. It didn't help that I was a black sheep in a Muslim household. Mine tried to fix my problems according to lessons learned from a completely foreign life. You can't sleep? You need to! You are sad? Get up and go out. You can't do anything? Try harder. But let's leave that stone unturned for this narrative.

During that summer, I planned to seek financial aid and move out. I would try and find myself again, or whoever the new me was. I had retreated so far to the back of my head just to survive everything: my body, my family's thundering words, my violent and screaming brain, every figurative wall I had been hitting, the overwhelming feeling of being a failure, the guilt, etc. I thought, *I've been lucky and haven't had to do chemo until now; radiation is rough, but I could get by on my own.* But that wasn't the plan. The surgeries couldn't wait and had to be booked ASAP. The chemo was to follow very shortly after. And everything else went on the back burner.

I tried to be logical and just accept it, but I broke. I wanted to scream and flail my arms. Why wasn't anyone as horrified by this? Why are they not freaking out? Do they understand what I have to do? Do they understand how far I have to go inside myself just to get through this again? Do they get that the only line of defence I have here is myself? That the battle is against my own mind and body? Do they know that everything I experience the world through is about to be mutilated by disease in ways they can't imagine? I didn't even know that brain fog (or chemo brain) was a term, but I knew my mind was going to be under attack again. I knew I was about to feel a whole new world of incompetence, of imprisonment. I was barely coping with my chronic pain, how much worse was it going to get? I knew that as soon as they removed my breasts, I would wake up in yet another body.

That's what always happens: you go to sleep whole and buzzing with nervousness, you wake up and everything is off. You are so fully shaped on the inside, by how your body interacts with the world on the outside. Surgeons take away chunks and pieces of me, and it takes me months, sometimes years, to adjust.

I was in shock during recovery from a lumpectomy, and then dove into five months of chemo, the end of which was punctuated by the double mastectomy. And all I could do was just get through. But I couldn't fake as many smiles. I didn't have the energy to comfort what few friends I had left, reassuring them that it was alright that they only came by the one time during my eight months from hell. That it was completely understandable that they had busy lives. Of course I knew they were thinking of me. Of course I appreciated the thoughts and prayers. Of course.

I wasn't fine. I was in hell. I had been in hell for a long time and had only known small moments of superficial happiness. And the truth is, the further inside I retreated, the harder it became to enjoy little moments of happiness. It's like watching a couple in their honeymoon phase when you're just on the tail end of getting over a break up. I wasn't bitter, I just didn't care. Apathy was in my bones and blanketing everything, a numbness so deep, it was hard to escape. It was the only coping mechanism I had to get through these fifteen years. And it's sometimes the tool I revert back to using even now.

I found support along the way in organizations with programs which helped partially resuscitate my mind. I've met amazing people with stories of their own who are fighting their battles in their own ways. And I love meeting them and feeding off of them. I'm often described as bubbly, joyful, vibrant, and a social butterfly.

I'm a three-time cancer survivor. But I didn't just survive those cancers, I lived every single day of them. I'm still living with them, because they have shaped me, mind and body. I'm grateful for everything I have in my life, but I still struggle with thoughts of suicide every couple of months. I am still a social butterfly, but I have moments where I just need to retreat to the numbness, just to get by. I don't always know what triggers it, but sometimes I'm lucky and I just end up there, sometimes I experience the full wave of shock and panic before I can find my way to the numbness. That's an aspect of the PTSD, I suppose. I recently learned this is a major issue which goes undiagnosed for many cancer patients.

I thought I was just weak, but looking back at it, how could I not be traumatized? I love my family, but I could never live with them again. A single day can be packed with enough triggers to put me down and out for weeks. I love my job, my education, and life, but I am in constant pain and I struggle with things on a daily basis. On a moment-to-moment basis, really. The nature of this pain is something I can't get used to. It fluctuates, and sometimes it almost feels like a living thing, a parasite with which I have to share my body and mind.

Everything is on the upswing, and I am grateful for and celebrating every single part of my life that's healing and flourishing. But I'm at the five-year mark from my last diagnosis, and I've lost most of the weight...

Some people consider it to be the equivalent of suicidal tendencies when I say that I will never go through chemotherapy or radiation again. There isn't a person in the world who could convince me to pick quantity of life over quality at this point. Anyone could be hit by a bus at any time; if I get cancer again, that will be my bus.

Gently Fondling the Nylon-tipped Sticks of Death

Nikki Reimer

Every day I ride the bus, listen to his music, and cry. The crispness of the snare drum and ride cymbal in the song "Jerk Chicken"[1] seems to be a message. The sticks must be nylon-tipped, I think. I ride the bus in the rain and listen for him. On days when I have the strength, I walk home from the Broadway SkyTrain station and listen to The National. Either *Boxer* or *High Violet*. I discover that it is possible to walk with eyes closed. "It's a terrible love that I'm walking in."[2] I do this a lot when the music overtakes me. I close my eyes and walk heel-toe in time with the music. My body keeps me moving forward in space. I am not afraid to cry or sing along while I do this. I am not afraid of judgment. I am not afraid of falling. I do not fall. I have excellent mind-body awareness. My dance training has prepared me to walk in the rain with my eyes closed in the months after his death. I can walk all the way down Victoria Drive without seeing anything.

❊   ❊   ❊

I tweet:

   LOUDER MUSIC. SADDER MUSIC. LOUDER AND
SADDER. SADDER AND LOUDER.

   Many nights I am depleted after work even though my shift
is only six or seven hours long. At the midway point of my day I
am energetically and psychically empty and I have to coast till
it's time to go home. Gravity navigates me down the steep hill
from the college to the New Westminster SkyTrain station. It's
recently been renovated, with shops up top near the platform —
a grocery store, a bank, an Ardene. I go to Safeway, purchase a
block of Havarti cheese, plain or dill flavoured. I break off
chunks to eat on the train. I require the sweet fat in my mouth.
Umami. I am trying to trigger the smallest hit of serotonin in my
brain. "It takes an ocean not to break."[3] When I get home, I lie
on the floor, slowly finish the entire block of cheese.

❊   ❊   ❊

I begin a descent into symbolism. I am crafting my own mythology. It is made up of skeletons, incense, and pictures of trees.
It comes from the same place as the wind. It is wrinkled and
sweet-tasting. It feels like Dido's[4] hands. It has the sad baritone
of Matt Berninger. It is solitude. My brother said once about
Berninger, and The National's lyrics — "He lives in New York.
And he feels *really* bad about it."

   Now I live in grief. And I feel *really* bad about it.

❊   ❊   ❊

Is/Was

Our noses were different. His more Slavic: longer and wider, with the ski-jump ridge at the bridge. Mine shorter and fatter like Dad's side of the family. My cheeks are fatter, but we have the same smile lines, or rather our smile lines had the same angle. If you traced one and laid it on top of the other they would match. My lips are fuller on the bottom, his fuller and wider on top. He had a little dimple on the left side of his mouth. My chin is pointy like a witch, his chin is rounder and wider. His hair is golden brown, mine ashy brown. His brows are closer to his eyes. Our eyes are the exact same shade of azure blue, a darker tone of Dad's wedding suit. We have the same funny, sunken eyes: one thick crescent-shaped crater under the eye and two folded wrinkles of skin above it. The lids are thick on the top and crinkle at the outer edges. He has the broad shoulders of a man. My shoulders are narrow and hunched. I slouch to protect myself. His eyebrows are thicker than mine, but a more golden tone. His forehead is taller, but the bone structure is the same. So are the little wrinkle patterns. In the mornings now when I put on foundation I see for a split second his undertaker made-over forehead — same bone structure same pore structure same wrinkle pattern same coverage of too-tan makeup. This square inch of skin looks the way his dead forehead looked, and this is how my forehead will look when I am dead. I flash forward and back through my own death all the time. I am trying to be prepared. His skin had more of a yellow undertone and in the summer, he became quite olive. My skin is purple undertone, I have rosacea, and I am very pale. He tans, I burn. When he was a toddler I could high-kick over his head with a half-inch to spare, when we were thirteen and nineteen we were the same height, and when he was grown he was four inches taller than me. We both have wide hips and long slender fingers. His hands were larger and more cisgendered masculine than mine, but the metatarsal structure was the same: long and thin and visible beneath the skin. I suppose either of us could have been a pianist if we'd had the right disposition. In pictures I have seen since he left, I notice that we had the same repertoire of unconscious facial expressions; we made the same face for disgust or contempt or bemusement. I changed his diaper once or twice when he was a baby, and we bathed together when he was two and I was eight, until the unfortunate incident with the poop. I haven't seen him naked since he was maybe about six. I remember that he has a birthmark on his bum, but I don't remember what side. Once when I was drunk in Vancouver and a friend was recounting a news report about uncircumcised men being at higher risk for contracting HIV, I called him on the spot to warn him. I apologized later for crossing a line, but he laughed and said not to worry, it was funny. Our hair is fine and thick at the same time. When it is freshly washed, it curls and frizzes and jumps and glows like a halo. I think he hated this and maybe that's why he rarely washed his. In some pictures, he looks more Ukrainian, and in some pictures, I look more Ukrainian.

I worry that he will not recognize my face when I am old.

※　※　※

One time we decided that if we'd had a third sibling they would have been the exact opposite of everything that we both were. So: confident, business-minded, corporate, professional, good with money. I wonder if one of the babies Mom lost was this mature and with-it sibling, in contrast with our unhinged selves that bled creativity and angst. We'd likely have fought a lot with him or her. We hate authority figures. We hate being told what to do.

※　※　※

NOT FAIR

I dial up Mom on Skype and am weeping so hard she can't understand me.

"What?" she says.
"I want to die," I sob.
"Well that's not fair to me."

※　※　※

Wild one won't you please come home
You've been away too long, will ya?
We need you home, we need you near
Come back wild one will ya?
How can we live without your love
You know that could kill ya
And how can we carry on
When you are gone my wild one.[5]

※　※　※

Death is a shockwave in the ocean. At first it topples everything. The wave is generated from the impact of the absence. And the spirit of the person ripples out into his entire community. And crosswaves ripple back. In this way, the person remains present even though they are ostensibly gone. They are in the waveforms. They continue to ebb and flow. Sometimes they flow back out to their loved ones when you'd swear they were gone completely. The form is smaller but it continues. For a long time, it continues, and the waves are a comfort. But eventually the wave dies. Then they are gone completely.

It's not fair to think that anticipated death is easier on the mourner than unexpected death, but I do think this, because with anticipated death there is a period of pre-mourning. His death is different: Chris had some drinks and watched TV with his girlfriend, went to bed. When she woke up he was dead.

We are in a temporarily lost boat, Dad says. We are standing at the bottom of a crater. We are under the tsunami. We are in the riptide. We are beneath the earthquake. We are the tornado.

Grief comes in waves and layers of sorrows that are sometimes difficult to parse out. Shock at what has happened. Dashed hopes for the future. Things I still needed to tell him — about life, about art. The funny story he was going to tell me later about this souvenir or that show. Books I wanted him to read, music he could have shared with me. The ways I could have helped him navigate the difficult rites of passage that mark an artist's mid-twenties, and never did. I never helped him. That we will never be aunt or uncle to each other's hypothetical-un-born children. That we will never care for each other in old age and sickness the way we watched our grandmother nurse her brother who was dying from bone cancer at St. Paul's Hospital in Saskatoon. Hectoring the nurses. Shifting his body to check his bedpan. Such strength and tenderness. That I am now left to be sole heir, attorney, executor to our parents' lives and objects. That when I die there will be nothing left at all of our family.

It's all you, says Dad.

HOME/NOT HOME

This city needs more coffee shops. It was not properly explained to me that a typical Calgary summer is twenty degrees Celsius and rain, for months.

I misplaced the notebook I was writing in when he died. It was purple.

I want to reach the state of Buddhist enlightenment where I am able to feel at home even in circumstances that are very anxiety-producing for me, but I am very far from this. It was not until we hung some of the pictures and paintings, four weeks after we'd moved into the little rental saltbox in Killarney, that I began to relax. Then early-September turned to mid-September, and the house still had no heat. And my sphincter tightened again, acid reflux burning up the pipes.

The human body is organic and never in stasis. Like every organic substance and under the right conditions it will begin to rot.

How much rent does a person have to pay in order to not have to deal with rot in the structure? Mould in the appliances?

※　※　※

I step breathlessly into the liquor store at two minutes to six on the holiday Monday of the August long weekend. Ask the man if the store is still open.

"For a Mars Volta fan, absolutely!"

He's smiling. What he's said hasn't registered. I don't even know the band.

"I have the same shirt. It's awesome."

Remember what shirt I am wearing.

Think — I took this shirt from my brother.

Do not say — I took this shirt from my brother.

No one wants to hear the next sentence.

※　※　※

Is it possible to divest oneself of enough of one's possessions so that one is ready to die at any moment, and if so, would one then begin to live, fully and completely, or would one then sit down and cease to live?

The things are what remain after death.

I am thinking of my grandfather's socks still folded neatly in his sock drawer fourteen years after he died, which my then twenty-one-year-old brother took home and started to wear. Always mismatched — one brown and one grey. Or one black and one blue. Thin man's dress socks from Kmart or Sears, circa 1980, maybe? The quality of even cheap goods back then. Things that endure vs. things that don't.

We put him in his favourite checked dress shirt and a pullover blue sweater of our Dido's. New brown pants that he liked. I don't know if we gave him socks, or shoes. Not that it would have mattered, as he would soon cease to (be) matter.

※　※　※

My problem is that I have trouble focussing. Maybe I have ADHD. I need meds, different meds, better meds.

My problem has always been that I'm arrogant when it would behoove me to be humble, and self-hating when it would be best to self-promote. I lack humour in times of frivolity and make light of situations that call for sober thought.

My problems are tonal. My problems are situational. I'm bad at my job because I don't live for marketing.

My looks are going. I'm getting the Slavic jowls that run through the Ukrainian side of our family.

Our people are gorgeous in the prime of youth — high cheek-bones and clear blue eyes that could cut steel — but we lose it in age. Our cheeks fill out and sag, lines that frame either side of the mouth, the bookends of the face sliding ever lower. Evolving into the dumb peasants from whence we came.

His looks were just starting to go before he died. The last time I saw him, he was just starting to bald at the crown of the head, though he was only twenty-five. He was getting fat too, like me, no longer able to fit into his favourite vintage-store brown blazer, an identical jacket to one of Dido's. He'd replaced the buttons with band pins — Sigur Rós and Beneath These Idle Tides. His face was puffy. And he died before he lost it all, still a young man's hands unnaturally folded in prayer position in the rental coffin. The skin puckered because his blood had been removed. But at twenty-one — at twenty-one we were both of us beautiful.

No that's a lie, he was always the beautiful one.

※　※　※

The carnivalization of my grief.

The big fat bellyfication of my grief.

Learning to love my grief.

Learning to love my grief more.

The performativity of this mourning is egregious.

I made him up. He is dead. He was never real. He is dead.

Write an obituary for every job he's ever held.

You may have noticed that I haven't started any digital community projects.

That's because I'm a self-involved asshole.

The problem is that I have to let him go.

And I don't want to.

I don't want to.

Chris, I don't want to.

"I'm unstable!"

Languages. The language of The Dead. I hear dead people. I heart dead people. I translate dead people. Shut up about your dead people, Reimer.

※　※　※

What is culture? Family tradition. I spent a lot of money attempting to buy myself comfort after he died.

The more degrees removed you are from your own cultural heritage, the more likely you are to outsource expressions of that culture, which is why we found ourselves attending Tuesday night Ukrainian dance lessons and purchasing fundraiser pyrohy.

※　※　※

I often feel that I am saying the word NO with my entire body. Resisting movement. Trying to squeeze time still by spending all my time aimlessly internet surfing. Stuffing my feelings down with food.

※　※　※

I felt itchy and irritable for longer than I could remember, from the beginning of childhood, a feeling that the world chafed and stabbed at my body, the fit was wrong, my cells were wrong, a vestigial unhappiness, an anxiety I would identify thirty-four years later as the sense that every situation called for a different version of myself than whomever I was currently presenting.

※　※　※

When people die, they leave a lot of stuff behind.

※　※　※

I'm thinking of how grey and papery my grandfather's skin looked in pictures taken at Christmas 1991, four months before he died. And how in pictures from Christmas in 2011 my brother's face is puffy, swollen, and grey. His eyes are two black, sunken circles. And I didn't see these pictures till afterwards, but he looked like death, he had two months left, we knew Dido was sick, but no one knew till Chris didn't wake up, and I'm trying to understand why this photographic foreshadowing is only apparent in retrospect.

❊ ❊ ❊

The point is to love as fervently as possible, even and especially when it hurts.

❊ ❊ ❊

How to stay grounded and connected to my writing and not give all my soul to my job.

❊ ❊ ❊

Walking home from the train station one day his thoughts suddenly in my head — *You need to have more fun in life* — the phrase enters in my own mind's voice, but the words are unmistakably his.

I know, you're right, I know, I say out loud.

❊ ❊ ❊

Later on, we'll be quaint and twee.

I AM STILL FINDING THE MINTS FROM MCINNIS & HOLLOWAY I DON'T THINK YOU UNDERSTAND.

Chic louche / chic gouache.

❊ ❊ ❊

This is never going to be ok.

※　※　※

I need to reclaim / respect the Baba Yaga I am become.

※　※　※

After four days in Montreal, leaving my dear university friend Janice's cozy Parc Ex apartment felt like stepping back out of the womb again. I could tell it was going to be a long flight because we left an hour late, I had to pee before they finished the safety instructions en français, and the lady in front of me kept coughing like she had a bronchial infection. After Mile End, the coffee at Starbucks was so terrible I just threw it out. Hashtag-first-world-whatever. I'm bored of my own internal monologue. I miss Janice already. My grandfather died in an airplane, but I'm a pretty relaxed flyer. I guess I think fate wouldn't take the third generation by the same method, though by that logic I should take up smoking. The sun set while we taxied. The businessman beside me appears uptight. Now there is a lineup for the washroom, and I have to poop. I feel sorry for the businessman, but I can no longer control my farts. I just wrote "faults" when I meant "farts." Farts.

※　※　※

He is very far away now. I can't reach him. My dreams are fuzzy.

I wanted to write a redemption story so I could live a redemption story, but I kept spiralling further down into my own wound.

The day is grey and bleak. Snow on the ground, but it might get up to three degrees. I feel dizzy and sick — not sure if it's the coming off the old meds or adjusting to the new meds. I wanted to be free of antidepressants for the first time since I was nine-teen years old. My status update on Facebook was going to read "Big Pharma Free for the First Time since 1999! Send me a cookie!" but my brain began to feel like water and I couldn't cope, couldn't drive, couldn't move, couldn't focus.

I'm not so much writing now as transcribing.

Last Christmas I wanted to use the time off work as a stay-at-home writing residency, but I was too fucked up to do any-thing beyond drink heavily every day and make angry posts on social media. That my day job involves social media is a bit ridiculous — I keep waiting to be found out and fired.

His music is the only thing that really matters to me.

※　※　※

A montage sequence of Christmases past, present, and future. His hauntingest tracks form the soundtrack. In the first clip, we put out cookies and milk for Santa at the old house on Wood-mont Drive. In the last clip, I am an old woman, wrinkled and bent with osteoporosis. I serve myself Earl Grey tea with a bit of milk. I bite into a shortbread cookie. He emerges from the shadows, a handsome young man with messy brown hair. He takes my hand. The mug falls and shatters. "Hallmark Produc-tions" runs across the screen. Fade to black.

Last Christmas I existed in a state of inchoate rage, a primal howl.

This year I feel detached, observant. Zero feels.

※　※　※

I never have much of a maternal feeling, but none of the rela-tives believe me when I state that I don't and will never want kids — because no one believes that children have fully-informed thoughts of their own — so when I'm around twelve, goaded by my great-aunt and second-cousins, I make a bet with my brother for one-thousand dollars, signed and dated, that I won't have babies. Me aged forty is the best-before date of the bet; he would have been thirty-four.

There is a period of time, between the initial aftermath of grief and shock, and before the miniature trials of Job to follow, when I become fixated on the idea of having a baby who will somehow be the reincarnation of Chris, and who will carry on the family lineage that is going to die with me. Genetic continuance has never been a concern before; now it is an oppressive responsibility. When told of his death my very first bargaining thought, clutching the linoleum in my kitchen and dry-heaving, was to wonder how long he'd been dead and if we could recover sperm from his testicles. If we could reproduce him in a test tube.

Death makes monsters of us all.

Around this time when I am weighing the thoughts of making a baby: me — with my lifelong crushing depression anxiety suicidal ideation, my undiagnosed ADHD-lack-of-impulse-control, my useless spiralling decades, my endometriosis migraines vasovagal syncope when my cervix is opened, my short patience and short temper, — a woman about whom my husband once said, "Nikki, if we had kids, you would stack them into a Banker's Box to sort out later..." I visit a medium whose office is on the second floor of a shabby, aging building on Seventeenth Avenue in Calgary, across from a liquor store. There is retail on the main floor, and apartments above. She gives me a terrible tarot card reading, tells me that I am supposed to travel and have a baby, that the baby will be my brother. At one point, she turns on the fan on the floor, which is supposed to detect the presence of spirits. It clicks and whirrs, stalls and then starts again. I wonder if anyone actually falls for this shit. I pay her eighty dollars cash for the performance. At the end of the session, as I am counting out her money, I try to make small talk, ask how she got into tarot cards. An expression passes her face, her real face, a look of pity and contempt. Her mask slipped — she doesn't believe what she's doing either. Then she recovers. Maybe the change is only microseconds long, but I see it in slow motion. I see everything real under the web of artifice that humans have constructed to keep from going insane, and it is exhausting.

※　※　※

Most days it feels like it would be all too easy to step right out of this corporeal casing and fly away. Just crack open this bone cage and go. I wouldn't think twice. My body smells like skunk and mushrooms. This happens, apparently, to women in their thirties. A hormonally-shifted pungency, worse than adolescence. I'm almost overripe. Ready to burst. Pomegranate Noir is the name of the fancy perfume sample in my purse. I envision the perfume, my purse, my body juicy and cracked open on the sidewalk. I understand how easily he did it, shedding his body's shell and stepping off into the astral plane. With enough concentration I think I could manifest this. Just take the stairs out of here. I could step right out of this shell and go.

1. Church of the Very Bright Lights. *Gang Crimes*. Church of the Very Bright Lights, 2013. Digital album.
2. The National. *High Violet*. The National, 2010. Digital album.
3. The National. *High Violet*. The National, 2010. Digital album.
4. Dido, or Gido, is grandfather in Ukrainian.
5. Thin Lizzy. *Dedication: The Very Best of Thin Lizzy*. Mercury Records, 1991. Digital album.

Qwerty

Laurie Lewis

Swaying and moaning in the day, raging at night.

A day then: I woke suddenly, sensing there was something floating in my mind, there were some words that wanted to be stated. I think it had something to do with aging...with being old; perhaps with death, with the pace and blandness of the past months, the rage and madness; with the liberation of age.

Perhaps it's me I'm running away from. Perhaps I don't have to keep looking at the black hole. Perhaps I can learn to read and walk and loaf about, to watch the world go by. Perhaps there is nothing and nobody to take care of but this little old lady who used to be me. Perhaps I can learn to do that as I slide into my bony, aching nineties, staring the future in the face.

Why am I doing this? Why don't I just go for a walk! The sun is shining. Why am I sitting here in front of these keys? Hands poised, eyes front, coffee just over there, near my right hand.

I could say I write to find out who I am and what I think. Perhaps that's true, though trite. But it's not my brain that gives me thoughts, ideas, it's my flying fingers. My fingers know the answers. I have only to ask QWERTY, the magic Ouija board of my life.

In the beginning, back in New York, when the keys were on a big grey Underwood and I typed film scripts to earn the rent money, that was when my fingers learned words, learned to talk. I had to fling the carriage back at the end of every line. That was the best part, that ferocity. I was full of anger then, and the great fling at the end of every line, after the bell sounded, was liberating. A physical blow, that fling. "Take that!" It got to be a habit. A habit of anger perhaps, a necessary habit in tough times.

I have softened since then, I am happy to say. I no longer feel the need to rage into my QWERTY board. Now it is more like a dear old friend, someone I have known for years, useful and kind. The QWERTY board has been part of my life for over seventy years, but only recently have I begun to feel possessed by the peculiar backchannel, up from the keys into my brain. As though my mind is elsewhere, just waiting. Perhaps it is. My fingers know what they are doing, where they are heading. I don't seem to hear the words, or even to think them. Just put fingers on the keys, settle, and be calm. Look out the window maybe. Let the fingers have their way.

When they finally pause in their incessant tap-tap-tapping I can pay attention, look at the screen. There it is, the magic of actual words, chattering at me from the glittering screen/page, talking into my eyes. This hour spent with QWERTY in the mornings seems to tell me who I am, what I am thinking and feeling, what I care about. Just let the flying fingers loose on the keys… talking to me now of my long life, of troubled times.

In this way, possessed by this energy through my late years, some stories got written, a book or two, some essays. Now and then a poem took its odd shape, sounded its observation or alarm through my fingertips. Words got saved or lost. Sometimes long, chatty letters went to friends or relatives. Files often lost themselves in the brains of my computer, coming to the surface years later to surprise me with their knowledge of the person I used to be, telling me what I used to think, used to feel.

Now, my fingers still search for the keys, still want only to set their words onto those flat surfaces. The modern keys are shiny and square – a different tactile experience, even more pleasant now, without the fierce physical energy I used to need.

At night sometimes, sleeping, I feel those fingers moving: QWERTY, QWERTY, QWERTY. I trust these keys. They will tell me, always, truthfully, exactly how I feel, what I am thinking, what is happening in my world. These days I can't seem to trust my inarticulate brain to tell me anything, or even to tell the truth. Only when I read what the flying fingers have written will I know — only then, when the Ouija board of my life speaks to me.

I sometimes wonder what I have been doing for the past few years. Living in some kind of space, some kind of limbo neither here nor there, not noticing, not really paying attention. And yet my QWERTY board has remembered things my mind has not.

Mourning – After

After my husband died, in the spring of some years ago, I seemed to ricochet about, colliding with events and people, raging. All around me other people were dying; other friends, family of friends; death seemed like the disease-of-the-month. I spent all summer, it seemed, alone in my little house by the lake. Every day a week.

The weather was turning warm, my visitors were few. Memorials for those endless dead ones kept me alive, gave me a reason to comb my hair, brush my teeth, put on clean clothes. Time folded over itself uncertainly all summer, all fall, as I raged. I went to memorials in other cities and tried to look sane. I smiled and drank. I didn't drive at night.

I napped in the afternoons, long and dangerously. Drifting into unknown lands — deserts and shorelines, never mountains.

Always somewhere flat, with bewildering skies, perhaps threatening.

It was my job to appear sane then, that spring. I wrote for sanity. The computer seemed my only companion, my friends distant — physically, emotionally. Also, my mind, perhaps. Distant.

I seemed to be deliberately cultivating chaos. In my writing workplace, my writing space, I couldn't settle. I carted my laptop from room to room — working in the big wing chair in the living room, sitting at the patio table, sprawling on a lawn chair, propped up in bed late at night. Fleeing the office desk, with its good lighting. I scribbled little notes about ideas and left them all over the house, where I wouldn't be able to find them, wouldn't be able to remember them. Sometimes I wrote them carefully into a notebook, and then I lost the notebook and started another one. Then lost that one too. Out in the garden, I had a little writing shed with a big window and a comfy chaise — a calm and secluded place to write. Sometimes I went there, but my restlessness drove me out, drove me to escape from serenity, that dangerous land. In serenity lay terror.

GRIEF, MOURNING, RUNNING AWAY

My grief is caused partly by the solitude, this sense of boredom and loneliness. This endless calm from too many deaths, too much grieving. After the raging will come the bland calm, perhaps. Perhaps I will be lucky.

I flee from solitude. And into solitude. I have developed a technique for running away. I must hide from all this, from the emotions of death, the uncertainty and questions, the truth. The consequences.

In my city I drive downtown to a book launch in a large room with windows full of sun. I sit next to a woman I know well. I nod my head up and down, the way I know I should, and I make something like a smile. I hope it's like a smile. As long as I don't make eye contact it might be okay to be here. My eyes dart about, to the corner, to the window, to the piano. I slide my gaze over the people. There are a lot of them, but I never lift my eyes above chest height. The food is good, as always. That's reassuring. I feast on bread and cheese and feel I am doing something good for my mind, something soothing for my body. Bread is gentle. Cheese is yielding. It doesn't ask anything of me, this food. It helps me and doesn't ask me to do anything. Perhaps a glass of wine? No, not this time, not today. Water, water, I am obsessed by the need for water.

The author says some words about his new book. Someone plays the piano. I do my rituals: buy a book and stand in line to have it signed by this author-friend. He is tall and his hair is newly cut; his scalp seems covered with sleek black paint. He smiles at me, he hugs me, signs my book. He's friendly but distant, therefore safe. That's why I am here. To be safe. "My husband died," I say to him. He looks as startled by this as I am, and I spin away. More bread, more cheese, more water. And then I flee. I drive home, having been saved, for this hour at least. For this day, perhaps.

Then it's another day, and someone takes care of my feet, scrubbing away calluses, erasing corns. I can't even say what's wrong with this day, but I'm wary. There is danger here somewhere. Slide away, slide away. Be safe. Drink water.

I have managed to slide past my eighty-seventh birthday, and many old friends, old acquaintances, old loves, are dead. Sometimes I feel like an elephant in mourning, standing around swaying and moaning, stomping the earth, with a wordless rumble deep in my body, deep in the earth, vibrating across the planet. My friends are dying. In the last couple of years, six of them went. Actually five friends and a husband.... The words come in a dream: *unutterable sorrow* repeated and repeated, inconsolable grief. I feel as though it's my job just to be here, just to mourn, and to spread the news along to the herd.

Funerals: I'm afraid of getting too good at them. It's a skill I didn't want to learn, this funeral thing, this weeping, this laughing, this hugging friends. We come together to do this thing. To weep, to hug. I wear a dark suit, small earrings, little makeup. Restraint is a basic requirement in the halls, in the chapels, attending to the funeral meats.

※　※　※

I can't even see my clock for the stack of books beside my bed, let alone the radio...this new untidy pile. Annie Dillard, Grace Paley, Murakami, Penelope Lively. All presents. And some Chardonnay, a present too. It's close to midnight and I should be sleeping but I got too excited on the first page of Annie travelling to an eclipse in Japan, and already I know I'll never sleep tonight. Because it's the night again and all the lives I didn't live are here with me, living here in the dark. Perhaps it would be better without the Chardonnay, but it would still be the night again, the dark again.

Annie Dillard has begun to talk of the place that is farthest from any other place, where people are the most remote from each other. I think about that remoteness. The nights feel like that. Some of the days, too. Remote. The time stretching ahead.

But my elephantine memories are accessible — at least part of the time — and I need to pass them along to the rest of the herd. That's what I'm doing. Just passing along some memories.

About Ellen's Death:

At KGH she fretted and we made her tea, just the way she liked it. I carried it to her in a china cup, on a saucer, because she liked that. Not a mug, a real cup and saucer. She looked so pink and healthy – all the oxygen they have given her.

Once again, death had been driven away.

She's not ready yet, she said. She's been trying to write the third act, she says, but there's so much distraction here. The medical people poke at her, the food is dreadful, the actors auditioning for the lead are not very good. But somehow it will get done. We all know the third act will get written, for each of us.

About my husband's Death:

To the nursing home twice a week I used to carry a thermos of coffee — half decaf, with lots of sugar. My husband was determinedly precise for thirty years, after he stopped being a drunk. And then those weeks of fading away — of pain and opioids, of morphine, and medical marijuana.

"I think I may be dying," he wrote in a notebook. "But I don't think I have the strength to do it."

The light in his eyes goes out, comes back, goes out, comes back. He's bland, for the first time in his life.

About Virgil:

I had planned to take him out for dinner, just the week before, at his request. We had a day and time, a reservation at a good restaurant. "You'll have to drive," he said. "I can't walk and I can't drive." But another duty of care usurped our date. And suddenly it was too late. Here he was at home, asleep, or something like it. A hospital bed, a nurse on hand — a legal requirement, as he starved himself. His choice, that. Music, quiet. Some art nearby in case he opened his eyes. We stood beside his bed chatting, forgetting that he might hear us.

About Ken:

I sit on the edge of his bed, reach out and pat his pale, bony hand. He has always been a man of great dignity, and yet here I am, being familiar and possibly condescending...no, it's not that. It's treating him rather like a child, like a naughty boy who has rather carelessly let himself get this dreadful cancer, who has through inattention let his bones disintegrate.

I mean no disrespect, and I hope he knows that, but I can't seem to stop myself. I can't seem to maintain the kind of formality we always had in our relationship, which was, after all, a business friendship, vaguely literary. And here he is, his eyes closed, sleeping or not sleeping. There's not much difference it seems, between those two states. His boney skull, pallid, seems newborn, infantile, a few bristles of white hair softening the clean globe of skin.

I tell him I have enjoyed working with him in the past years. I tell him I will write to him. A lie, I know. There is no response, in any case. He is sliding away into a pale, quiet space. A week later I hear that he has gone, quietly, without theatrics. As was his way in life. Don't call attention to yourself, don't make a fuss.

HIDING

I think I am hiding from grief. But also from rage. The rage comes lashing out, rage that I try to hide. It leaps out, a fierce cat, a tiger. Rage at little slights, at unkind words, at unkind thoughts. Everyone, now, must love me, must care for me, I am so wounded by death. No one is allowed to be angry with me. Just be kind, just love me, I am wounded. If you don't love me, I will rage and rage and rage and never forgive you.

Sweet River of Red

Bruce Meyer

While visiting a university to give their annual lecture, I was invited into the anatomy lab. In a block of Lucite with all the flesh, bones, and organs removed, the inner river of blood vessels and capillaries was held together with latex inside the clear plastic. I saw the intricacies of a brain's cardiovascular system. There are more than one hundred thousand kilometres of arteries, vessels, and capillaries in the human cardiovascular system. Isolated from flesh, bones, and organs, the pattern these channels chart resemble a Lichtenberg figure — the tracing of tree-like branches and stems lightning leaves behind when it strikes a person or an object. We bear the spark of life in more ways than we know. The conduits within each of us that carry our blood throughout our bodies also resemble the paths major watercourses cut in the landscape. Beneath everyone's skin resides the map of a continental watershed.

When the blood that flows through that map becomes too sour or too sweet, it poisons the continent it is meant to sustain. As I lay on a hospital gurney, I thought about my visit to the anatomy lab. The doctor had just diagnosed me with Type 2 Diabetes. She said I was dying, that my blood, the inner river, was poisoned beyond the point where it could be reversed. That my body was dying, and there was nothing I could do to stop it. You will only suffer more if you fight it, they said, adding that my organs would shut down one by one. "Lie back and let it happen," the nurse and intern both told me. I refused. The process of dying was far too fascinating for me to surrender to it.

Three months before that night in the emergency ward of Barrie's Royal Victoria Hospital, I had been helping my mother move from the house in which I had grown up. Over the space of fifty years, as my father worked to pay the mortgage and each member of my family went about the business of rising, schooling, eating, and sleeping — the obliviousness to life that is the beauty of life — the house filled with the detritus of our presence in it. My father's enemy every summer were the grubs that hid below the grass of his perfect lawn. He also despised the sparrows who built nests in the light over the garage door. He fought the aphids that lived upside down on the underside of rose leaves, and the ants and mice that gnawed their way inside the house to eat our food. I am certain my father saw our house as his castle under siege.

To combat the plagues that came against us, my father collected and used poisons. He was of that generation that believed an enemy could be fought by using chemistry as a weapon. By the time he has passed away from a combination of Alzheimer's and a bad heart, the boxes with the names for his chemicals had long disappeared. Unmarked containers of foul-smelling, brown liquids lined the shelves of a store room off his basement workshop. During his final year, we discovered that he had been secreting his store of unknown lethal materials in the store room, but when we asked him what the yogurt containers and honey pails held, he simply shook his head. He could not remember. They were all meant to kill something.

One container on a high shelf had fused with the wood. I gave it a twist, and a shower of brown liquid rained down on me, splashing into my right eye. I immediately stuck my head under the tap of the laundry tub, but it burned as my eye swelled. With only hours to go until the house had be vacated, I had to put up with the pain in eye. Immediately after we settled my mother in her new condo, my wife and daughter and I left for a week in Muskoka. There, a spider got behind my glasses one windy afternoon. It bit the lid of the right eye. I tried to shrug it off. I went to Manitoulin Island for five days, even farther away from where I could have gotten the help I needed. The pain grew more and more intense each day. A pharmacist in a small town on the island suggested pink-eye ointment. It didn't work. By the time I returned to Barrie, the pain was excruciating. The eye was ready to roll out of my head: I went to the hospital.

An emergency doctor examined the eye, but she didn't have the necessary scope to peer in and see if there was any internal damage. She ruled out pink eye immediately and called an ophthalmologist. His solution to the problem, without seeing me, was to put me on a dose of prednisone. Prednisone is an anti-inflammatory that prescribed in small doses reduces inflammation in the body. It is given widely for all manner of cures and ailments. In small, brief doses, it works well. In large, prolonged doses, it is lethal. I was prescribed forty milligrams a day. The following week, I went to visit the ophthalmologist. "Stay on the prednisone until we figure out the problem with your eye." That was September.

By late November, I was feeling awful. Everywhere I went, I thought I could smell garbage rotting. I thought the pungent odour was a result of the rehabilitation of the city dumb that was under way. I had gained forty pounds over the three months, and was famished even after eating a large meal. My head throbbed. My urine stung to the point where I could not pass it. Climbing stairs in my house or at work was next to impossible. I would have to stop and rest at each seventh step. I thought I was going to explode.

My family physician couldn't work me in for an appointment on short notice because I was suffering from nothing more than being overweight and exhausted. At the walk-in clinic, the doctor asked me why I was there.

"I think I need a blood test. I think I might be diabetic. I've got a number of the symptoms."

He looked at me. "I can smell you from across the room. Diabetics smell of rotting fruit. You're the worst case I think I've encountered."

I passed some urine into a cup. He took a piece of what looked like litmus paper, then asked if anyone was with me.

"My wife can come for me," I said, "I don't drive."

"I am calling you an ambulance. You're going straight to emergency." He picked up the phone and the doctors and my wife were waiting for me when I arrived at Royal Victoria.

An elderly man on another gurney asked me what I was in for.

"Blood sugar," I said. "How about you?"

"Ticker," he replied as they wheeled him away.

The nurse appeared in my cubicle and pricked my finger with a lancet. My blood sugar level read 27.6.

"Did you know that's a lethal blood sugar level?" she said, shaking her head. "A person dies if the level goes past thirty."

The doctor on call was busy with the old man, who had gone into distress.

I lay back on the gurney. I could hear every word from the next stall, and not only that, could hear conversations from the nursing station down the corridor. I listened as a man was telling his wife how he had hurt his back while curling; how a teenager thought he'd caught the flu from his girlfriend; how the husband of one of the nurses was drywalling the basement and making a mess of it. I could hear every small sound in the ward. My hearing had gone into overdrive.

The doctor appeared and took another blood sample. While I had been waiting in the cubicle, my wife had fallen asleep on a chair in the corner. The doctor woke my wife and was whispering to her that my blood sugar was so high that I probably would not live through the night. The physician came to the side of the bed and took my hand, and without any notice pricked another finger.

"You should be dead by now," the doctor said bluntly. "Your blood sugar is 33.4. Thirty is the point where internal organs are damaged and shut down. We're going to give you some insulin, but I can't guarantee we'll get the sugars down enough in time."

"In time for what?" I asked. I looked at my wife. She was crying. "It's okay," I said, trying to reassure her. "It will take more than a sugar pie to kill me. Go back to sleep. I'll call you if I croak." I smiled at her. She shut her eyes. She seemed more afraid than I was.

The nurse who had told me to lie back and let it happen returned to the cubicle to take my blood pressure. "As I said earlier, my advice to you, is that you simply lie back and try not to fight it." Another nurse joined her as if an extra body would ease the reality of the news.

"I don't think this is my time," I said. I wasn't being brave.

"We'll make you as comfortable as we can. We're going to inject insulin directly into your stomach. You're also going to get an IV, and I'm leaving instructions for how you can ramp down on the prednisone. If you get through this, you can't go cold turkey on the prednisone. That can kill you just as quick."

The nurse puffed my pillow and brought me an extra cotton flannel sheet. The way she tucked it around my legs made think it was intended to be my winding sheet. The image of John Donne's marble statue in St. Paul's Cathedral in London flashed

through my mind. Donne, the poet of love and wit, the sermo-
nizer who said that "no man is an island," even if he has a poisoned body of water course inside him, stands in a niche of the
cathedral, a sheet pulled tight with only his face emerging from
the vestments of death. When the cathedral burned in 1666, it
was one of the only objects to escape unscathed from the
flames. It was now my turn to pass through what had come to
test and temper me.

An emergency room at night is not made of the fire of hell.
It is a place of sounds, a dark, purgatorial realm. People are suffering. They moan. They weep. The old man next door fought.
I could hear his heels battering his mattress. I could hear the
crash cart revving up, then the snap of the electrical shock. I
heard the doctor pronounce him dead. I had just said hello to
him in triage. Time of death was 4:32. Between the layers of
sounds that were now mere whispers in the exhausted silence
that comes before dawn, stood a darker, more solemn phantom
silence, a presence that spoke to me through its absence of life.

I sat up in bed and reached for my leather satchel. I never go
anywhere without my satchel. It usually holds a book for me to
read, several favourite fountain pens, and my Moleskine notebook.

I took out the notebook, and a pen, and began to write. I was
held in the thrall of a thousand thoughts racing through my
mind. I could picture my body as the watercourse of a newfound continent, a place where no one had set foot because no
one understood it was there, at least not me, until now. Something was impelling me to embrace every idea that was entering
my mind. I was on the verge of discovery. I wanted to say everything. I had become the world, and the world was inside me. I
was Alexander Humboldt on the Amazon, overcome by a world
beyond anything he had learned or imagined, so familiar to
those who were part of it yet so vast and different and unfamil-

iar that his mind and heart leapt in awe as he encountered things beyond his ability to put to words. That was the world of my cardiovascular system, the sweet river of red, all one hundred thousand kilometres of it in artery, vein, and capillary, that had me in its current as I rushed ahead into the unknown jungle of thoughts I had never experienced before.

As I was writing, my hand moving faster than I thought possible as I filled page after page with poems — I had never experienced such a rush of imagination — the nurse parted the curtains and my wife opened her eyes. She looked at me, astonished. "I thought the doctor told you to lie back and just let things happen."

"I can't," I said. "I'm alive like I've never been. I am a poet. I write poetry. I teach it. Poetry is life for me. I carry a book of poetry with me everywhere I go. And for the first time, I feel I know what poetry can do. I can feel every word. I can hear every thought in my brain. I know it sounds like I'm tripping, but I can taste the colour of the things I am writing about. My senses are one sense, not five, and everything is happening at once, and I have to write it down or it will go missing." The nurse shook her head. I had the feeling she thought I'd gone looney. She readied the lancet and the blood meter of my tray table. My wife sat up and looked at me as if I was daft.

At that moment, I remembered something Elizabeth Bishop had said — "Poetry is a million things happening at once." Poetry and I were dancing for our lives. It needed me to embrace the words and ideas, and I needed it to fill me with a wonder that was new, and bright, and glistening like a dense, green jungle whose every leaf was gleaming after a steaming rain at dawn. I was emerging from a state of numbness in which, I realized, I had been living — that's the best I can describe it — and I remembered the morning when my wife and I were on a Caribbean cruise and we anchored off St. John and I watched the green island take shape from the grey fog in the first light of dawn. I had stood on the deck of the liner as I waited for my wife to emerge from our cabin, and as the fog gradually gave way to the dawn, the details of the island became more and more distinct. That was a moment when I understood clarity as an epistemological experience. In the hospital cubicle, that emerging focus, that finite recognition spread to my other senses. I realized what it was to be alive.

The nurse pricked my finger again. The story of *Sleeping Beauty* is almost a parable of the blood sugar test, but instead of falling into a sleep each time they tested me, I became more awake. I had fought to stay alert through it all, fought to live, and not merely to live but to be a conduit for what life could say. I tried to find the words to explain what had gone through me — not just the blood sugars that were now down to 16.8, a level at which I could be released to go home and finally get some rest — but what I had been part of. I know now I had been conversing in a new language with the world and was struggling to speak it and translate what it had said to me. I couldn't.

In time, with the prednisone out of my system, I lost the weight — too much at first, which was hard on my system — and then, I lost the diabetes. My doctor looked at my blood tests.

"You've free of the diabetes, but we're going to leave you on the metformin. We've discovered that the drug you've been taking for your Type 2 is an anti-aging medication. It slows the oxidization of your system. All the tests indicate that you are physically younger than you were two years ago. If I have your permission, we'll leave you on the drug because it can't do you any harm, and the long-term results may be beneficial."

"When I almost died that night, I had a very strange experience," I said. "I almost understand it now." My doctor nodded. During a previous experience I had tried to describe the brain rush that overtook me that night. The more I attempted to put the experience into words, the less coherent I sounded. She just smiled and nodded as if to say, "I'll take your word for it."

Since that night in the hospital two years ago, I cannot stop writing. The words and the ideas just keep coming, but I could not describe what it was that overtook me that night until a few weeks ago. That is when I found my explanation for the experience in the emergency ward.

I went to Mexico, not to one of those coastal tourists resorts that I can't stand, but into an old, sleepy, almost forgotten colonial city at the foot of the Sierra Madre. One afternoon, my host asked if I wanted to go into the mountains. "You will see a beauty you cannot explain," he said.

The mountains were a half hour away. They loomed larger as we approached, turning from grey mirages in the afternoon heat to purple waves, then green dragon's teeth. In the arms of the canyon, he pulled his car off the twisty road. We walked through the overgrowth, parting the branches of the trees. Millions of butterflies of all varieties flittered from branch to branch on the trees overhanging a stream known as an arroyo. They lit on my head and on my hands and arms. They were beautiful — blue, yellow, orange, red — every colour imaginable, and they were so profuse in the air that I had to hold my breath for fear that I might inhale one.

My host walked into the middle of the arroyo, and we began to follow its course uphill. He pointed to a cave in the side of the mountain where the river was pouring forth in a white plume from deep inside the sloping heights. I couldn't figure out how water could gush out of a cavern so high up the incline, but there it was, cooling the air, sounding its roar as it flowed faster than my beating heart over the stones at its lips, and each stone was alive and singing to the world.

Death's Long Embrace

Jill Yonit Goldberg

*Man's origin is dust and his end is dust. He
spends his life earning bread. He is like a clay
vessel, easily broken, like withering grass, a fading
flower, a passing shadow, a fugitive cloud, a fleeting
breeze, scattering dust, a vanishing dream.*
— Mahzor

In his outstretched hand he has a gun. I am sure of it. From
inside the closet where I hide, I watch him through the inch
where the door will not fully close into the frame. I imagine the
menace of death wrap her arms around me; my skin prickles at
her warm breath on my neck. Later, it doesn't matter that the
man who had broken into my apartment in the middle of the
night isn't actually holding a weapon. What matters is that in
those few moments, between the time I wake to the sound of
heavy footsteps on creaky floorboards in my empty apartment
where he should not be, and the time he yanks open the closet
door and grabs me, I have decided two things: I will kill any
attacker before he kills me, and I will likely die tonight.

I will likely die tonight. I wait in the closet as the footsteps
grow closer. Finally sound becomes form and a man appears in

the doorway of my bedroom and hovers there. He is tall and broad with messy hair, and strangely, he is wearing a jean jacket and glasses like any neighbourhood hipster, but I've never seen this man before. Before he enters my bedroom, he hesitates, backs away, and then returns, as if unsure, practicing. I swear I can feel the air heave with malice. My heart explodes a thousand times. I try not to breathe.

I will kill him before he kills me. In my hand I hold my cordless phone. I begin to dial 911, though to be honest, I really want to call my mother. When I press the talk button, the beeping noise is thunderous in my ears. Fearing that the noise of the phone will give me away, I hang up. He turns toward my hiding spot in the closet.

I will likely die tonight. I see the faces of my mother, my father, and my brother. I say goodbye to each of them. I am sorry that I recently fought with my brother. I feel strangely guilty knowing this will destroy my mother. I hope they will find my body.

I will kill him before he kills me. Eyes. Throat. Groin. Put your thumb all the way in his eye socket. Rip out his Adam's apple. Kick him so fast that he can't grab your leg. Then kick him again.

※　※　※

I will likely die tonight. I will kill him before he kills me. I will likely die tonight.

※　※　※

He opens the closet door, and, seeming not to know I am huddled below eye level, he fondles skirts, dresses, blouses, as if looking for a sign, maybe trying to get a scent of me. He lowers

himself to the floor of the closet and gropes in the darkness. He
does not make eye contact, does not seem to see me. When he
grasps my leg, it almost seems accidental. Still, I charge upright,
I make fists, and I scream my rage and fear. For an instant, I
meet his eye, and he says these words: "I just want to touch
you." I bolt to the door of my apartment — his attempt to block
me is only halfhearted — and I hurl myself down the flight of
stairs to the street even as I still believe he might be holding a
gun, might yet shoot me from behind.

In the all-night bagel store a half block away on Rue St.
Viateur, I duck behind the counter, a pink-flannel-pyjamas-clad
banshee with the phone still in my hand. I sputter to the men
there.

"Help me. He's coming."

I haven't noticed that through the bright blue, knitted stock-
ings, my feet are soaked from the late-March melt. The men
offer me warmth, words, a chair; they call the police who come
and take me back to my apartment, which is suddenly a crime
scene. A female officer takes a statement, urges me to pack a
bag, not to stay the rest of the night in my place. He could come
back, she says. By 4:30 AM, I am at a friend's place drinking hot
tea. I am safe.

I do not yet know that I may never feel fully safe again.

That morning — it is a Wednesday — I go to work in time to
teach my 8:15 class on post-war Japanese literature. We discuss
the novel *The Woman in The Dunes* by Abe Kobo, as if this were
all perfectly normal. As weeks pass, I swear I will not develop
PTSD, yet I find myself gasping for air when, one night, I witness
a man looking through the lit window of a nearby home. He is
watching a teenage girl who, unaware, talks on the phone,
winds her ponytail around her finger. He leaves in a silver
Subaru station wagon. I ring the doorbell and explain. Her
father. It was only her father.

Just after midnight, a woman screams from the nearby park. I spring from bed, dialling 911 before I can think, a hammer in my hand. I am surrounded by threat.

※   ※   ※

I will likely die tonight.

※   ※   ※

This is the thought that is now tattooed on my brain, as if a relic of some obscure hazing ritual. It is the thought that loosens the hinge on the invisible trap door behind which sits the amygdala, a primitive bundle of grey matter just waiting to be activated, waiting to find easy pathways into the brain through which to send out an urgent, flashing message: danger, danger, danger.

No one has the key to lock the door back up, or even the map to find the door. And once that door's been opened, the amygdala purrs all on its own. You don't have to do a thing.

※   ※   ※

Danger, danger, danger.

※   ※   ※

There are many myths of trauma.

People talk about being traumatized. Traumatized by a crowded bus, a bad haircut, a mouthy co-worker.

Trauma is not feeling sad, though, or even shocked. It is a recurrent nightmare that seeps in multiple times every night, stalking you with the intent to kill. It is waking paralyzed — cemented to the bed — electric with terror. It is getting off at the wrong metro stop and wandering around as though dazed. It is the feeling that you wear your nervous system like a sensitive exoskeleton atop your skin. Brittle. Rattled by everything. It is watching yourself disintegrate.

They talk about post-traumatic stress as a "disorder," as if it is outlandish to have a dramatic reaction to death having sat down beside you and looked you in the eye.

They talk about healing from trauma with yoga, light therapy, meditation. As if any of these things — if you just try hard enough, believe enough — could get you back to where you were, who you were in the time before.

I remember a therapist's words as a cudgel to my heart. The "post" part of PTSD means it never truly goes away. The episodes may grow shorter, further apart, but given the right stimulation, the danger signal will come back to life in an instant. Your brain is now a tinderbox waiting for a flame.

The idea of healing, then, is a chimera. I think of the rhyme about Humpty Dumpty whose pieces couldn't be put back together again. It dawns on me that I will never go back to being the person I was before. I will never be the person I would have been if it hadn't happened. What was taken from my future self? What experiences will I never have because of what happened? How much time did I lose being a complete fuck-up who stopped sleeping, and spent every hyper-vigilant minute wondering when the feeling of imminent death would ease? All these years later — twelve to be precise — I consider these questions, and from a place so deep inside of me I can't name it, grief rises in my throat, a tsunami. These are the days when I feel I cannot stride, but only creep ahead in this life.

Still, this is better, much better, than the early days and nights when I believed death would have been preferable to life in the aftermath.

Who was I before that night? Who have I become? Sometimes I think I can feel the difference in good ways. Perhaps my empathy to others has been heightened by my increased awareness of how close to the edge, how fragile we really are, how our minds — what we think of as being so solid — can be altered with one careless stroke of fate, or how our lives and all the networks that sustain them can shatter into pieces, crumble away into the dust of history without anyone seeming to notice. I see this now when I look in the eyes of those who struggle, and I can say with honesty: I know.

There are other alterations I see in myself, parts of me I am still integrating as mine.

I am quietly obsessed with escape routes. Show me a room, a building, and I'll show you the escape hatch, the quickest, most covert way out.

I read articles online with titles like "What To Do If You're Being Shot At."

Weapons terrify me, yet I am now secretly drawn to them. As research for the novel I am writing, I went with my American husband, who grew up around guns, to a firing range in Inglewood, LA, and learned to shoot a .38 caliber police special. A Smith & Wesson. It was a thick, heavy revolver, and as I pulled the trigger, my knees juddered. I hated it. I loved it. I hit the target. In my mind, I turned a new image over and over: me hiding in my closet, waiting for the man to find me, my hands wrapped around a deadly weapon. That scenario would have ended terribly. Violence — especially gun violence — sickens me. Still the fantasy — the gun in my hand, the fearless knowing that I am in charge — this quickens my breath, makes me half-close my eyes in the excited way of embracing a lover. I still carry my orange membership card from the LAX Firing Range in my wallet.

In the drawer of my night table, I have a small collection of weapons: knitting needles (I don't even knit), a small Japanese saw, a chisel with a sharp edge, and, to remind myself that I am only assuaging a fantasy, that none of this is really necessary, I have a keychain in the shape of a ghost with eyes that light up and make a wailing noise at the press of a button. I keep my drawer organized so these things are always near at hand.

If it happened again, I tell myself, I would be ready.

It must be obvious that none of these thoughts, these obsessions, is comforting, or indeed, healing. In a tangential way they remind me of the behaviour my mom's cousin, Phil Goldstein, who survived the holocaust. He died only a few years ago in his early nineties, and every time I saw him eat — for as long as he lived — he saved half his meal for later, always waiting for the war — or in his case Auschwitz and Birkenau — to come back to finish him off. My preoccupation with readiness is a trap: every time I check the contents of my night table drawer or subsequently check each closet in my home to make sure there's no one there, these actions I take supposedly to protect myself, in fact re-stimulate the whole trauma network that lingers in my brain, ready to flame to life again.

※   ※   ※

Danger, danger, danger.

※   ※   ※

Some nights — especially when I am alone — it takes everything I've got, every fragment of discipline to convince myself, in spite of my very salient fear that someone is coming in through the balcony window, there are better ways to cope.

In the aftermath I've read everything I could about PTSD. I've tried to control my feelings by understanding the biology, the symptomatology. If I could understand what was happening in my brain, I thought, I could cure myself. I attended a lecture where a research psychiatrist described giving electric shocks to the feet of mice in order to traumatize them so he could cure them. Part way through his talk, I stood up in a room full of rapt audience members, and left, astounded by how little this doctor appeared to understand about the raw demands of trauma. I turned to other sources.

I have studied Buddhism, read Viktor Frankl, Primo Levi, Hannah Arendt, and Camus. I have recited out loud and multiple times, alone in my kitchen, the poem "Kindness" by Naomi Shihab Nye who writes:

Before you know what kindness really is
you must lose things,
feel the future dissolve in a moment
like salt in a weakened broth

※　※　※

That line — "feel the future dissolve in a moment" — pummels me with its resonance every time. Yet, Shihab Nye takes the greater view: our sorrows are not unique. They are ordinary. They are the very thing that make us human. She writes:

You must wake up with sorrow,
You must speak to it till your voice
Catches the thread of all sorrows
And you see the size of the cloth

※　※　※

It took a long time before I could take comfort in seeing my pain as part of anything greater than myself. I am not proud of any of this: in my anguish, I have cursed fate (an idea I don't believe in), and God (while I think belief in her is useful and perhaps beautiful, I am not, myself, a believer), and many of those who tried but could not help me. I have thrown lit matches in the direction of love, and scavenged for further misfortune to make myself abject. I have believed I was pitiable, alone, born as Blake wrote, to "Endless Night." I have longed for time to stop.

In believing in the importance, the specialness of my suffering, how many millions of people did I dehumanize by seeing the agony of others as somehow less real, less worthy than mine? The evidence was all around me: it doesn't take special powers of perception to notice that every day is a litany of tragedy for the many, not the few.

Perhaps it is something about living in the developed world and being middle class that filled me with the belief that life would, and should be a series of met expectations, and actualized dreams, and, therefore, left me shocked by the force of a traumatic event, and — even worse — by the losses of home, employment, and relationship that rode along with it. Even as the nightmares came less often, and the most acute wounds stopped bleeding, grief kept right on making me feel like I woke every morning face down in a puddle.

Viktor Frankl wrote that to survive suffering is to find meaning in it. Camus advises us to imagine Sisyphus happy. The Buddha proposes that the source of all anguish is desire, and that we must seek its cessation. Eventually, from my darkest place, I began to consider that even as I suffered with PTSD and depression, I retained the freedom to interpret my suffering as meaningless or meaningful, to imagine it as permanent or, like all things, fleeting, to see my condition as unique or ordinary.

What does it mean for suffering to be meaningful? It means that I am able to gather solace in knowing that suffering is a universal condition, and I am able to offer solace to others by simply being present and witnessing. It means I am aware that it is suffering, and not its absence that challenges me to be the kind of person I most want to be: perseverant, strong, moral, compassionate. It also means that I am tasked with the work of learning to soothe my own pain through acceptance, by ceasing to want my life to be any other way.

I don't propose that some hybrid pill of Buddhism and existentialism is the holy grail of antidepressants, or that any of this can still an overactive amygdala. But I find relief in the ideas that we are, all of us, condemned to the uncertain conditions of life (and the very certain condition of death), yet we are also all free to choose whether to carry the burden of our circumstances with despair or with the dignity of knowing that misery too can provide purpose, solidarity, and the opportunity to, ironically, make ourselves lighter by ceasing to resist the perils that life will inevitably bring.

In my own tradition, there is a story about a Polish rabbi: Rabbi Simcha Bunem of Pershyscha who lived from 1765 to 1827. Though he was a rabbi and a leader of Hasidic Judaism, his teachings were not written down, but transmitted orally. His most famous is this:

> Everyone must have two pockets, with a note in each pocket so that he or she can reach into one or the other, depending on the need. When feeling lowly and depressed, discouraged, or disconsolate, one should reach into the right pocket, and there find the words: "Bishvili nivra ha'olam" or "For my sake the world was created." But when feeling high and mighty, one should reach into the other pocket and find the words: "Anochi afar va'efer" or "I am but dust and ashes."

※　※　※

It might seem that during my worst moments in the aftermath, as I watched my old life fall away, that I needed to read over and over the words about the world being created for me, to remind myself of my value, my place among my peers whose lives all seemed so much richer, so much easier than mine. Yet, banished as I was from what I came to call the pink bubble of ease, what I really needed was to remember: I am but dust and ashes. For it is this knowing, this humbling of myself that has allowed me to accept the normalness, the banality of my distress, and to stop insisting that life itself is obliged to bend to my will. There is no answer to the cry *why me*? Because in the view of the universe, the cosmos, and all the randomness that entails, the idea of "me," or of "self" doesn't rank as terribly important.

Why me? Indeed Why not me? In a world of refugees, illness, violence, and poverty: why not me?

There is additional meaning in this admission of my own insignificance. I do not need to berate myself for my "disordered" response to trauma. I am but dust and ashes. I do not need to have some great, triumphant comeback. I am but dust and ashes. I can see and accept the unimportance of my pain because I am but dust and ashes.

I am, like so many others, small, staggering over a craggy landscape, now seeking moments not where I can find, but where I can make meaning through a kind gesture, a look of understanding exchanged with my fellow boulder-rollers.

By being confronted with the big questions: what does it mean to be human? Where is meaning found? I have seen past the flimsy veil of control we all cling to as a way to believe our lives are ordered. What I see now is that life is not transactional. There are no certain rewards for hard work or good behaviour. There is this moment. This breath. That is all. It's not just that

I notice the little things more: the sunlight that skips and trembles on ocean waves, the spring air heavy with the scent of lilacs. I've always noticed these. Now I know that this is all there ever may be, and I wrestle to have that be enough.

There are so many dialectics to navigate: having survived the feeling of imminent death, I know I will face it again some day, yet I can choose to live with hope. I make all kinds of plans for the near and distant future, still I know that the daily rituals of sweeping the floor, and stroking my cat behind her ears, are more reliable repositories of joy than any dream I project on the future, which may always be but a receding mirage.

Today I live with the trauma. It is inside me — literally a feature of my mind — and I walk with it, hold it as both a gift and a burden, a knowledge that pierces finely: I am part of the cloth, not separate from it. My life is but dust and ashes. From that I am free to make what I choose.

When Something Awful Happened

Sarah Lyn Eaton

I didn't know I was in a coma. That's important. Some patients wake from a deep drug-induced sleep with no memories at all, but I was living in that other reality. I was in my own hell. The cocktail of fentanyl, methadone, ketamine, morphine, and versed I was on to keep me in the coma just happened to cause nightmares, paranoia, and hallucinations. My brain was desperately trying to process what was happening to my physical body. I remember everything.

I walked out of a black fog into the middle of a dozen stories-in-progress. Each one felt real and I felt real in them. Where I was, I was tortured and assaulted over and over and over. I was flayed. I made bargains with crossroad beings for more life. I made wrong decisions. I made wrong decisions out of cowardice that caused the deaths of other people. I was set on fire over and over until I couldn't find an ounce of bravery. I almost succumbed to the madness of it. It felt like it was never going to stop.

Something stalked me from the shadows and I discovered the meaning of skin crawling and blood running cold. I learned real terror. Writing appeared on the walls, tempting me and teasing me with the potential for another go-round. What would it be worth to me?

I begged. I pleaded. If Rumpelstiltskin himself had appeared before me I would have granted him whatever wish he desired of me if he would only spin my horror into light.

Somewhere I remembered I was a creature of magic. And I knew, based on my Buddhist metta work, that the greatest magic in the world is love. But in order for that love to shield me from the pain, I had to believe one-hundred percent that it would. That it could. Not ninety-nine. Not ninety-eight. It had to be one-hundred. It was the first blind leap of faith I'd ever taken.

I took a deep breath and reached further into the darkness. I sank deeper into the pain to get through it, without knowing what was waiting on the other side. Without knowing if there was even another side, I accepted that there was, whether I could comprehend it or not. I chose to believe.

I dug deep. Really deep, to find that primal love, that instinctive love and kindness we're born with. I was sweating. I was bleeding. I believed the torture world was real even as I sought some kind of relief from it.

I found a thread, made of green light, floating in a darkness. When I touched it, my heart warmed. It expanded. It became a bubble of light around me, cloaked just beneath the surface. No matter what happened to me in the coma, I clung to that light like a buoy in an ocean of pain. I surrendered to it as the storms raged, matching pitch with my perpetrators' rage.

Because the love held me. It fed me. It gave me strength. And the things they did to me no longer hurt me.

I thought about my wife and my family. Every person in my life I have ever had love for flashed through my heart. It sustained me. It built onto the spell. I flew backwards in time, to my childhood and I hit a wall where I ran out of people. I knew there was more to love and I pushed through the barrier.

My concept of love shifted. It wasn't just an emotion shared between people. My call to arms widened. All of my favourite places in nature showed up. The neighbourhood stray cats. The weeds growing in the sidewalk cracks. The creek beds. Planting seeds and growing gardens. Birdsong. The way clouds move across the sky.

I was in love with all of it. And it was the heartbeat that I grabbed onto. No matter what was happening to me, love allowed me to bend without breaking.

※　※　※

There was a moment in the coma. I was running from a fire and toward it at the same time. It was urgent I get there before it happened, to save people I loved.

My eyes were closed. The smell of the soft, supple Cadillac leather told me where I was. I smiled despite the lump in my throat. I listened to the music of the asphalt flying underneath the wheels. I relaxed for the first time in the months of my unrealities. I was safe. Tears welled in my eyes.

Eleven years gone, my Grandpa Riddle sat beside me, driving into a dark night. He cleared his throat and I started shaking. He reached his right arm over and wove his calloused fingers in with mine. The familiar smell of him filled the car, too.

My heart expanded a dozen times in my chest. I heard his breath. His laugh as he chuckled at my astonishment. I felt his palm against mine. And my heart constricted. I missed him so much.

His eyes were on the empty road and the black sky.

My great-grandma blew her nose into a handkerchief on my other side. I gasped. After twenty-one years without her, I knew her by touch. Skin smooth and cool like silk. Nothing could hold back my tears.

My two beloveds. We drove for a while in silence. Mother, son, and granddaughter.

"Where are we going?" my grandpa asked.

I had a choice. I could have stayed with them. I hesitated for a nanosecond. I didn't know what was going to come out of my mouth until I heard myself say it. I didn't want to leave them. I was so afraid. And yet...

"I'm not ready," I said.

I didn't even know what it meant. I didn't know what I was returning to. I only knew the words were true.

I could have chosen to go with them. And I might have made that choice. I was ready for the pain to stop. I thought I had endured enough. But...

"I'm not ready yet," I said.

My grandpa nodded. Great-grandma Elsie squeezed my hand. I made a choice.

※　※　※

I woke in a bed in a strange space. I wasn't wearing my glasses so everything was blurred and out of focus. I didn't recognize any of the voices I heard. My heart thundered in my throat. Machines were beeping and people were pulling at lines coming in and out of my body. I couldn't feel anything below my breastbone. I couldn't move my legs.

After I woke in the hospital, the hallucinations continued. It was a while before I understood where I was and why I was there, but I knew one of the horrible things I had experienced was real.

But which one?

I had been airlifted to the ICU of one of the top burn centres in America. Over half of my body, mostly from the waist down, was covered in third and fourth degree burns. I lost muscle and skin. They weren't sure I would live. They weren't sure the grafts I needed would take. They weren't sure I would keep my legs.

They asked me if I understood.

"Something bad happened," I answered.

I was weak. I couldn't sit up. I could barely swallow. Lifting my head was an exertion. I was a writer and woke to find my hands wrapped with gauze into tight balls to keep the burned skin from contracting. I was a singer whose voice was barely a whisper due to weakness from fighting the ventilator.

I suddenly wasn't sure living was the right choice.

I didn't understand I had been in a coma for weeks. I wasn't retaining new information. I couldn't remember what happened to me. I couldn't remember the last three seconds. I couldn't see a future.

I could see spirits standing around my bed. I recognized some of their faces. Great-grandma Hattie. Great-great-grandpa Hiram. My shadow world bled into the waking one. The living nurses and technicians moved through them but the ghosts were vigilant. They laid hands on me. I couldn't tell if they were healing me or claiming me.

I was convinced that I was slowly burning to death, that my brain was spinning out while the electrical synapses shorted. I believed that my life was flashing before me. I waited for the angelic chorus, the bright light, and the tunnel to appear.

I thought I was dying.

※　※　※

Hospital rounds happened regularly with the same questions:

Can you tell me your name?

Do you know what day it is?

Do you know where you are?

I couldn't remember my name for quite some time. There

was this horrific chasm that opened beneath me screaming that I should know that answer and yet all I found when I reached for it was a void. An absence with no trace of what was there.

I couldn't feel my legs. But I could see them. I could touch them and my palms felt them. The doctor said it was because all the nerves burned away quickly.

I remembered that. I remembered screaming. I remembered those three seconds of agony.

I didn't remember more than that. But, despite the gravity, there was also elation at having something real to hold onto. I was on fire. I remember.

"Hey, baby," my wife swept into the room.

I cried. She cried. I apologized profusely for whatever had happened. She didn't care. She promised we'd figure it out. She said my surgeon was sure they could save my legs. I believed them because I wanted to.

I also wanted to close my eyes and go away. I wanted anything other than I-almost-died-after-being-on-fire-and-now-we-had-to-rebuild-my-body to be true. I knew what it meant. I'm smart. I knew the surgeries and rehabilitation and physical therapy and hard work it would take to walk again, if the grafts took. I knew I would have to sit in a state of lucid limbo while we waited between surgeries. There was a chance, as a diabetic, that I wouldn't heal the way my surgeon hoped I would.

I gripped the rails of the bed, trying futilely to move my body, when a thought snuck in. What if I had stepped a little more to the right on the porch? What if I had been just a foot out of reach and this had never happened?

A quaking began in my body. A parallel world where I was unscathed made its way up to my neck, to my traumatized nervous system. I understood that one thought could undo the very delicate scaffolding I had built to protect myself. I almost freaked out.

But the fire happened. No amount of wishing or pleading would change that. I shut the intruding thought down.

I took a deep breath in and exhaled. I let it go. It didn't matter. Wondering wouldn't change anything. According to the arson investigator, it was a freak accident. There were toxic fumes that caught fire.

I was in the wrong place at the wrong time. Something awful happened and I happened to be there when it did. It wasn't personal.

I became the fire. I survived the fire. Somehow I was alive. I chose to leave death behind. How could I not choose to live now? Just because it would be hard?

In the hospital, I accepted that what was happening was really happening. I decided in the next second to trust my team completely. I was in their world and they knew what they were doing. So I let it go. All the fear, worry, terror... I let it all go. I greeted the next nurse's round with a tearful smile instead of a fearful face.

What needs to happen next?

What do I have to do today to get better?

I surrendered again. I let go of tomorrow. I asked them what I had to do each morning and didn't think beyond that. That's how I survived.

※　※　※

Immobile in the bed with my hands bandaged, I didn't have access to a phone. I didn't have a cell phone. I didn't have television as a distraction. I had a CD player, but it was across the room and I couldn't reach it on my own. I didn't have a laptop. I had no personal technology, no window into the world. My life revolved around lights up, lights down, and meal times.

I underwent seven skin graft surgeries in seven weeks. The

skin they used they harvested from my unburned flesh. They
came in every three days to change my dressings. They peeled
back the medicated gauze and scrubbed off the dead cells and
tissue. All my nerves had burned away, but the air on muscle that
was never meant to feel it was utter agony. The nurses had to
give me more fentanyl every fifteen minutes. It barely touched
the pain. I apologized for screaming.

I didn't believe I could endure it.

I was afraid. I wanted to not be in my body so badly, but I was
still freaked out about the coma and lost time, so I didn't not want
to be in my body either. I compromised. Using meditation tools,
I slipped gently to the right so I was in my body but not in what
was happening while they worked on me. They found when they
let me meditate, I only needed half as much pain medication.

In the limbo space, love came to me in the guise of a bison,
lowering himself to the ground beside me so I could hold onto
him, bear into him. I fell into the mountain of him. And the
earth held me while they scraped at my legs. Morning glory
vines wrapped around my limbs. The scent of aloeswood and
sweetgrass swept the room. All was sacred.

And I flashed through all of my favourite places in nature,
some I had forgotten about. And then places in nature I had
not yet seen in waking life blew through me and my soul said
one thing very clearly.

I'm not done yet.

I didn't have to hold onto the love anymore. It was in me. It
was part of me. I was made of love. We were all made of love.

It was easy to see by the light of day.

※ ※ ※

At night, the darkness was oppressive. The nightmares crept in.
I knew them for what they were, but they still filled me with

real terror. The nurses put on Bach's cello music for me and I wrapped myself into the notes. I spun it like thread. I wove it into my body.

I needed connection. I needed to connect to my physical self. I meditated on my body in the dark. I meditated on multiplying skin cells and knitting them together. I fought the nightmares that told me lies by focusing on binding the cells together, one at a time. It kept me mindful of the impact of the science on my body. Of all the hands that worked on saving me. And all the people who supported them so that they could do the healing they did for me.

My love blossomed into gratitude. I smiled. I thanked everyone who worked on me. When they came in to force my leg muscles to move, I said thank you. When they came to scrape the dead tissue off and reapply the Xeroform, I said thank you. When housekeeping cleaned the bits of me off the floor after a dressing change, I said thank you.

I thanked all the nurses who performed my dressing changes because they knowingly took a job where they have to cause people in horrendous pain more pain in order to heal them. That's a hard career choice. So I thanked them. How big their hearts must be to tolerate patient screams and pains while pushing them further. I saw the love these strangers had for me. They sincerely wanted me to live.

And that made me want it, too.

I couldn't get out of bed without help. I couldn't stand up. I couldn't feed myself. I wasn't sure what kind of life lay ahead of me, but I had already chosen life multiple times. I couldn't deny that.

※ ※ ※

I don't resent the fire for doing what fire does. I learned to use my hands again. I learned to walk again. I have walked around bonfires. I have lit matches. I am not afraid of the elemental. It was not personal. I breathe that in and out like a mantra when I am around it. I do not want to be afraid. It's a choice.

I don't take anything personally anymore.

I know I walk brighter. I wear my grace every day. I am mindful of the world in a way I couldn't see before. Everything is magic, everything is possible. I take nothing for granted.

I can feel the awe in people's hearts when they see me. People see me as a miracle. It's overwhelming. I just did what I had to do to survive. I did what was necessary. I did one hard thing at a time. So the awe is overwhelming. It's hard to be the centre of it.

There wasn't something special about me that made it possible for me to overcome what other people couldn't. I made a series of choices that each required a moment of bravery.

I don't regret it.

I am the most me I have ever been.

Family and friends were certain I would be damaged and broken by the trauma. I might have been. I thought I was going to be. But I wasn't. A fearlessness lives in me now. Not a devil-may-care-I-cheated-death kind, but one that comes from knowing myself to the core and back. I know what dark spaces still lurk inside me. I know where they are. I know I can endure far past the point I previously thought possible. I hope I don't have to but I know I can overcome anything.

Living no longer feels like risk taking.

I want to experience everything. When I plant my garden, I want to pull those grubs and salamanders from the soil. I want to find the worms a better spot to thrive. When I have lunch with a friend, I want to make eye contact and stay present with them. When I take a walk, I sit on the park bench and watch the chipmunks and squirrels for a while. When I hug someone, I want them to know how I feel about them without needing words. I also say the words so that the people I love know I love them.

I'm still in recovery. I'm starting to think every day I step further away from the fire will be a day of recovery. I still make small choices every day. To get out of bed even though I know stretching hurts first thing in the morning. To surrender to whatever hurdle presents itself. To be patient with my disabilities. To be patient with the people who try to rush me.

I hope I can always meet those moments with bravery. I have so far, though I get tired. I get frustrated. And I retreat into nature to recharge. I don't know what the future holds for me. I know there will be more pain. I accept that there may be pain for the rest of my life.

I don't want that to harden me. I believe that is a choice. I have made mine.

I am no longer afraid of the process of death. It is an inevitable necessity. And its timing isn't personal. Sometimes death comes and you are the one who is there. I'm not afraid of it coming back for me. We've travelled a hard road together. Death is more an old friend than a monster.

Twenty-Five Aprils in the Post-Mortem Bar

Tanis MacDonald

hey big hello from your previous life

It was any day on Facebook when I received this PM. Like many people over fifty, I have had several previous lives, and wondered which one the writer was greeting me from.

hi it's me haha so glad to have found you

It was D. I had thought he was dead.

it's been forever

My spreading shock of recognition was not just because I saw his name appear on my screen, but because being hailed by the dead felt so damned familiar. It was a moment that had played in my dreams for decades before the dead/not-dead slid into my PMs.

※　※　※

My mother died three years ago. The death of a last living parent comes to us all eventually, but it's not a moment that comes to us all in the same way or under the same circumstances. After long weeks of caring for my mother, after her death and her funeral, I settled the estate and had my first Christmas without family because everyone fell away like parts of a multi-stage rocket as soon as my mother was dead. I don't know whether they burned up on re-entry to the atmosphere. After all that, I stood in my kitchen watching the snow falling and thinking about who else I knew who lived familyless in the world. The numbers were low. Many of my friends still had living grandparents as well as parents. I envied the luxurious connections I thought they enjoyed, and still felt an odd relief that I now moved through the world without that cocoon: parent-free, family-free. I thought of my gay male friends from the 1980s and 1990s with whom I had such intense relationships and knew some of them could have advised me, at length, about how to proceed family-free with style and élan, but they had been dead a long time. Twenty-five years or more. *Hey big hello from your previous life.* I stood in a kitchen of a house I paid for with work I had never discussed with my dead friends in my twice-previous life. I wondered if any of them would recognize me.

※　※　※

I have been doing a fairly bad job of believing my mother is dead, though I catch myself wondering why I haven't talked to her for a long time, if we are having a fight, if I am stubbornly refusing to talk to her for some petty reason. Then I remember she's dead, and then I think that I'm going to have to wait it out, because surely that "being dead" gig can't last forever.

※　※　※

Some people go to grad school in their twenties. I did not. Instead I worked in AIDS activism and on several palliative care teams from 1988 to 1995. Then I burned out. Then I went to grad school.

Burn out. Stay lit.

A few years ago, I was at a World AIDS Day event when a representative from a local HIV support organization said that there was no such thing as AIDS anymore. I knew I was supposed to be happy; instead I made it to outrage in record time. What I heard yoked to the news of the control of the virus was a corresponding wipe of a history that included my friends' lives and their deaths and the hard-won visibility of those years. I knew that the speaker's intention was to gesture to where we are now in terms of new treatments that make living with HIV much more possible in North America. The antiviral cocktail had kept D alive and PMing *it's me haha.* But I was still headachingly furious.

※　※　※

Elaine Scarry notes in her introduction to *The Body in Pain,* that "the derealisation of artifacts assists in taking away another person's visibility" to the point that "what is quite literally at stake in the body in pain is the making and the unmaking of the world." I had lived, but derealisation was a bastard.

※　※　※

Going to grad school had a result. In one part of my life, I am an elegy specialist and a Canadian literature professor, and while CanLit has been a justifiably shouty place in recent years, over in elegy studies, it's pretty quiet. I'm tempted to call it silent as the grave, to make macabre puns, but perhaps it's enough to say that I go to elegy studies to still my mind. This is the habit every-one — other than me — worried about when I started studying the elegy as a genre in 1999 after six years of AIDS work: how far down the death-writing rabbit hole would I dive? Dissuaders came in all shapes and styles; I was scoffed at, quizzed about my research, and interrogated about my motives. Professors rolled their eyes and suggested with asperity that my feelings were not fundaments of doctoral study. The books that would become the classic texts of affect theory, books in which feelings were the text, were being written by young female academics all across the world, but these books would burst into flameflower a little too late for my dissertation. When Sara Ahmed's *The Cultural Politics of Emotion* came out in 2004, I would be vindicated, but I would also be nearly finished my study by then. Between 1999 and 2004, it was just me and Eve Kosofsky Sedgewick and Jahan Ramazani. I also read a lot of Freud, which was useful if only because reading Freud explained all the eye-rolling and made me do it myself.

※   ※   ※

"Mourning and Melancholia": Sigmund, keep your pathology off my affect.

※   ※   ※

Between 1988 and 1995, I saw and wrote about and spoke publicly about many deaths. The effect is now one of intimate abundance; like my mother, my dead friends seem to be people with whom I am a bit on the outs. Gotta give him a call soon, I think. In April, I think, after the term work is done and it's warm enough to sit on a patio. I'll call him then, and he'll call me a jerk and then we'll laugh and I'll drive into the city and we'll meet for coffee.

※   ※   ※

In grad school, when the faculty discovered my past in AIDS work, I heard a flurry of suggestions that I trash my elegy project and instead write a study of Canadian AIDS literature. I parsed that idea like a sentence with a misplaced modifier. I said no, but what I meant was, field of cultural production be damned, my past is not a consumable object.

Keep your affect off my pathology.

※   ※   ※

One twilight in that city of doctoral study, J and I were driving past the park when I spotted a mailbox. "Pull over and I'll mail this letter," I said. I zipped across the street, dropped the stamped envelope in the box, and took two strides back onto the road when a van took a right turn onto the side street without reducing its speed off the main road. Visibility was bad in the lowering dark. The wind generated by the van's passing snapped my baseball cap off my head. I was that close. It was over in a second. The driver of the van had not touched the brakes, and I had not seen the van coming. A stand of Douglas fir was five-hundred yards to my left, trees that would soon hold herons' nests again. The previous spring, we had stood beneath the trees, J with his telephoto lens, focussing far above us on the newly-hatched herons' big heads on their thin swaying necks. But now in the twilight, the Douglas firs grew quietly, and my death rattled down the street on the hood of the van.

※   ※   ※

Back in my PMs, D wrote that he was looking for me because he had been going through old papers and found a poem I wrote twenty-five years ago about the death of a mutual friend. I was on a palliative care team who had cared for W in the final months of his life, and I tried — so badly, so imperfectly — to write that experience. I wrote a lot of these poems at the time, frustrated that I had neither the writerly craft nor the affective reach to say what I wanted to say. These were poems I could not show to many people because my friends and I were young and unpractised at death. People outside the community sometimes made it clear to me that their status as young marrieds or new parents meant that they had no room to read of the death of my friends.

※　※　※

The making and unmaking of the world.

※　※　※

I sometimes made, in my truth telling, a social pariah of myself. I was at an old high school friend's house and he showed me a recent photo of his godfather, a prominent figure in the arts community and an out gay man. The photo showed him several pounds lighter than when I last saw him with a large lesion from Kaposi's sarcoma on his right hand. I said "I'm so sorry to see he's ill." My friend's head snapped up and he said, "He's not. What are you saying?"

※　※　※

If you're long-lived, you may see the hot-button topics of your youth, the policies against which you railed and protested and conducted die-ins and annoyed people with at dinner parties, the things that made people say "man, she's so pushy" or just "shut up already," you'll see these policies defeated, then forgotten, then your history buried, then resurrected in the questions of people who, like you, wonder how we moved so quickly from being pariahs to protestors to dinosaurs, and if you're like me, you will feel another kind of grief for the erasure of your terrible but terribly politicizing and highly volatile history with illness and dying and living.

※　※　※

D wrote: your poem is a real witness to what happened and I felt a fiery flush of shame run down my spine. I found a copy of my poem and reading it, the flush didn't go away. The poem has every embarrassing earmark of my early years as a writer way, way out of my depth, a writer grappling with impossibility and failing. Even with those conditions, that poem is still a better witness than me.

※　※　※

Twenty-five Aprils have come and gone.

※　※　※

We are both over fifty now. D gave me his health update, which included getting cancer and recovering with lasting effects. I told him about my degenerative disk disease, which is bad some days and seems like nothing on others. He was shocked. When we were both thirty and the AIDS crisis was in full roar, I was the owner-operator of a "good body": that is, an uninfected body. D had trouble catching up with disease — any disease — as a reality for me. It made me shake my head at the irony of the female body being thought "invulnerable" for one second, let alone more than twenty years, anywhere in our capitalist, corporatist, colonial patriarchy. And I shook my head because I also knew what he meant.

※ ※ ※

I looked again at the photo of the man with AIDS in my high-school friend's hand and didn't know how I could see it and my friend couldn't. His voice was tight when he shouted *you think you know everything* and *you don't know anything* and *who do you think you are* and I said *okayokayokay sorrysorrysorry* and he said *yeah you'd better be*. When I attended his godfather's memorial service six months later, my friend was nowhere in sight, and he didn't answer his phone when I called and never returned my calls despite all the messages I left. So I never got to say I'm sorry I said it before you were ready, I'm sorry he died, I'm sorry I couldn't read your distress signals, I'm sorry I knew, I'm sorry I scared you.

※ ※ ※

The worst thing about my mother being dead is that I can't talk to her, a fact that became horribly apparent when I wanted to call her to tell her about this supremely awful thing that was happening to me, but the awful thing was her death and it was happening to her and not to me. The second worst thing is that there is no one left to talk to about her.

※ ※ ※

My mother had a big scar on her right shin and always wore pants to hide it.

I stopped working in AIDS care and activism in 1995. While all professors count their own aging in the milestones they passed by the time their students were born, this one is my personal mind-bender: that my students, born between 1996-1998, now constitute an entire generation between the aging me and my perpetually young friends who died before 1995.

※　※　※

At the end of Craig Lucas's 1990 film *Longtime Companion*, three surviving characters of the group of friends and lovers we've followed throughout the film walk a beach on Fire Island. They've lived through a confusing and painful decade of diagnosis, panic, caregiving, and grieving, and they muse about what it might be like to see the AIDS epidemic become a memory, a thing of the past. The female character says, "it would be like the end of World War II." Her utterance is instantly followed by a fantasy sequence in which hundreds of men and women — their resurrected friends, returned to them young and healthy — come running onto the beach for multiple joyous reunions. And just as instantly, the beach is empty again and one of the three survivors says, "I just want to be there to see it" and the lyrics of Zane Campbell's song "Post-Mortem Bar" come up loud over the credits:

> We'll go down to the post-mortem bar
> And catch up on the years that have passed between us
> And we'll tell our stories.
> Do you remember when the world was just like a
> carnival opening up?

When I saw this film in 1990, this ending was variously received among my friends and colleagues as a) heartbreaking, b) too sentimental, c) an enraging manipulation of our realities by

Hollywood into a trope that appealed to our parents' generation and not to us, and d) a way to make queerness commercially saleable while reinforcing bellicose metaphors for illness. Susan Sontag had published *AIDS and its Metaphors* the year before. Somewhere, Tony Kushner was writing *Angels in America*.

※　※　※

I am a regular at the post-mortem bar. It's my local.

It would be wrong and useless to parse who I loved the most. But I'd be lying if I said that I don't think about it.

※　※　※

One of the anxieties that haunted me in those years — the shape of which I can just discern from where I stand now — was how I would remember. In the midst of a mass dying, I was terrified that I would forget people, what was important about their lives, the details of their faces or their quick wit or their sweetness. I was afraid of forgetting because I saw how quickly death could blot out specificity. The future yawned before me; what would I do with the years that my friends would not have? Memento mori didn't feel profound. I felt stupid with the fug of it.

※　※　※

I was there to see the end of the era. For the record, it wasn't like the end of World War II. It was more like the end of communism and I wasn't supposed to talk about living under the regime. Or it was like finding myself on another planet and wondering how everyone else knew how to breathe the air.

※ ※ ※

One day in 1986, I woke with a searing pain in my neck and down my right arm, and six days later, had a tumour removed from my neck. The tumour was determined; it had chewed through the spinous processes of two vertebrae and was moving in on a third. My mother, afraid of flying, got on a plane and visited me every day in the hospital. She was there the day my ex phoned my hospital room, a man insensitive enough to open the conversation about whether or not I had cancer with, "What have you done to yourself?" My mother saw the look on my face and took the receiver from my hand, lifted it and said, "My daughter doesn't want to talk to you." Then she smashed down the receiver like she was determined to shove it into the bowels of the earth, or into his face.

※ ※ ※

I didn't have cancer. The tumour had been aggressive but benign. The surgeon's face as he told me looked like he didn't get to say that often. He had kind and calm eyes and made a neat scar up the back of my neck that now is just a bit silvery when the sun hits it, like a zipper.

※ ※ ※

I knew my mother was dying the moment I laid eyes on her three years ago in August. She couldn't find her balance getting up from a chair. Her eyes didn't quite focus. She mistook me for her sister, her mother, and once for my father, dead for eleven years. She was in a great deal of pain and I got her to the hospital, where they ran tests and pronounced her fine. I knew she wasn't and insisted they keep looking. No one dared roll their

eyes at me, especially not the interns who smelled my profes-
sorial authority and answered all my questions like any visit to
my mother's bedside was a test situation. It was. I was a nightmare relative, the one everyone wanted to avoid: an authorita-
tive non-scientist, a feminist, and a lone caregiver. I looked at
doctors in their white coats and saw people my students' age. I
asked them what year of study they were in. I read my mother's
chart every day and noted the bad spelling of the doctors and
doctors-in-training. I waited for them to tell me not to read it;
they never did.

But none of them passed the test; no one knew what was
wrong with my mother and they wanted to send her home. They
were, every one of them, obsessed by the old but massive scar
on her right shin. I am giving them all a failing grade, except for
the red-haired nurse from Croatia who always knew my mother
would not leave the hospital. She and I understood each other.
The doctors found the cracked rib that had nicked my mother's
lung only when her lungs were filled with fluid. They operated,
but it was too late. My mother, a fifty-year cancer survivor, fell
in her living room on the Prairies and drowned three weeks
later. Needed systems, guttered out.

※   ※   ※

In Jan Zita Grover's *North Enough*, Grover charts her move to
the woods of Minnesota in 1997 after years of working as a
palliative caregiver in San Francisco's AIDS community. In the
essay "Cutover," Grover pinpoints the need to think together
about two kinds of devastation, ecological and epidemiologi-
cal, weaving together what Kim Stafford calls, "the double
killings of our time." The "cutover" of Grover's essay pairs the
clear-cut of trees in northwestern Wisconsin with the death of
thousands of people, many of them gay men, in the early years

of the AIDS health crisis. Grover describes changing the bandage on her friend Perry's leg and seeing the organics of his body as earth:

"...a leg no longer smooth, intact, encased in a tan skin. A leg now erupted, returning to orderless matter. It did not look like a leg. It looked like freshly turned soil, dark and ruptured... Its world was entropic: moist, swirling with energy turned on itself, no longer producing orderly structure. Dermis, epidermis, capillary, vein, artery, ganglion. Gone. Instead, hyperbolic replication that guttered out needed systems, flooding cells. Drowning them."

Reading the lesions from Kaposi's sarcoma as a bodily text, Grover offers the clear-cut as a metaphor of annihilation: trees and people, environmental and cultural devastation as policy choices. If truth is the first casualty of war, expedience is the first excuse for the clear-cut.

※　※　※

My mother had a four-by-six inch rectangle of flesh removed from her right shin in 1963. She had a malignant melanoma and underwent an early form of chemotherapy, which involved being dosed with a chemical derivative of mustard gas. It made her grossly, violently ill for weeks, but it worked. She came home from the hospital to be my mother.

※　※　※

I gave a talk about Grover's book at a medical humanities conference, and the young man who chaired the panel caught me as I was leaving and thanked me for mentioning Kaposi's sarcoma. I asked why that infection in particular interested him. He hemmed and hawed a bit and didn't want to answer, but eventually said he was a gay man of twenty-eight and a medical student, and he had never heard of KS. "What's your area of study?" I asked. He answered, "Epidemiology."

※　※　※

Angels in America is back on Broadway.

※　※　※

I reread the poem that D remembers and I see every flaw, including my extreme anxiety about forgetting. Don't worry. I won't reproduce it here.

※　※　※

Grover again: "Now middle-aged, I find mortality doubly in my possession, keeper and kept. The diminishment of this landscape mortifies and disciplines me."

※　※　※

I mean I won't reproduce the poem. The anxiety reproduces itself.

※　※　※

When I was young I thought memory would fade like a photograph, but now I know it sharpens and elongates, an icicle on an uninsulated house in a long winter. My worries about forgetting were unfounded. I remember. All I needed was a few decades to recall Peter's eyes and John's cowboy boots and Barry's strut and Dave's jokes and Ted's wonky eyeteeth when he smiled that March we stayed at the Chateau Marmont, which was too fancy for the likes of me. The first time I met Wilf, we were both eighteen and my neck was unscarred and long. The first time I met my mother, I cried for three months. They called it colic, but I think it was relief.

Works Cited

Grover, Jan Zita. *North Enough: AIDS and Other Clear-Cuts*. Saint Paul, MN: Graywolf Press, 1997.

Kushner, Tony. *Angels in America: a Gay Fantasia on National Themes*. New York: Theatre Communications Group, 1993.

Longtime Companion. Dir. Craig Lucas. 1990.

Scarry, Elaine. *The Body in Pain: The Making and Unmaking of the World*. New York: Oxford UP, 1985.

Sontag, Susan. *AIDS and its Metaphors*. New York: Allen Lane, 1989.

Options

Vera Constantineau

I see death as the only certainty in gender equality. I am a woman, but my brothers died, my sisters died, my mother died, my father died, friends of both gender, relatives of other strain, co-workers — the list is long and age is irrelevant in all cases: dead is dead.

I remain breathing the air, carrying my stents around in my heart, flexing my arthritic bones, rechecking annually, my previously cancerous bladder and my previously cancerous vaginal threshold.

In spite of the many occasions when the door was knocked upon, I did not answer. Never fall for that old line: opportunity will knock more than once. While my husband was days into recovering from open heart surgery, I had a heart attack. We are now the scary couple no one wants to hang out with. I jest.

What have I learned from this life of knocked doors? I've learned a lot about positivity and I know it's pure bull. Nope, that's not strong enough, I say, fuck that noise. I know you can be as positive as a woman in her third trimester taking an over-the-counter pregnancy test, but if it's time for you to go then bye-bye, baby.

Does death still scare me? Hell, yes. Have I decided to go

forth in spite of that? Of course, what choice do I have? Unless, as one of my relatives did, you take matters into your own hands, choose your time and exit, forthwith. That's not my way.

Once a doctor offered me a drug therapy she said would make both the pain of my arthritis and the unsightliness of my psoriasis, things of the past. Unfortunately, this drug would shave a few years off my life, but hey, wouldn't I like to give up some of the ugly? Live a better life while I was here? I said no, I would not give up even one day of my life. Nope, that's not strong enough. I said, absolutely not! I want to live every day. If I suffer, so be it. She was peeved, I could tell by the sudden redness in her cheeks, the way she pulled out her cell phone and looked at the screen while taking a few cleansing breaths. This is my life. She's still my doctor, she still has new drug therapy ideas, but she doesn't try to sell me on them anymore. I am not amenable to drug interference. If that's another person's choice I say, you go ahead, believe in the possibilities of a drug that will change the you, that is you. I will rely on the me that is me.

Years ago, the night before my first hip replacement, I was certain I was going to die. I was weak from years of dealing with arthritis and I was chronically anemic. I spoke to my husband about the possibilities; we held each other and cried until visiting hours ended and he went to the hotel to try to sleep. I spoke to my primary nurse that night and told her my fears. She said it wasn't up to me to live or die. In the early morning, close to 5:00 AM, I was wheeled into surgery and received my new hip. When I woke up my primary nurse's face was hovering over me and she smiled. Her first words were, "You see? You didn't die."

Still, the fear. I'd witnessed my brother wheeled into heart surgery, and while under anaesthetic, he had a stroke. I saw him hooked to machines that blinked and beeped, another machine breathed on his behalf. And in that moment, I mourned him. I was sure he was going to die. Then, one day I went in and he was awake. It was obvious he was damaged. He couldn't speak and he'd forgotten who I was. I know this because during the first minute of my visit to his bedside, he showed me his catheter without any embarrassment. This was not something he would have done in a million days of greetings. His face was impassive, as if he was showing me a freckle on the back of his hand. On my next visit he was sitting on the side of the bed and he smiled at me, nodded his head just the way he always did, and out of excitement I rushed forward to hug him. I scared him badly; he wheeled and crouched at the top of his bed like a wild animal. I had to talk him down softly. For weeks I watched him progress, regress, progress. He eventually went for speech therapy, for physical therapy, and recovered enough that he could leave the hospital. Death lost that one, but five years later, came in the night.

What no one tells you about the bedside wait is this: you will anticipate each breath. I learned this from my mother's death. That she would take long breaths in and hold, then release, no one said that would happen. That the inhale would pause for longer and longer until we were sure it was done. And she would exhale. She was always a trickster. Telling silly jokes, playing silly games and singing silly songs. She gave us all the backbone we needed. She knew us all, all eleven of her children, as individuals and often tailored the advice for us alone.

When I pointed out the small lump in my cervix to my gynecologist, she looked and said, "Hmm." She asked her nurse for something with teeth. That didn't sound good. Wasn't good, but in the aftermath, I learned to live my life in snatches. First, three months at a time between checkups, then six months between checkups, then yearly until finally I was released. For several years I sailed calm seas. Then my sister, the one who'd always been a laugher, a crafter, a Christmas fanatic, was diagnosed with Alzheimer's disease. There is death and there is

death. During her building to the silence years, she had fantastical trips of all manner. She made up the best stories, "I walked
back from Toronto today and since I wasn't tired I headed up
to the Green Bush for the afternoon." Miles to go before she
slept away her days, forgot her daughters, slipped into nothing.
Then there was death.

My favourite brother and I had traditions. We'd take a
backroad ride every spring and he would pick a lady's slipper for
me. Until his last spring. I surprised him one afternoon and I
think it is fair to say, he surprised me. I picked him up, cajoled
him into the car, drove us to our favourite spot and when we
found a clump of lovely yellow lady's slippers, I pulled over. He
didn't want to get out to pick one. In hindsight, I realize he was
likely afraid he would topple into the shallow ditch. I quizzed
him and he insisted he was fine. He said he'd been dieting. I
ought to have known. A month later he was in the hospital
having a circle of tests. Then the answer came. The afternoon
he was diagnosed with liver cancer, he called me. And here's
what I learned about death from him, denial will set in almost
immediately. We were lucky, he and I. I got to tell him I loved
him and told him I would miss him when he said there wasn't
much time. Once the denial arrived, he was looking ahead,
chatting up the pretty doctor, thinking there might be a cure.
The night he died, he lay quietly in a hospital bed, not quite
with us, but not yet gone. When our niece was leaving for home
she joked, "You be a good boy." And he smiled his mischievous
smile, said he would try, in such a voice I realized he was, in
that moment childlike. He seemed to me to have gone back in
time. Then he did go fully back, to a place where he was only
energy released into the stillness of the room. It flays us all.

Shortly after that brother's death, another sister was diagnosed with Alzheimer's disease. Show of hands, who thinks life
is fair? Not me. Over the next couple of years, it was as if I was

reliving some of my first sister's fantastical tales. Then, a darkness came. This sister began to have bouts of paranoia and anger. She forgot her husband, she forgot me, but she remembered our youngest brother. He was able to get her into his car the day she struck off for home, from home. Was able to take her to the hospital, supposedly to be examined, but in fact to be placed in a locked room for her own safety. She has outlived her husband, both the one she remembers and the one she doesn't, but then, she doesn't know. There is death and there is death.

What do I know? I know that arthritis, heart disease, and cancer haven't killed me yet. I know that I have one fine sister left and we talk every day. I have a sister who is walking the halls of the nursing home with an ankle bracelet to keep her safe. I know, a few months ago, doctors diagnosed my youngest brother with the early stages of Alzheimer's disease. Know what else I know? I know death can come for me wearing any one of a number of names, cancer, heart failure, stroke, Alzheimer's, so whichever exit strategy takes me, death will be a surprise. Can a woman get any luckier than that? Gender equality has arrived in this one inevitable way. Would we change it if we could? I wouldn't.

I'm going to live every day, and laugh as much as I can. Eat what I please and throw my words into the wind. You want my life, Death? I'll wrestle you for it.

The School of Possibility: Living and Creating After Surviving

Lisa Neighbour

He who is educated by Dread is educated by possibility...
— Søren Kierkegaard

The meaning I extract from Kierkegaard's words is that, once you are made aware of the fragility of your life, and that all your worst fears can come true, you are permanently transformed by this knowledge. The process of transformation is different for each person, but anyone who has experienced it will, from then on, understand reality in a completely new way.

THE SURGERY ARTIST

In the fall of 2005, I went for a check-up. My doctor and I have known each other for many years, and my health had never been a source of worry for either of us. We usually chatted about art, and friends, and the economy — but this time she stopped and gave me a funny look. She said: "What's this?" and prodded my chest right above my heart. She showed me a bump under my skin I hadn't noticed before. My doctor insisted I shouldn't worry, but I worried without restraint for the next two months. There's no objective way for me to describe being diagnosed with cancer. Time seemed to have been suspended. Everything became surreal, and I was thoroughly disoriented, as if I'd suddenly found myself starring in a horror movie. It seemed like language and images were arranged like orange safety cones around the site of an enormous cave-in, a site where entire trees, streets, and houses had vanished in seconds, leaving a ragged darkness with constantly moving edges.

> *The knowledge of death is reflective and concep-*
> *tual, and animals are spared it. They live and they*
> *disappear with the same thoughtlessness: a few min-*
> *utes of fear, a few seconds of anguish, and it is over.*
> *But to live a whole lifetime with the fate of death*
> *haunting one's dreams and even the most sun-filled*
> *days — that's something else.*
>
> — Ernest Becker

It's not all that rare to survive a close call with death. And yet, the experience of being ill marked the turning point where I became fully aware of my mortality. My reasons for making art, my methods, and my beliefs, have all been profoundly affected. I decided to examine my experiences through the model of a rite of passage. Arnold van Gennep describes the purpose and the stages of these rites in his 1909 book *The Rites of Passage.* His words go to some length to bring order and understanding to the jumble of fear, rage, pain and disbelief brought on by a serious health crisis. The stages vary in their details from culture to culture. But, in almost every example, the sequence of events, and the end results, are remarkably similar. Rites of passage often have three stages: Separation — characterized by being removed from the community, changing one's appearance, a journey, an ordeal or punishment; the Liminal Stage — during which the subject has an ambiguous status and may experience a symbolic death, be in disguise, or break taboos; and finally, Reincorporation — which may include a celebration and emblems of identity, at which point the subject returns to the community and assumes a new status.

I was first separated from normal life by receiving a diagnosis, and becoming isolated from society in the hospital, where I removed my familiar clothing and jewellery, and was given a temporary identity bracelet. Next, I was anesthetized and embarked on a liminal voyage between life and death. After awakening and returning home, I took some time to heal physically, and adapt emotionally to my status as a survivor. My old identity seemed to have been erased, and replaced by an incipient new persona. I felt and acted differently, and my community treated me with a certain amount of awe. The emblems of my new identity were several scars directly over my heart. I imagined that they had been drawn there by a mysterious person I called "The Surgery Artist."

> *What can be salvaged from the shipwreck of*
> *existence proves not to be a possession withdrawn,*
> *in whatever way, into interiority but rather the self-*
> *possession achievable through the process of*
> *self-discovery and self-appropriation.*
>
> — Hans Blumenberg

In coming to terms with such an abrupt rift in my world, a metaphor helped me to assimilate the experience on a subconscious level. The idea of an ocean voyage made sense to me as a symbolic representation of my illness. The arrangement of a hospital waiting room resembled the piers of a seaport. Here the ships were prepared for departure, and the relatives of the passengers were left on the shore waving, as the ships pulled up anchor and turned toward the open water.

I have a distinct memory of that moment, just before I went under the general anesthetic. Before arriving at the hospital, I'd spent sleepless nights saying goodbye to everything and biting my nails. But as the drugs took effect I felt a strange and joyous thrill, very similar to pushing off from land in a kayak or a canoe. I realized that no matter how far into the unknown this voyage took me, I carried my home with me. Several times later on, during lengthy treatments and recovery, I felt as isolated as a ship in the middle of the ocean. And yet, at that point I left off worrying about how the voyage would end.

> *The man with the clear head is the man who*
> *frees himself from those fantastic 'ideas' (the charac-*
> *terological lie about reality) and looks life in the*
> *face, realizes that everything in it is problematic,*
> *and feels himself lost. And this is the simple truth*
> *— that to live is to feel oneself lost — he who*
> *accepts it has already begun to find himself, to be*
> *on firm ground. Instinctively, as do the ship-*
> *wrecked, he will look round for something to which*
> *to cling, and that tragic, ruthless glance, absolutely*
> *sincere, because it is a question of his salvation, will*
> *cause him to bring order into the chaos of his life.*
>
> — Ernest Becker

Like the shipwrecked sailor clinging to debris, I learned that I'm not really in control of anything. I also learned that fear is a tool that can help you to see what is real. If you can look at what you fear head on, the reflected light illuminates huge tracts that were once in darkness. As it turned out, the order that emerged from my chaos was found right inside "terror, perdition, annihilation," as Kierkegaard had recognized so clearly.

KNIVES AND LAST WORDS

Returning to work as an artist confirmed my sense of the permanence of these transformations — brought on as they were through a combination of abrupt revelations and months of numbingly slow progress. Soon after resuming studio work in the summer of 2006, I began to have dreams of knives and sharp weapons, and battles where I was fighting for my life. I also noticed knives when I was cutting vegetables in the kitchen, carving woodblocks, using a mat-cutting knife, and so on. These actions became hugely significant in a way they'd never been before. I became obsessed with knives without knowing why. It was only when I started using knife blades in my work that I began to understand where the obsession was coming from.

The experience of "anesthesia" (which comes from the Greek words for "without" and "sensation") is almost like a gap or a hole in the continuum of life. If all goes as planned, the surgical patient remembers nothing afterwards. In the absence of direct experience and memories, I reconfigured anesthesia and surgery as a mythical battle. I knew I had been through something, but whenever I tried to examine the experience consciously, it melted away into the shadows. During my encounter with The Surgery Artist, I couldn't defend myself from attack, but somehow my body was remembering the event like a trauma or an assault. The gap in consciousness felt like amnesia brought on by an event still too disturbing to assimilate.

Fig. 1
"Don't let it end like this.
Tell them I said something."

Fig. 1: Last Words of Pancho Villa, died 1923.

Once I knew I had cancer, I tackled illness with a kind of "pick-and-shovel" attitude, trying to plan for my death through paperwork; making a will, listing property, investments, bequests, insurance policies and so on. After the paperwork was organized, I tried to write a last message, in case I died. I wanted to leave behind a "summing up" in words. Although I worked at it for weeks, this task proved frustrating, maudlin, and eventually so absurd I laughed at myself, which was a good thing. I gave up, and instead began researching what other people said when they composed their last words. At times when events take an abrupt turn into the unknown, it is comforting to examine how others have coped with similar situations in the past.

Fig. 2
"I'm just going home like a. shooting star."

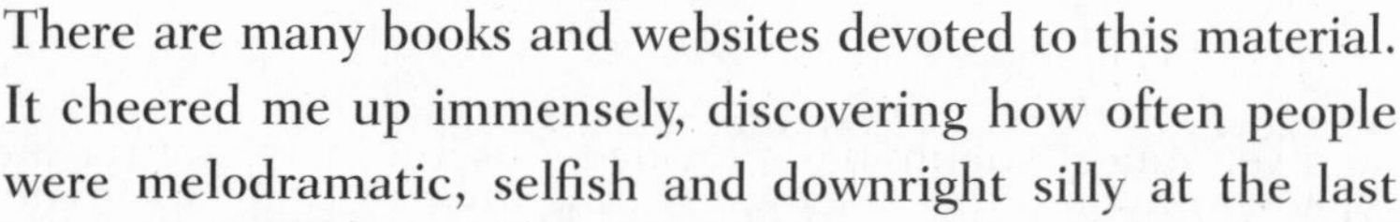

Fig. 2: Last Words of Sojourner Truth, died 1883.

There are many books and websites devoted to this material. It cheered me up immensely, discovering how often people were melodramatic, selfish and downright silly at the last moments of their lives. When someone dies without building an empire, or giving birth to children, or adding their name to history in some way, after a few years nobody will remember they existed. I think the need to leave a memorable final message is directly related to the fear of being forgotten. If you compose the perfect epitaph, maybe people will remember it, repeat it to one another, and through word of mouth remember you as the person who said it. Many of the last words I found were ridiculous and embarrassing, and all too revealing of the dying person's last attempt to assert control. Some expressed a poignant grandiosity, or surprise, and occasionally bitterness. I was relieved to see many people found composing their last words almost beside the point.

Fig. 3: Last Words of Joan Crawford, died 1977.

Fig. 3
"Dammit...
Don't you dare
ask God to
help me."

Among the last words of famous people were some that revealed uniquely human moments of courage, love, humour, and a sense of awe at the enormity of the event. In theory, dying involves less anguish and doubt when religious faith ensures your arrival in paradise soon afterwards — but you must believe. If you don't have spiritual beliefs about death, then you're left to confront your mortality with some of the other basic psychological defences: sublimation, humour, intoxication, and madness.

I wanted to somehow capture that shocking moment when the illusions of personality fall away, and we can catch a glimpse of the real. I knew it and felt it, but I couldn't speak about it. It's surprising how many potentially deadly weapons are used in our everyday lives. The blade of a knife, an object both disturbing and yet almost subliminal, provided a useful metaphor for the ideas I was struggling with. I wanted to acknowledge that any-time, our lives could come to an abrupt end. You could take a paring knife and with a few stabs and slashes end your own, or someone else's life as surely as with a dagger.

Fig. 4: Intaglio Print from Kitchen Knife.

Those potential stabs and slashes are embodied in a beautiful, familiar, and useful tool. Knives are metallic and mirror-like. The juxtaposition of domestic life and sudden death seemed to materialize in that one object. I began buying lots of knives. The clerks at Value Village were about to report me to their version of Homeland Security. I started out by wiping the knives with ink, and printing them like etchings. The outlines of the printed knives contained evidence of wear and tear, scratches, brand names, and nicks along the edges. I thought their surfaces resembled drawings or mappings of events. They contained traces of so many things that had been severed, bisected, and chopped.

Fig. 5: Intaglio Print from Kitchen Knife.

Eventually it occurred to me I should engrave last words right onto the knife blades. I took some of my blades (wrapped up in a box), to the mall kiosk where they engrave on pens and lighters. I kept them hidden in my bag, not wanting to alarm the engravers, or the mall security guards. As it turned out, the engravers were quite enthusiastic when I explained what I had in mind.

One of my sources was the Texas Department of Criminal Justice website, which contains a gloriously morbid archive of hundreds of condemned prisoners' last words. A strange form of afterlife is maintained there, inside our digital version of the collective unconscious. Although the prisoners may not have been aware their last words would end up on the internet, you can tell they wanted their words to be heard and remembered. Someone in the Department of Criminal Justice must have started the archive, envisioned a purpose for it, and then talked the department into creating the web page and maintaining it. Perhaps it was meant as a deterrent, but the information it contains is quite obsessively detailed.

Fig. 6

"I love you Chiquita. Peace, freedom, I'm ready."

Fig. 6: Last Words of John Amador, executed in Texas, 2007.

Some of the prisoners expressed an earnest faith, joyous apprehension, even relief that their imprisonment was nearly over. I envied them a bit. I asked myself: How will I be able to face death without faith? Am I completely without faith? These questions continued to circulate in my mind with some urgency. My research into last words included Japanese death poems, written by Zen monks and haiku poets before, or during their final moments.

Rain clouds clear away   Ame harete
above the lotus shines   hasu ni shinnyo no
the perfect moon.   tsukiyo kana

— Seishu (d. 1817), *Japanese Death Poems*

When I reflect on these haiku poems, I have to admit they seem self-consciously profound, to the point of being kitschy. It's this quality of neediness that I find irresistible. The wistful, sensuous beauty of Zen poetry comforts the living. Evidently, the authors believed the world would go on without them, and the poem would exist after they were gone.

Fig. 7

"My life
came like dew
disappears like dew
All of Naniwa is
dream after dream."

Fig. 7: Last Words of Toyotomi Hideyoshi, died 1598.

MEMORY IMPLANTS

Through research into the last words of poets and prisoners, I was reminded of the aphorism of Hippocrates, (as translated from Greek to Latin by Seneca) which refers to the study of medicine:

"*Ars longa, vita brevis, occasio praeceps, experimentum periculosum, iudicium difficile.*" This can be translated into English as, "Art is long, life is short, opportunity fleeting, experiment treacherous, judgment difficult."

Each translator interprets this differently. The idea that an artist's work could become a monument to, or a memento of their lives, is a strange one to me. Whenever I hear someone going on about archival paper, acid-free framing, climate-controlled storage, and the longevity of art materials, I wonder why the artist is so concerned about the survival of their work after they're gone. It seems few of us, whether we are writers, criminals, Buddhists, or artists, can easily accept the idea of vanishing without a trace.

Some works of art have an ability to create what I call "memory implants." Once you've experienced these works you'll find they have embedded a permanent marker in your memory. It's not like an ordinary memory of colours and compositions, but more akin to a special link or association. Although evoking memory implants is probably a by-product of interesting work, rather than a goal of the artist, it points toward the intrinsic possibility that an artist's creations can take on a life of their own. Instead of a public legacy (such as having books published about your work, and retrospective exhibitions in museums), memory implants sustain the artist's work through the experiences of individual people. A legacy is formed out of fresh insights and quirky associations. If there is a gift that can be bequeathed, it is contained in these beautifully random, yet meaningful sparks of connectedness.

ORNAMENTAL DAMAGE

The idea of deliberately limiting the longevity of artworks has an extensive history. By using impermanent materials, by staging time-based events and performances, or by assembling objects that immediately or eventually self-destruct, various artists have made it clear their priorities do not include preserving their works of art indefinitely. Along with questioning an artwork's role as a memorial to the artist, they also critique the ways that art attains market value through incorporating precious and/or durable materials. Conversely, ephemeral works may acquire value in other ways. I became interested in using materials that have the same uncertain and brief lifespan as the human body.

When you acquire a new scar, it can feel like a defacement of your body. After some reflection, and time passing, scars can be integrated and accepted as ornaments, symbols, and signs of healing. This process is affected by whether you chose to be scarred as part of a meaningful ritual, or got them after an injury or surgery. I began using a scalpel-like instrument to inscribe images on to the surface of fruit. The feeling of cutting was creepy, but turning the cuts into images of ships made sense to me. I was beginning to make a conscious connection between the scars on my body, and the process of using knives as a subject and a drawing tool. It helped me to see that something I was ashamed about, and had felt sad about, could be transformed into a source of insight, and eventually pride.

The fruit I used was a large citrus fruit called a pomelo. When one of my friends studied to be a tattoo artist, the first "skin" they practiced on was that of an orange or grapefruit. This idea stuck with me as being something both strange and compelling. The fruit rotted away, but the learning experience was preserved in the hands of the artist. I carved into the pomelos and dried out the peels, which shrivelled up and distorted the drawings. The carvings went through a kind of alchemical transformation; the end result was an enigmatic version — edited, altered, and then completed, as much by chance as by intention. The ripe fruit was transformed into a wrinkled shell, with the drawing imbedded in it like a hieroglyph.

Fig. 8: Carved Pomelos

DIRT AND SPIRIT

Man is literally split in two: he has an awareness of his own splendid uniqueness in that he sticks out of nature with a towering majesty, and yet he goes back into the ground a few feet in order blindly and dumbly to rot and disappear forever. It is a terrifying dilemma to be in and to have to live with.

— Ernest Becker

A fresh pomelo seems so sturdy and perfect, but it is made of the same materials we are, and it will soon decompose. By drying the peel, and eating the fruit itself, I was both preserving it and transforming it. Consuming it preserved the fruit by incorporating it into the energy of my body, which lives on. Drying the peel was also transformative and suggested the alchemical process of "desiccation." When the liquid of life is drained away, the essence of the peel is purified and concentrated.

According to Ernest Becker, fear of death is an intrinsic part of human nature. We are living creatures made up of minerals and organic matter that will, sooner or later, dissolve back into the earth. The other ingredient, one that is inextricably joined to the dirt, is our sentient spirit. Coming to terms with this strange paradox is one of the most difficult tasks we face in our lives — if we face it.

Beyond the Fear of Death

My experience at the edge of nothingness, the vivid sensation of being in a boat pushing off from shore, has affected how I experience transitions ever since. I re-experience it when I'm on the verge of sleep, or about to undertake a difficult task that makes me nervous, or at times when I have to say goodbye to someone I love. My resistance to new experience (the desire to stay on dry land, so to speak) is resolved by a spontaneous release of tension that feels very much like jumping off a cliff into the ocean - a mixture of joy, exhilaration, and profound awareness that there's no turning back. I have realized that throughout my life I was seeking this same kind of knowledge — an unconscious perception of the truth, the bones under the flesh of ordinary consciousness.

The main ingredient traumatic events have in common is that they point out the astounding fact that everything we create, everything we believe, everyone we love, in fact anything that has meaning in our lives (including the fact of our own existence) will come to an end at our death. However difficult the after-effects of illness may be, they contain the seeds of a new way of living. I have recovered my health but lost my naive faith in a benevolent universe. Although the exact date of my death has been postponed, the certainty of it has been emphasized and illuminated. Not being able to forget about it, or to become completely aware of it, leaves me searching over and over for an appropriate language, a representation, a precise embodiment of a thing that is essentially inexpressible. Yet, it also contains the key to an unlimited source of renewal and inspiration — the school of possibility.

WORKS CITED

Becker, Ernest. *The Denial of Death*. New York: Simon and Schuster. 1973.

Blumenberg, Hans. *Shipwreck with Spectator, Paradigm of a Metaphor for Existence*. Translated by Steven Rendall. Cambridge: The MIT Press. 1997.

Hoffmann, Yoel. *Japanese Death Poems*. Tokyo: Tuttle Publishing. 1986. Texas Department of Criminal Justice. tdcj.state.tx.us/death_row/dr_executed_offenders.html. Accessed October 10, 2018.

Hom, Susan K., ed. *R.I.P.* New York: Sterling Publishing Company Inc. 2007.

Iverson, Margaret. *Beyond Pleasure, Freud, Lacan, Barthes*. University Park: The Pennsylvania State University Press. 2007.

Kierkegaard, Søren. *The Concept of Dread*. Walter Lowrie, transl. Princeton: Princeton University Press. 1957.

Nietzsche, Friedrich. *Twilight of the Idols*. Translated by R.J. Hollingdale. London: Penguin Classic. 1990.

Robinson, Ray. *Famous Last Words*. New York: Workman Publishing Company. 2003.

Van Gennep, Arnold. *The Rites of Passage*. Translated by Monika B. Vizedom and Gabrielle L. Caffee. Chicago: The University of Chicago Press. 1960.

Acknowledgments

This anthology was edited and published on the ancestral and unceded homelands of the Musqueam, Squamish, and Tsleil-Waututh people in what is currently called Vancouver. I recognize their histories of survival and am grateful for the lessons I am learning here.

Thank you to the authors who shared their stories, including the astounding pieces I was unable to include here and am unable to forget. Our correspondence has been a beautiful experience of building community. Each submission affected me and helped me consider what the point of editing is and how I might begin to shape an anthology on such a strange topic. I respect the efforts it took to craft these essays: bringing these personal stories public, re-experiencing the painful moments was a somatic and mental challenge for many of you. Thank you for trusting me to take care of your words.

Thank you, Anvil Press — Karen, Cara, Jess, and Brian — for bringing this book into the world.

I am lucky to have a generous writing community of authors. Many of them carried me along through my healing and in spreading the news of this anthology. Julie Okot Bitek retweeted my daily calls for submissions and helped me connect with several authors, all with her trademark gorgeous blast of humour; I urge you toward her own work on grief and trauma. A major comfort, instigator, and conspirator in my appeal to use art to understand fear and illness is angela rawlings, whose guidance on my two books of poetry (*serpentine loop* and *Trauma Head*) was indispensable. Rachel Rose walked me through these steps, quite literally, during our active visits. Ali Blythe was, again, a sounding board I needed for ideas large and small. Alex Leslie's talks rooted me through this process. Thank you, Melissa Bull, for unshakeable literary sisterhood. Thank you, Zena Sharman, for good reminders. A special thank you to Mikaela Asfour for editing her father's interview into the piece here. To say this connection is meaningful sounds trite, but I am profoundly moved to have her be a part of this. Her editing also turned my wide-ranging interview with Joe Average into the essay herein and was a puff of air in my sails.

To T.C. Tolbert and Pam Houston, who took precious time from their own creative work to think about ours: gratitude!

Thank you to my mainstays, Robert, Beba, and Ivar, for softening the world's hard edges. And to Dr. Tenley Albright and Dr. Tudor Gardiner for their intellectual, emotional and moral guidance.

Ultimately and always, to the healers, the healing, the helpful. I know of no other way to come through this than to turn to each other.

— Elee Kraljii Gardiner

Contributors

Adrian Matthew Zytkoskee is a widower, a parent of two beautiful children, and a teacher at the University of Nevada, Reno's School of Medicine. Specifically, he teaches writing for healing purposes and is currently researching the correlation between reflective writing and the development of empathy. If you are interested, you may find more of his writing at mateoanonymous.wordpress.com.

Aislinn Hunter is the award-winning author of seven books including the novel *The World Before Us* and *Linger, Still,* her third collection of poetry. The dead and the revenants of the dead figure largely in her work. She lives and writes on Coast Salish Territories.

Amanda Earl is an Ottawa writer, publisher, editor, and visual poet. She's the managing editor of Bywords.ca and the fallen angel of AngelHousePress. *Kiki* (Chaudiere Books, 2014) is her first poetry book. More info is available at AmandaEarl.com or connect with Amanda on Twitter @KikiFolle.

angela rawlings is an interdisciplinary artist using languages as dominant exploratory material. Her methods over the past fifteen years have included sensorial poetries, vocal and contact improvization, theatre of the rural, and conversations with landscapes. rawlings' books include *Wide slumber for lepidopterists* (Coach House Books, 2006), *o w n* (CUE BOOKS, 2015), and *si tu* (MaMa, 2017). rawlings loves in Iceland. More: http://arawlings.is

Becky Blake is a two-time winner of the CBC Literary Prize (for nonfiction in 2017 and short story in 2013). Her work has appeared in publications across Canada, and her debut novel *Proof I Was Here* was published by Wolsak & Wynn's Buckrider Books in Spring 2019. She recently celebrated her fifth "birthday," post-transplant.

Ben Gallagher is a poet and essayist, currently splitting his time between Toronto, ON and Scotch Village, NS. He is pursuing a PhD at the Ontario Institute for Studies in Education, researching poetry pedagogy, occult curriculum, and the environment. He is the co-founder of Listening Parties, an irregular reading series, and is the coordinator of the Toronto Writing Project. Recent work can be found in *Sewer Lid, The Puritan*, (parenthetical), *Arc, Prairie Fire*, and *Lion's Roar*.

Bruce Meyer is author or editor of more than sixty books. *The First Taste of It: New and Selected Poems*, appeared in November 2018, and a new collection of poems, *McLuhan's Canary* will be published in November 2019 with Guernica Editions. His most recent book is a collection of short stories, *A Feast of Brief Hopes*. In 2019 Guernica Editions will release a book

---

of essays about his work. He teaches at Georgian College in Barrie and at Victoria College at the University of Toronto.

C. M. Faulkner is a criminal defence trial and appellate lawyer. She holds a BFA (Hons.) and LLB from a major Canadian university. This is her first published work in creative nonfiction.

Elee Kraljii Gardiner is the author of *Trauma Head* (Anvil Press, 2018), a chapbook of the same name (Otter Press, 2017) and *serpentine loop* (Anvil Press, 2016). She is co-editor with John Asfour of *V6A: Writing from Vancouver's Downtown Eastside* (Arsenal Pulp Press, 2012) and founded Thursdays Writing Collective, a beloved non-profit creative writing program for Downtown Eastside residents that ran for a decade and for which she edited and published nine anthologies. eleekg.com

Emma Smith-Stevens is the author of *The Australian,* a novel (Dzanc Books, 2017). Her fiction and essays have appeared widely in both print and online publications including *BOMB Magazine, Literary Hub, Subtropics,* and *Conjunctions.* She holds an MFA from the University of Florida and lives in New York.

Fiona Tinwei Lam has authored three poetry books and a children's book. She edited *The Bright Well: Canadian Poems on Facing Cancer* and co-edited the nonfiction anthologies, *Love Me True: Writers on the Ins, Outs, Ups & Downs of Marriage,* and *Double Lives: Writing and Motherhood.* Her poetry videos have screened at festivals internationally. www.fionalam.net

Harry Langen (1952-2017) was the author of the self–published *The Dead Sea Revelation*, as well as an investigative journalist, and publisher (*The Wendy King Story*). He founded numerous print and online publications, the last of which is *The English Bay Banner*, and contributed frequently to the letters pages of major Canadian newspapers. He was a member of Thursdays Writing Collective and wrote this piece in a hospital bed shortly before his precipitous death.

Jane Mellor writes poetry and prose. Captured through vignettes viewed from real time as well as imagined, she incorporates a rhythmical cadence into her work that brims emotion. A 2007 graduate of Simon Fraser University's The Writer's Studio, Jane has published one book of poetry, and under a pseudonym, writes and has published six books of provocative fiction she branded #ModernTrash. Jane is more than honoured to be included in this courageous anthology.

Jennie Chantal Duguay is a disabled queer femme and disability justice organizer. Her poetry and creative non-fiction have appeared in *GUTS*, *CV2*, *Hematopoiesis*, *The Capilano Review, Monstering*, and *The Peak* magazine. She lives on unceded Coast Salish territories in Vancouver, Canada.

Jennifer Van Evra is an award-winning Vancouver journalist and University of British Columbia writing instructor. Her work has appeared in dozens of publications including *The Globe and Mail, Vancouver magazine, Metropolis, Mother Jones*, and the *Harvard Business Review*. She has also been a CBC reporter and producer for nearly two decades, and is the recipient of UBC's John K. Friesen Excellence in Teaching Award. Find her at jennifervanevra.com, or on Twitter @jvanevra.

Jessica Michalofsky's previous fiction, nonfiction, and reviews have been published in *Brick, Geist, Joyland, The Globe and Mail, The Malahat Review, The Quarterly Conversation, LemonHound, The Rumpus*, and *Bookslut*. She lives in Victoria, BC.

Jill Yonit Goldberg reads, writes, and dances the tango in Vancouver where she also teaches literature and creative writing at Langara College. Her writing and photography have been published in *subTerrain, Tikkun Magazine, Flyway, The Globe and Mail*, and *F(r)iction* magazine where she won the 2015 Tethered by Letters poetry prize. Jill is the past chair of CCWWP (Canadian Creative Writers and Writing Programs), and she is working on her first novel.

Joe Average is a sixty-year-old Vancouver-based artist. In the 1970s, he started exploring photography focusing principally on documenting people. In 1984, he was diagnosed with HIV, prompting him to put his aspirations into action by making a living from his artwork. Using vivid colours and bold lines as structural elements, Joe created highly stylized paintings. In 2010, he started photographing again creating a series of self-portraits to document his struggles with lipoatrophy. Joeaverageannex.com

John Mikhail Asfour (1945 - 2014), born in Aitaneat, Lebanon, wrote five volumes of poetry in English, including *Blindfold*. He edited and translated the landmark anthology *When the Words Burn: An Anthology of Modern Arabic Poetry*, and co-edited with Elee Kraljii Gardiner the anthology *V6A: Writing from Vancouver's Downtown Eastside*. His latest translation, Faraj Bayrakdar's *Mirrors of Absence*, was published posthumously.

Kateri Lanthier's poems have been published in Canada, the US, and England. Her poem "The Coin Under the Leftmost Sliding Cup" won the 2013 Walrus Poetry Prize and was included in *Best Canadian Poetry 2014*. She is an Adjunct Professor, MA in English in the field of Creative Writing, University of Toronto. She is the author of *Reporting from Night* (Iguana, 2011) and *Siren* (Signal Editions, Véhicule Press, 2017). *Siren* was longlisted for the 2018 Pat Lowther Memorial Award. Poems from *Siren* have been reprinted with the permission of the publisher.

Kerri Power's writing has appeared in *The New Quarterly*, the *Newfoundland Quarterly*, and the *Bywords Quarterly Journal*. Kerri received her MFA in Creative Writing from the University of British Columbia. Originally from St. John's, Newfoundland, she lives in Ottawa, Ontario. She can be reached at power.kerri@gmail.com

Kiera Miller has an MFA in Creative Writing and a Master's in Library and Information Science from University of British Columbia. Her writing has appeared in literary journals, anthologies, magazines, and newspapers in the US and Canada. She was fiction and nonfiction editor of *Prism International* and has worked as a librarian in the US and Canada. She wrote three history books for kids to be published by Full Tilt Press. She lives in Port Townsend, WA.

Laurie Lewis is a Fellow of Graphic Designers of Canada and is editor emerita of *Vista*, the publication of the Seniors Association in Kingston, Ontario. Her memoir, *Little Comrades*, published in 2011, was a Top 100 Book of the Year. She is currently working on a collection of essays and stories about age, but is not persuaded the title *Mouthy Old Broad* will have much commercial appeal.

Lisa Neighbour was born in Montreal, Quebec, and now lives and works in Toronto, Ontario. She graduated from OCA in 1982, and received an MFA from York University in 2009. Her recent exhibitions include: Sparrow Night, Museum London, London, Ontario; Gumball Machine of Fate, Various locations, Toronto, Ontario; #*&ʌ%$!! I Broke My Glasses! Sointula Art Shed, BC; Smithereens, YYZ Artists' Outlet, Toronto, Ontario; This is My Punishment, G Gallery, Toronto, Ontario, and, Pilot X: Death in the City, Le Gallery, Toronto, Ontario.

Maureen Medved's writing has been published, produced, and adapted internationally, garnering nominations and awards. Her novel *Black Star* was published in 2018 with Anvil Press. Her screen adaptation of her novel *The Tracey Fragments* opened the Panorama program of the 57th annual Berlinale and won the Manfred Salzgeber Prize and has since featured at MOMA and numerous film festivals. Maureen is Associate Professor in the Creative Writing Program at the University of British Columbia.

Mikaela Joy Asfour is a writer and editor. She graduated from the UBC Creative Writing MFA program, earned a scriptwriting certificate from Algonquin College, and a BA in psychology from McGill University. She was shortlisted for the 2018 *Geist* Erasure Poetry Contest, and her work has appeared or is forthcoming in *Poetry Is Dead* magazine and *Room* magazine.

Moira MacDougall's artistic life began as a serious student of classical ballet and modern dance. It is poetry however, that has wed her love of movement and rhythm with voice and linguistic performance. She is published in Canadian and American literary journals. *Bone Dream*, (Tightrope Books, 2009) was her first collection of poems. Her second manuscript, *Vanishing Acts*, was published in March 2019 by Pedlar Press. She is the current poetry editor for *The Literary Review of Canada*. She lives in The Beaches in Toronto, Ontario.

Nikki Reimer lives on the traditional territories of the Treaty 7 peoples in Southern Alberta. Published books are *My Heart is a Rose Manhattan, DOWNVERSE*, and *[sic]*. She is a founding co-director of the Chris Reimer Legacy Fund Society. cjjrlegacyfund.com / reimerwrites.com / @NikkiReimer.

Rabi Qureshi is a Special Events Coordinator who lives in Toronto. She is a three-time cancer survivor, a feminist, and an advocate for mental health. She has a love/hate relationship with tomatoes. This is her first publication.

Rachel Rose's most recent collection, *Marry & Burn* (Harbour) received a 2016 Pushcart Prize, and was nominated for a Governor General's Award. Her memoir, *The Dog Lover Unit: Lessons in Courage from the World's K9 Cops*, was just shortlisted for the Arthur Ellis award for best non-fiction crime book, 2018. Her Poet Laureate Legacy Project anthology, *Sustenance: Writers from BC and Beyond on the Subject of Food,* supports refugee and low-income families with fresh, locally grown produce through the BC Farmers Market Nutrition Coupon Program. http://rachelsprose.weebly.com/

Rebecca Fredrickson lives in Williams Lake, British Columbia, where she teaches English at Thompson Rivers University. She is currently working on two projects: a poetry manuscript and a novel. The poetry manuscript (*Arrow Creek Diary*) is simultaneously an ecological manifesto, a meditation on poetics, and a collection of observations about grief. The novel (*The Asparagus Fields*) is set in the Kootenay Region of Southeast BC, and it is about things that disappear and sometimes reappear, including objects, people, animals, and love.

Sarah Lyn Eaton is a writer who has survived both flood and fire in the Southern Tier of New York state, with a penchant for dystopian stories.

She lives with her wife where two rivers meet. Sarah Lyn collects rock and works at being a source of every day kindness. She is currently recovering from serious injury. Her published stories can be found in *Pantheon* magazine, as well as the anthologies *On Fire; Dystopia Utopia; Fracture: Essays, Poems, and Stories on Fracking in America; The Northlore Series, Volume One: Folklore, What Follows;* and, *Elf Love.*

Susan Briscoe (1966-2018) published a book of poetry, *The Crow's Vow*, and taught college English for several years. She was born and lived most of her life in Montreal where she wrote her blog, The Death Project, at susanbriscoe.wordpress.com. She was also the proud mother of two grown sons.

Métis multimedia writer **Susan Cormier** has won or been shortlisted for such awards as CBC's National Literary Award, *Arc* magazine's Poem of the Year, and the Federation of BC Writer's Literary Writes. Her short films have screened around the world at festivals including the Montreal World Film Festival, the herland Feminist Film Festival, and Berlin's Zebra Poetry Film Festival. Her current projects include producing the Vancouver Story Slam monthly storytelling show and *Back Down the Rabbit Hole*, a research film project about youth bullying. She lives in Langley, BC.

Tanis MacDonald is the author of three books of poetry and one of creative nonfiction, *Out of Line: Daring to Be an Artist Outside the Big City* (Wolsak & Wynn, 2018). She was a finalist for the Gabrielle Roy Prize in 2013 for *The Daughter's Way* and was the recipient of the Robert Kroetsch Teaching Award in 2017. She is also a co-editor, with Rosanna Deerchild and Ariel Gordon, of *GUSH: menstrual manifestos for our times* for Frontenac House (2018). Widely known as a scholar and a reviewer, her fourth poetry book, *Mobile*, is coming out with Book*hug in Fall 2019. You can find her at www.tanismacdonald.com.

Vera Constantineau lives in Copper Cliff, Ontario. She writes creative nonfiction, poetry, short fiction, and for years wrote a humour column. Her work has been published internationally in anthologies, magazines and e-zines. Her story, "Betting on Death" was podcast by Toronto's Event Theatre, read by actor, Tony Nardo. Vera has read her work on the CBC's national and regional broadcasts. She is a member of the Canadian Author's Association, Vice President of the Sudbury Writers' Guild, a member of Haiku Canada and a Charter Member of the Manitoulin Writer's Circle. Vera recently published her debut collection of short fiction titled *Daisy Chained.*